Guided Inquiry Design® in Action

Guided Inquiry Design® in Action

High School

Leslie K. Maniotes, Editor

Libraries Unlimited Guided Inquiry Series

LIBRARIES UNLIMITED™

An Imprint of ABC-CLIO, LLC

Santa Barbara, California • Denver, Colorado

Library of Congress Cataloging-in-Publication Data

Names: Maniotes, Leslie K., 1967– editor.
Title: Guided inquiry design in action : high school / Leslie K. Maniotes, editor.
Description: Santa Barbara, California : Libraries Unlimited, an imprint of ABC-CLIO, LLC, [2017] |
   Series: Libraries Unlimited guided inquiry series | Includes bibliographical references and index.
Identifiers: LCCN 2016034667 (print) | LCCN 2016048151 (ebook) | ISBN 9781440847110 (paperback) |
   ISBN 9781440852855 (ebook) | ISBN 9781440847127 (ebook)
Subjects: LCSH: Learning. | Motivation in education. | Information literacy—Study and teaching (Secondary) |
   High school teaching. | Information technology.
Classification: LCC LB1060 .G84 2017 (print) | LCC LB1060 (ebook) | DDC 370.15/23—dc23
LC record available at https://lccn.loc.gov/2016034667

ISBN: 978-1-4408-4711-0
EISBN: 978-1-4408-4712-7

21 20 19 18 17   1 2 3 4 5

This book is also available as an eBook.

Libraries Unlimited
An Imprint of ABC-CLIO, LLC

ABC-CLIO, LLC
130 Cremona Drive, P.O. Box 1911
Santa Barbara, California 93116-1911
www.abc-clio.com

This book is printed on acid-free paper ∞
Manufactured in the United States of America

Contents

Preface

An increasing groundswell of teachers, librarians, and administrators are discovering Guided Inquiry Design® for successfully transforming learning in their schools. Teachers report that Guided Inquiry Design has consistently led students to deep learning, research independence, and academic success that has had a powerful impact on the learning environment of the entire school.

The Guided Inquiry series includes two foundational texts: *Guided Inquiry: Learning in the 21st Century,* 2nd ed. (Kuhlthau, Maniotes, and Caspari, 2015), which explains what it is and why it is important now, and *Guided Inquiry Design: A Framework for Inquiry in Your School* (Kuhlthau, Maniotes, and Caspari, 2012), which describes how to do it. *Guided Inquiry Design in Action: High School* is the second in the series to show what it looks like, following *Guided Inquiry Design in Action: Middle School* (Maniotes, Harrington, and Lambusta, 2016). My studies found that the Guided Inquiry approach to teaching and learning is particularly suited to meeting the intellectual and emotional needs of high school students (Kuhlthau, 2004). As students engage in the inquiry process they gain competence and independence for successful living and learning in an expansive information environment.

Dr. Leslie Maniotes, coauthor of the two foundational texts in the Guided Inquiry series and lead author of the *Guided Inquiry Design in Action* books, has conducted extensive professional development training and consulting for learning teams of teachers, librarians, and administrators across the country and abroad. These teams have designed units of study for guiding their students through the eight phases of the Guided Inquiry Design process. As they use this approach over time, we see significant evidence of substantial curriculum innovation and enhanced student learning. These learning teams are being recognized in their schools, districts, and nationally as innovative leaders for collaboration and instructional design.

Guided Inquiry Design is a framework for designing, guiding, and assessing inquiry learning that is tailored to the specific needs of your students in the local context of your school. It is not a prepackaged program for all to follow in set lockstep. Instead it gives you a dynamic framework to create units of study by applying your professional pedagogical expertise and your understanding of the specific needs of your high school students. It expects and empowers teachers to use their expertise to create highly motivating units that engage students in learning and inspire teachers to teach. This book draws on the expertise of noted researchers and expert practitioners for detailed explanation of unique components of Guided Inquiry for high school students.

The example units in this book will give you ideas for designing units for the students in your school. Each unit was designed by a team of high school teachers and librarians who participated in the Guided Inquiry Design training workshops led by Dr. Maniotes. These examples show what Guided Inquiry looks like in the context of these high schools from different regions across the United States and abroad. The units demonstrate the variety of students that benefit from this approach, from high academic achievers in a college preparatory independent school to those in an alternative school for students at risk of dropping out before graduating. The units also illustrate a wide range of curriculum content learned through Guided Inquiry incorporating the social studies, science, and literacy.

There is a pressing need to transform schools for learning in the vast information environment of the 21st century. Guided Inquiry is meeting this need in many schools by engaging students in the process of learning from multiple sources of information. There is a growing cohort of educators adopting the Guided Inquiry Design framework. Much has been accomplished in the years since we first introduced Guided Inquiry in 2007, but we are still learning and developing this approach to teaching and learning. This book is an invitation to join the initiative by using the Guided Inquiry Design framework for designing inquiry learning for your high school students and sharing your results. Become part of this endeavor to improve learning for students in information age schools.

Carol Collier Kuhlthau, Professor Emerita
Rutgers, the State University of New Jersey

References

Kuhlthau, C. (2004). *Seeking Meaning: A Process Approach to Library and Information Services.* 2nd ed. Westport, CT: Libraries Unlimited.

Kuhlthau, C., L. Maniotes, and A. Caspari. (2012). *Guided Inquiry Design: A Framework for Inquiry in Your School.* Santa Barbara, CA: Libraries Unlimited.

Kuhlthau, C., L. Maniotes, and A. Caspari. (2015). *Guided Inquiry: Learning in the 21st Century.* 2nd ed. Santa Barbara, CA: Libraries Unlimited.

Maniotes, L., L. Harrington, and P. Lambusta. (2016). *Guided Inquiry Design in Action: Middle School.* Santa Barbara, CA: Libraries Unlimited.

Guided Inquiry Design® in Action: High School

At the high school level, educators often feel stuck in the middle of having strong pressures to innovate practices with new models of instruction (like inquiry-based learning) that engage students alongside continued pressure to cover content. Guided Inquiry is an instructional design framework that supports deep content learning through an inquiry-based model. Through Guided Inquiry Design®, high school teachers and librarians collaborate together to ensure that students learn deep content, information literacy, and literacy practices; engage socially; and learn how they learn. This book is a compilation of materials to show how Guided Inquiry Design can be used to achieve a high level of learning at the high school level.

This book is an important addition to the Guided Inquiry series. This is the second in the series to showcase how Guided Inquiry Design looks in action. The first centered on middle school, and now this text focuses on inquiry-based learning at the high school level. *Guided Inquiry: Learning in the 21st Century* describes the research behind the design and offers a research-based rationale for why Guided Inquiry is necessary for all students in the information environment of the 21st century. *Guided Inquiry Design: A Framework for Inquiry in Your School* presents the design framework and describes how to design inquiry units using the research-based process. In that text, samples are provided as exemplars to contrast and define each phase, so that people can understand the reasoning behind each of the eight phases. The objective of those two books is to increase educators' understanding of Guided Inquiry Design and be able to begin to design prototype units of study.

This book fills the need of high school practitioners to see Guided Inquiry Design in action within the high school context with complete units so as to get a better sense of what Guided Inquiry Design is and can be. Guided Inquiry Design is an ever shifting and growing practice, and we are hopeful that this book will support readers' development and knowledge of inquiry-based learning and how to implement it at a high level.

This book is arranged as a practical tool for implementing Guided Inquiry in the high school context. It is a companion text to *Guided Inquiry Design: A Framework for Inquiry in Your School*. The design book describes how to use the design process and provides a variety of instruments for designing each phase. This text reveals each phase within a unit of study so the flow of the inquiry is exposed to show what it looks like in action. The units in this book have been specifically designed and successfully implemented with high school students at a variety of schools from an elite private school in Canada, to large American high schools, to an alternative school for students at risk of not graduating in a credit recovery program. We are proud to showcase that Guided Inquiry Design is not for one type of learner or one type of

1

school and can be successfully implemented in many different contexts. We hope that this will encourage your implementation and success with the model.

In this book we cross the boundary of practice to provide background on what's needed for designing inquiry-based learning at the high school level. The first chapters of this book describe some key components of instructional design for inquiry: the Guided Inquiry Design model, concept-based considerations, and recognition of the role of students' emotions in learning within an inquiry context. The next section includes descriptions of instructional strategies from practitioners in the field that are critical to the instructional design. Finally, we give some full examples of units with handouts and protocols for you to use as is or adapt for your students and need.

This book begins with the Guided Inquiry Design process so when you are using this book for planning and designing purposes, you have the design model and short description of each phase at your fingertips. The bullet points for each phase are meant to serve as a guide and reference point for teachers collaborating to design inquiry-based units. Deeper student learning is achieved when the learning team targets the activities for learning at each phase to ensure they are grounded in the concepts described in these bullet points. You may notice that this chapter is the same as is found in *Guided Inquiry Design*. *Guided Inquiry Design* includes a deeper description of each phase in Guided Inquiry and should serve as the best reference for a complete description of each phase in action. We strategically placed this short description here for your use and reference as you begin to design your own units or as you are reading and implementing the units found in this book.

In this age when facts are at our fingertips, the push and shift in teaching is to move beyond facts and arrive at deeper learning. In Chapter 3 Jean Donham has tapped into an essential piece of the instructional design for inquiry-based learning. In this chapter Jean describes how to frame learning around concepts rather than topics or facts. She shows us how learning about concepts opens up the learning. A concepts-based approach is more meaningful and has more relevance as it increases students' ability to transfer what they learn to other disciplines, areas of life, and other learning situations.

The research-based strategies to support learning through inquiry are the Inquiry Tools that were first described in *Guided Inquiry Design* (2012). In Chapter 4 we get a look into a model Guided Inquiry program led by Anita Cellucci, librarian. In this chapter Anita describes how she organizes the learning to achieve student engagement and assess student learning at Westborough High School. Over the years of implementation Anita has fine-tuned her orchestration of the Inquiry Tools to support students, embed technology in use, and enhance reflection in the learning.

Confusion, frustration, uncertainty, and confidence are all emotional responses to inquiry learning that students experience. Kuhlthau's research has long stood out as one of the first to look at how emotions are deeply connected in constructing new understandings through research. In Chapter 5, Dr. Carol Kuhlthau, Distinguished Professor at Rutgers University, strips away the thoughts and actions that occur through inquiry to focus solely on the student's emotional journey. Through this close look at feelings, she uncovers the responses that we can provide to support students' knowledge construction through inquiry-based learning.

Everyone who knows about Guided Inquiry has read about Kuhlthau's 6 Cs from *Seeking Meaning* (2004). These are six research-based strategies that help us to guide student learning through inquiry (see our other books for more information). One of the 6 Cs is conversing. In Guided Inquiry Design, students converse with one another, but also with their inquiry guides or the members of the Learning Team. In Chapter 6 Heather Hersey, a self-proclaimed Inquiry

Sherpa and former student of Dr. Carol Kuhlthau, describes how she uses conferences to guide student learning. Heather has been studying the Information Search Process (ISP) in practice for years in her high school library. As a result, she has fine-tuned her practice of student conferences within the Guided Inquiry Design process. Here, Heather shares her wisdom, organizational structure, and examples of how to manage this important structure to guide students' deeper learning through this "Zone of Intervention" in inquiry (Kuhlthau, 2004).

In the second part of this book are four exemplary units of Guided Inquiry Design. The first unit, Chapter 7, is from Westborough High School and was one of the units the team designed at the CiSSL Summer Institute. Over the course of its implementation, this unit has gone from a two-person team to include the entire ninth-grade team. Marci D'Onofrio, science teacher, and Anita Cellucci, librarian, are the original team members and have worked tirelessly to craft this into a complex unit with all the Inquiry Tools to ensure deep process and content learning in the sciences.

Chapter 8 includes a second unit from Canada. Marc Crompton, teacher librarian, and Jennifer Torry, English teacher from Saint George School in Vancouver, BC, teamed up to take a fresh look at *Romeo and Juliet,* layering a conceptual lens of relationships on the text. The unit artfully uses the Guided Inquiry Design process to guide students to weave in and out of reading the play to examine the relationships within that text. The students are able to extend those ideas into the real world and make connections to relationships that they encounter as they research different kinds of relationships relevant in their lives.

Chapter 9 is a deep description of a unit on National History Day (NHD) by Kathy Boguszewski. Kathy, in her role as librarian, has worked with social studies and language arts teachers for years on the implementation of the National History Day project at the high school level. Having a deep knowledge of the ISP and Guided Inquiry Design, she recognized the benefit in shifting the NHD unit to align with the Guided Inquiry Design phases. Having had excellent results and response from students after doing so, she was excited to share this unit here, making this connection to the annual theme and helping others to enhance historical thinking.

The final unit, Chapter 10, is a truly integrated unit from an alternative school in Norman, Oklahoma. Buffy Edwards, librarian, led a team who typically used packets to teach. This time they collaborated to create a unique cross-disciplinary unit of Guided Inquiry Design where students could gain credits within different content areas, depending upon their need for credits for graduation.

As the examples and chapters in this book suggest, Guided Inquiry Design requires a shift in mindset and practice from traditional transmission teaching of the past into guiding learning based on a sound instructional design framework. Many schools are on that pathway to shifting, but continual pressures to teach content remain in high school. This book concludes with Chapter 11 by Leslie Maniotes on the leadership and systemic challenge of getting started and sustaining change with Guided Inquiry. This chapter provides guidance for you to create your own path over the course of a few years to shift your school to new ways of thinking in order to address and equitably meet the needs of your students today, in this information age. This chapter provides you some guidance in creating that shift.

Now, ten years since the first publication on Guided Inquiry, many educators are successfully using the approach with their students. This is the first book in the series to provide fully tested exemplar units including the use of embedded tools described in Guided Inquiry Design from start to finish at the high school level. These units came out of the collaborations between librarians and teachers who were working to develop their students' skill and knowledge through interdisciplinary units of Guided Inquiry Design. In each of these units students learn to question, research, draw conclusions, and think for themselves. These exemplars are meant to explicate the process even further and inspire educators to find a way in, to gather a team, and to design inquiry for their own students as they gain insight from these examples.

References

Kuhlthau, C. (2004). *Seeking Meaning: A Process Approach to Library and Information Services.* 2nd ed. Westport, CT: Libraries Unlimited.

Kuhlthau, C., L. Maniotes, and A. Caspari. (2012). *Guided Inquiry Design: A Framework for Inquiry in Your School.* Santa Barbara, CA: Libraries Unlimited.

Kuhlthau, C., L. Maniotes, and A. Caspari. (2015). *Guided Inquiry: Learning in the 21st Century.* 2nd ed. Santa Barbara, CA: Libraries Unlimited.

Maniotes, L., L. Harrington, and P. Lambusta. (2016). *Guided Inquiry Design in Action: Middle School.* Santa Barbara, CA: Libraries Unlimited.

Guided Inquiry Design® Framework

2

Guided Inquiry is based on principles of constructivist learning, the need to create a Third Space for optimal learning, and Kuhlthau's model of the Information Search Process (ISP) describing the dynamic process of learning from a variety of sources. Guided Inquiry Design® is a framework that describes how to guide students in each stage of the ISP. The shape of the design framework follows the flow of students' confidence, interest, and learning in the inquiry process. The basic tenet of Guided Inquiry is Third Space, a dynamic learning space that connects school learning to the student's world. It is the "watermark" of Guided Inquiry, a pervasive underlying impression that influences all aspects of the design and guidance throughout the inquiry process. The Guided Inquiry Design framework employs the six principles of constructivist learning throughout each phase of the design framework, which are based on the stages of the ISP.

Guided Inquiry is founded on research that reveals students' holistic experience in the process of learning from a variety of sources described in Kuhlthau's model of the Information Search Process (ISP) (Kuhlthau, 2004). Figure 2.1 displays how Guided Inquiry Design is mapped onto the model of the ISP. The design framework provides substantive direction for designing, guiding, and assessing learning in the inquiry process.

Model of the Information Search Process

Tasks	Initiation	Selection	Exploration	Formulation	Collection	Presentation
Feelings (affective)	uncertainly	optimism	confusion frustration doubt	clarity	sense of direction/ confidence	satisfaction or disappointment
Thoughts (cognitive)	vague————————————————————→focused					
				increased interest		
Actions (physical)	seeking relevant information————————→seeking pertinent information					
	exploring			documenting		

(Kuhlthau, 2004)

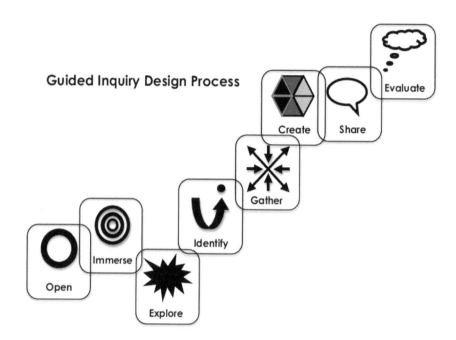

Kuhlthau, C., Maniotes, L., Caspari, A. (2012). *Guided Inquiry Design: A Framework for Inquiry in Your School*. Libraries Unlimited: Westport, CT.

Figure 2.1 The ISP and Guided Inquiry Design®

Guided Inquiry Design® and ISP

The Guided Inquiry Design process begins with **Open**, to catch students' attention, get them thinking, and help them make connections with the world outside of school (Figure 2.2). Next is **Immerse**, which is designed to build enough background knowledge to generate some interesting ideas to investigate. Then **Explore** those ideas for an important, authentic, engaging inquiry question. Next, pause to **Identify** and clearly articulate the inquiry question before moving on to **Gather** information. After gathering, **Create** and **Share** what students have learned, and then **Evaluate** to reflect on content and process and evaluate achievement of learning. Guided Inquiry is designed to encourage collaborative construction of knowledge with reflection and assessment of learning occurring throughout the process.

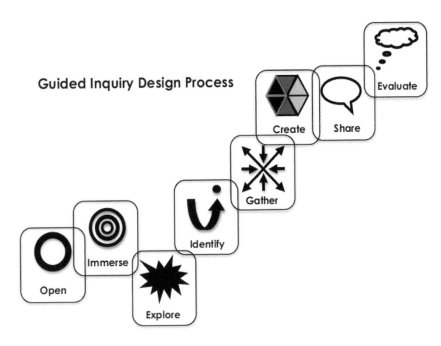

Kuhlthau, C., Maniotes, L., Caspari, A. (2012). *Guided Inquiry Design: A Framework for Inquiry in Your School.* Libraries Unlimited: Westport, CT.

Figure 2.2 Guided Inquiry Design® Process

Open

- **Invitation to inquiry**
- **Open minds**
- **Stimulate curiosity**

Open is the invitation to inquiry, the beginning of the inquiry process. **Open** is a distinct and important phase of the process that sets the tone and direction of the inquiry. Once the Learning Team has decided on the learning goals, they need to create a powerful opener that invites the learners in, establishes an inquiry stance, and introduces the general topic to engage the Inquiry Community.

The main challenge is to open students' minds and stimulate students' curiosity. The **Open** session inspires students to want to pursue the inquiry. The opener is designed to spark conversations about ideas and themes, pose questions and problems, and highlight concepts related to the subject. These conversations stimulate students to think about the overall content of the inquiry and to connect with what they already know from their experience and personal knowledge.

Immerse

- **Build background knowledge**
- **Connect to content**
- **Discover interesting ideas**

In the **Immerse** phase, the inquiry community begins to build background knowledge together through an immersion experience. The Learning Team designs engaging ways for students to **Immerse** themselves in the overall ideas of the content area under study.

The main task of **Immerse** is to guide students to connect with the content and to discover interesting ideas to explore further. Learners are guided to think about what they already know and what seems particularly interesting, curious, surprising, or troubling. As they build background knowledge, students reflect on ideas that matter to them and are worth further investigation.

Explore

- **Explore interesting ideas**
- **Look around**
- **Dip in**

In the **Explore** phase in Guided Inquiry students browse through various sources of information to explore interesting ideas and prepare to develop their inquiry questions. In this critical, early phase of constructing new learning, students need to explore ideas rather than accumulate facts. The Learning Team guides students to browse and scan a variety of sources. Students dip into a few sources to make sense of the information they find and raise lots of further questions.

In **Explore**, students survey a wide range of sources, read when they find something interesting, and reflect on questions that begin to shape their inquiry. Students often become overwhelmed by all the information and confused by the ideas that don't fit together. The Learning Team guides students to keep an open mind as they **Explore** and reflect on new information. Guiding students through exploring leads them to form a meaningful inquiry question.

Identify

- **Identify inquiry question**
- **Pause and ponder**
- **Decide direction**

In **Identify**, learners pause in the inquiry process to ask a meaningful inquiry question. In Guided Inquiry, they have had lots of preparation for this phase. Students are ready to identify an important question for their inquiry because of the time they have spent immersing and exploring to build enough background knowledge to ask many meaningful questions.

The main task of the **Identify** phase is for students to construct an inquiry question from the interesting ideas, pressing problems, and emerging themes they have explored in various sources of information. The team introduces strategies that enable each student to sort through information and ideas to clearly articulate a meaningful inquiry question that will frame the rest of the inquiry.

Gather

- **Gather useful information**
- **Go broad**
- **Go deep**

A clearly articulated question gives direction for the **Gather** phase. **Gather** sessions are designed to help students collect detailed information from a variety of sources. This information engages them in learning about their inquiry question. The Learning Team guides students in locating, evaluating, and using information that leads to deep learning.

The main task of the **Gather** phase is to guide learners to choose what is personally meaningful and compelling about their inquiry question in the information sources they find. The Learning Team guides students in a structured approach for managing their search. Students "go broad" to find a range of sources that will be useful in understanding their inquiry question. Students also "go deep" and choose a core of the most useful sources to read closely as they find connections and gain personal understanding.

Create

- **Create to communicate**
- **Reflect on learning**
- **Go beyond facts—interpret and extend**

After students have gathered enough information to construct their own understandings, they are ready to organize their learning in a creative presentation in the **Create** phase. Creating a way to communicate what they have learned through the inquiry helps students to articulate what is important about the subject and requires them to integrate the ideas more firmly into a deep understanding. The Learning Team guides students to go beyond simple fact-finding and reporting to summarize, interpret, and extend the meaning of what they have learned, and then **Create** a way to share their learning with others.

Create sessions are designed to guide students to reflect on all they have learned about their inquiry question, construct their own understanding, and decide what type of presentation will best represent the engaging ideas, controversies, and theories generated through the inquiry for a particular audience. The Learning Team guides students in creating a meaningful, interesting, clearly articulated, well-documented presentation that tells the story of what they have learned in the inquiry process.

Share

- **Learn from each other**
- **Share learning**
- **Tell your story**

Share is the culminating phase in the inquiry process when students share the product they have created to showcase what they have learned with the other students in their Inquiry Community. Students have become experts on the question for their Inquiry Community. They now have the opportunity and responsibility to share their insights with other students and contribute to the learning of others. Their inquiry products also may be shared with a wider audience, and what they have learned may result in taking an action.

Share is designed so that students share the products they have developed during **Create** to communicate what they have learned about their inquiry question in an interesting, informative way. An important component of Guided Inquiry is the collaborative learning that takes place when students share what they have learned in the inquiry process. The Learning Team organizes **Share** sessions to provide the best conditions for students to learn substantial content from one another.

Evaluate

- **Evaluate achievement of learning goals**
- **Reflect on content**
- **Reflect on process**

The **Evaluate** phase, which occurs at the close of the inquiry process, is an essential component in Guided Inquiry. Although Guided Inquiry incorporates assessment for determining student progress throughout all of the phases of the inquiry process, evaluation comes at the end when the Learning Team evaluates students' achievement of the learning goals.

The Learning Team also guides students in self-assessment of content learning and their progress through the inquiry process. Student self-reflection takes place while the entire process is fresh in their minds to reinforce their content learning and establishes good habits for learning through the inquiry process.

Process Used by High School Teams to Design Units of Inquiry

This process is used by Learning Teams of teachers and librarians as they work in collaboration to design units of study around core topics of important content in their discipline. To design units of study, Learning Teams come together in a simple design process. First, the team outlines the concept, the guiding questions for the unit design, and identifies the learning objectives for the unit in all five kinds of learning. Next, they consider how the learning goals might be assessed. (See Chapter 3 for more information about using concepts to drive unit design.) Then, they use the bullet points for each phase to support the design of the unit. Practitioners say that it is most important to carefully plan the first three phases of the unit in order to set the students up for success. Learning Teams go through and brainstorm together the best ways to **Open** the inquiry, **Immerse** students in content, **Explore** the ideas around the theme, and so on throughout the phases.

The units in this book are examples developed using that planning process. Of particular importance that should not be overlooked in design is that there is often more than one session for each phase of inquiry. In the beginning people may think that Guided Inquiry Design falls easily into one session per phase, but it rarely works out that way. The units presented in the coming pages include the core plans for the inquiry, knowing that there might be other plans in the units occurring around literacy practice or developing content knowledge or specific skills that are not represented here. These learning needs would vary by student need in the individual school setting and depend upon the Learning Team's determined goals for the unit. The units in these pages showcase the process from start to finish to show how the whole process works through each phase.

Process Used by Students to Learn How They Learn

In Guided Inquiry, student research is considered an integral part of inquiry learning. By providing a context for learning through research, students become aware that research supports learning about a personally compelling topic. This unique approach to inquiry learning emphasizes research as a core component of learning in the information environment. The design framework is also useful for students as a tool to understand the process of research, where they are in the process, and how they learn and work in each phase. Just as students come to know the writing process, knowing the Guided Inquiry Design process supports them to become independent researchers through inquiry and helps them learn how they learn. Posters, anchor charts, and cards of the Guided Inquiry process are beneficial as visual reminders of the phases to students. Students use these visuals as a reference point, as they build an awareness of the phase they are in, to support their own reflection and learning how they learn.

References

Kuhlthau, C. (2004). *Seeking Meaning: A Process Approach to Library and Information Services*. 2nd ed. Westport, CT: Libraries Unlimited.

Kuhlthau, C., L. Maniotes, and A. Caspari. (2012). *Guided Inquiry Design: A Framework for Inquiry in Your School*. Santa Barbara, CA: Libraries Unlimited.

Kuhlthau, C., L. Maniotes, and A. Caspari. (2015). *Guided Inquiry: Learning in the 21st Century*. 2nd ed. Santa Barbara, CA: Libraries Unlimited.

Syba Signs, http://sybasigns.com.au/guided-inquiry-products.

Employing a Conceptual Lens When Designing Guided Inquiry

3

Jean Donham

In the Guided Inquiry Design® process, students immerse themselves in a topic in order to build background knowledge and discover interesting ideas. The result of their immersion in a topic is readiness to explore those ideas further. At this point, students anticipate focusing their questions. How that focus is framed can be key to the quality of their inquiry. One approach to framing is to encourage students to shape their inquiry around a concept—a "big idea"—in order to generate a meaningful research question. A conceptual lens can "power up" the work our students undertake in the name of inquiry. In this chapter, we will discuss what is meant by a conceptual lens and how it can guide students as they proceed to explore information and formulate their inquiry questions.

Through the inquiry process, students progressively integrate facts, data, and information into bigger and bigger ideas—conceptual understandings. H. Lynn Erickson (2008) expressed the significance of this pursuit of conceptual understandings rather than seeking isolated facts when she stated:

> Kings, queens, dates, and the presidents and all their men: what significance do they hold for understanding our world or the human condition? Certainly as isolated bits of stored memory they hold little significance, but as key historical players in life's drama, their social situations, actions and reactions hold lasting lessons for understanding the human condition today and for predicting the world of tomorrow. (p. 24)

To arrive at "lasting lessons" students must be challenged to elevate their intellectual work to more cognitively complex levels—analyzing, integrating, and synthesizing their findings as they focus on "big ideas" that constitute concepts. This conceptual approach to inquiry draws students into enduring ideas that transfer across time and circumstance so that the relevance of the learning is increased; as a result, the learning can be not only more challenging but also more interesting for the students. For example, if students investigate the Holocaust as a specific topic, they may learn much about the particulars of that historical event. However, when they apply the conceptual lens of genocide, their understanding deepens as they compare the events of the 1940s in Germany to events of the 1990s in Rwanda or events of the 1990s in Bosnia or today's Syrian conflict or even the Israel-Palestine conflict. Not only does this perspective bring new insight into the Holocaust itself, but the issues inherent in that event gain relevance for students as they compare similar human conflicts in various areas and eras. Not only does the conceptual lens add to the intellectual complexity of students' investigations, it also adds relevance and interest.

The Shift from Topic to Concept

"The Endangered Species Act of 1973"

"Diesel Fuel"

"Martin Luther King"

These are the kinds of topics searched via Google as students write reports on a law, energy, or a famous American leader. However, these topical investigations will not inherently engage students in inquiry. They may be useful explorations for background building, but these are the topics that *begin*—not *complete*—the inquiry process. This is the work of students as they *immerse* themselves in a topic in pursuit of interesting ideas that will pique their curiosity. These topics, once explored, can lead to questions like:

"Why was the designation of eagles as an endangered species important to their recovery?"

"How do various fuels compare in energy use and environmental impact?"

"How did Martin Luther King exhibit characteristics that resulted in his reputation as a national leader?"

These questions share a common attribute. They all focus the inquiry around a concept—endangered species, energy, and leadership. In 2005, Loertscher, Koechlin, and Zwaan published *Ban Those Bird Units* in which they urged educators to move away from the conventional *locate—copy—paste—assemble* model of library projects. Earlier, Gordon (1999) had characterized a problem of "no-learning inquiry" when she stated, "Reporting has masqueraded as researching for so long that the terms are used interchangeably" (p. 2). Yet, the reports continue as students locate facts with less and less difficulty using a simple Internet search engine to gather what they need, transfer the facts to their word processor, and dress them up in favorite fonts and formats. By thinking about inquiry in terms of conceptual learning, perhaps educators can begin to shift toward deeper, more complex, and more interesting student work.

To begin, then, what is meant by a concept? Taba (1962) defined concepts as "systems of highly abstract ideas" (p. 178). Examples include revolution, interdependence, democracy, organism, or change. Such concepts share several attributes as identified by Erickson (2008):

- *Abstract:* Concepts are "big ideas" or generalizations that bond a set of data or information together under shared attributes. Consider the concept of adaptation, for example. Students might consider examples of adaptation like how the deer has adapted to human settlement or how the polar bear has adapted to climatic warming. By comparing various examples, new questions of *why, how,* and *what if* are likely to emerge as students seek understanding of the concept of adaptation, how the process works to change animal behavior, and what the interaction between the animal and its environment means. Indeed, they may even see the application of the concept beyond natural science to social science as they wonder how human adaptation to new environments—physical and social—is similar to and different from adaptation in the animal world.

- *Universal in application:* Because concepts are universal, students construct understandings that apply in other settings and provide ways of seeing their world that will apply not only in school but also in life beyond school. For example, investigating the concept of human migration provides rich opportunities for universal application, as students study the early migration of Europeans to the North American continent and pose questions about why they migrated; what they brought in possessions, skills, and values; and what they left behind or gave up upon arrival. Finally, applying these learnings to examples of today's migrating populations provides the opportunity for empathetic perspectives that might not have been so likely without the investigation into what human migration means in multiple contexts.

- *Timeless:* A concept survives across ages. In social studies, for example, when students examine a concept rather than a specific event, the lessons of history become clearer. Consider such concepts as revolution, colonialism, or leadership as lenses for understanding history across eras and nations. When students study the French Revolution, if they examine it through the conceptual lens of revolution, they can then compare it to more recent uprisings as the Hungarian Uprising of 1956 or the 2011 Arab Spring and gain new insights into the past and the present. In this way, history becomes more relevant when its lessons are applied to current world issues.

- *Grounded in observation:* Observation is a key skill for inquiry. The generation of questions begins by observing details, behaviors, changes, or interactions. Conceptual inquiry encourages students to observe patterns or trends in order to fit details together within the conceptual frame. Observations can be made through reading a book or article and engaging curiosity by asking, "What does this make you wonder?" or "What questions does this raise for you?" Also, real-world situations can afford opportunities for observations that pique curiosity. For example, for the **Immerse** phase of Guided Inquiry, a high school sociology teacher assigned students to learn about community by visiting a local diner and observing for one hour the interactions among people coming and going. Returning to class, the students focused on questions like, "What did you observe? What does it cause you to wonder about life in that community?" Observations can be recorded by asking students to keep a journal or to keep "field notes." Field trips, real or virtual, can be constructed as observation opportunities where the task for students is to return with questions—rather than results. If, for example, students study the governance of their city, they come to understand the laws that regulate their city—traffic laws, sanitation laws, noise ordinances. Once these observations are made, they can then begin to wonder how people's behavior is regulated in other communities around the world as well as their own as they develop an understanding of the meaning of the concept of the common good.

Essentially, the shift to concept- rather than content-based inquiry requires establishment of a *conceptual* focus. Concept-based inquiry invites students to learn how to organize information in logical abstract structures. Consider a typical history class studying World War II. Perhaps a topic to be investigated is the Japanese internment. What questions are students likely to ask to begin this investigation?

When were the Japanese interned? When were they released?

How many people were interned?

Where were they kept?

What were the conditions under which they lived?

This is useful information to engage students in the topic. However, once this background knowledge is developed, the inquiry task at hand is to generate an inquiry question on an issue related to this event in history. Here students will advance from *what, when, where* questions to *how, why,* or *what if* questions. These questions might be questions like, "How were the people removed to the internment locations?" or "Why were the Japanese Americans treated with suspicion?" or "What would have happened if the internment camps had continued beyond the war?" These are questions that still focus on the specific time and specific actions of this historic event. However, if students can be challenged to consider a conceptual lens to frame their inquiry, the inquiry can take on meaning beyond the specific event. For example, in this instance, students might be asked to investigate the Japanese internment through the conceptual lens of national security. Now, the inquiry questions are likely to become more abstract and more complex. Students might raise questions like, "How does a nation maintain its national security while also protecting citizens' rights?" or "Under what circumstances should a nation suspect its own immigrant populations for the sake of security?" or "What if today's Homeland Security Department chose to intern all Muslim Americans in response to the war on terror?" By incorporating this "big idea" of national security, students now are challenged to compare/contrast the World War II decision to intern citizens with situations in other times and determine relationships between times and events. They must now make judgments and speculate about possibilities that might not have arisen if their inquiry continued to include only the World War II experience. Clearly, they have advanced in complexity to application, analysis, and evaluation and beyond knowledge and comprehension.

Another example might be the typical report on countries in a region of the world. What questions will students ask?

What is the population?

What is the capital?

What does the flag look like?

What is the predominant religion?

What are the primary exports?

How many people are living in poverty?

What is the state of education in the country?

If we reframe that inquiry around the concept of economic development, their question might become, "What must this country do to become a strong global economy?" Students will still gather facts about education, poverty, and economic drivers, but now they must analyze those facts to determine what changes will be necessary to advance the economy of that country. Now, instead of gathering facts about the country, researchers are gathering facts and then applying their findings to propose solutions. They are gaining insight into the concept of economic development. Additional examples of the shift from content-oriented to concept-oriented investigations are shown in Figure 3.1.

Topic	Topical Questions		Concept	Conceptual Questions
Japanese internment	When were the Japanese interned? What provoked this internment? How long were they kept in internment camps? Were they the only people interned?	→	National security	How have nations attempted to ensure security? How does national security divide peoples within a nation? How does it unite them?
American Revolution	Who were the leaders? What battles were fought? What were the conditions under which the soldiers fought? What event(s) provoked the revolution?	→	Revolution	How does a government provoke revolutionary sentiment in its people? How are revolutions organized? How does a revolution bring about change?
Fuel	What is ethanol? Why do few cars use diesel? What do octane ratings mean?	→	Energy	How is fuel converted to energy? Why are some fuels better for the environment than others? How does a consumer decide what kind of fuel is best for his or her car?
Blood circulation	What is the function of the heart? How does the heart work? What are veins and what are arteries? How do they work?	→	Systems	What is the relationship between the heart and the lungs? Why do hearts fail?
Egyptian pyramids	What kinds of items have been found in the pyramids? How were mummies preserved? How were they transported to the pyramids? What did the ancient Egyptians believe about the afterlife?	→	Rituals	How do archaeological finds inform us about the beliefs of a culture? What do rituals tell us about a culture's values? How certain can we be about our understandings of ancient civilizations?

Figure 3.1 Moving from Topics to Concepts

Uncertainty

The shift from fact-finding to concept-based inquiry brings the risk of uncertainty. Often, there is a desire to know the answer to our query in advance—or at least to know that there is an answer. This risk inherent in uncertainty—or the anxiety it produces—often results in a preference for low-level questions that can be satisfied with factual answers (Harrison, 2004). Shifting inquiry in the direction of conceptual learning offers a vehicle for moving beyond low-level questioning to encourage students to posit ideas and speculation based on evidence they gain through their exploratory investigations. It is possible that students will arrive at questions for which they cannot find absolute answers, and both students and educators must be ready to accept that uncertainty and/or ambiguity. This is a powerful lesson in understanding that the outcome of inquiry may not be an answer, but rather another question.

An important factor when information seekers face uncertainty is the effect of time pressure. Nahl (2005) posited that time pressure can discourage and frustrate information seekers. A caveat, then, is to structure the time we schedule for inquiry so that we can encourage and nurture the perseverance that deeper inquiry demands. This may require that some aspects of the inquiry process be short-circuited. For example, the production of the final product may need to be simplified in order to shift the time to earlier phases (**Open, Immerse,** and **Explore** of Guided Inquiry) of the process; instead of an elaborate final product, a simple oral or written presentation of discoveries may allow for deeper investigation as students gather information. Or, perhaps some preselection of sources through a LibGuide or other method of bringing sources together for students may be a way to gain time within the gathering stage of investigation. Clearly, deeper investigation and conceptual questions will require time for information processing and reflecting.

Making the Transition to Concept-based Inquiry

The shift to concept-based inquiry is really a process of changing lenses. Instead of a focus on a particular event or person or item, the inquiry needs to be seen through the conceptual lens. For example, what was proposed as a report on a war becomes an inquiry into the significance of that war through a conceptual lens like power. What is the conversation between librarian and teacher to make this transition? It goes something like this:

Teacher: I would like to bring my students to the library to do some research.

Librarian: Excellent! What will they be researching?

Teacher: We have just finished a unit on the Civil War and I think it is important that we pause to consider the contributions that African Americans have made in our society. We have been pondering the question, "What difference did the slave trade make in American history?" So, part of the response to that question is to consider the contributions of descendants of slaves to American society. Each of them will be writing a report about a famous African American.

Librarian: That is interesting. Do I understand that they will be gathering information about an individual and writing up what they have found?

Teacher: Exactly. They will need to write a five-page paper introducing the person and his or her accomplishments.

Librarian: I wonder if there is a way to reframe their assignment so that they have to think a little deeper.

Teacher: Like how?

Librarian: Well, what if we take the concept of identity and ask students to describe the ways in which these individuals demonstrated ethnic or racial identity through their work. Might this require students to think at a more abstract and more complex level?

Teacher: That is an interesting idea. Slavery sought to repress identity, so this could be an interesting contrast to the lives of their ancestors. So, we say to students, "For the individual you are studying, as you examine the person's work, think about how that person exhibited, used, or exemplified his or her own ethnic or racial identity." We can talk in class about the concept of identity so that students have some attributes of the concept to guide their thinking. We can talk about how the history of a people defines them. I think this could be very interesting and actually connect even better to our class content. Thank you for this idea. We will start this investigation on Monday. OK?

Librarian: You bet! See you then!

High School Concepts from National Curricula

Each discipline has at its core concepts that help to organize the important understandings that constitute the field. When students engage in inquiry within a discipline using its concepts to frame their inquiry, they deepen their understanding of the discipline itself. While the following lists are not comprehensive, they provide examples of the concepts addressed in disciplinary national standards. Examining these standards may stimulate ideas for transitioning from topical to conceptual inquiry.

Next Generation Science Standards
(See http://ngss.nsta.org/AccessStandardsByTopic.aspx)

Structure
Ecosystems
Sustainability
Energy
Evolution
Force
Interaction
Systems
Stability and Change

National Curriculum Standards for Social Studies
(See http://www.socialstudies.org/standards)

Culture

Change

Identity

Bias

Stereotype

Common Good

Ritual

Assimilation

Interdependence

Scarcity

Conceptual Reframing

What is the effect of this reframing? Relevance for the student may be one benefit. Facts about a country may be helpful when one is preparing to travel there, but the concept of economic development can be transferred to other settings—even students' own state or city. They can begin to see the relevance of their inquiry work when it is framed around a concept that has potential for transfer to other settings, other times, or other problems. The concept of economic development is more interesting than gathering facts. Too often, we give students inauthentic exercises to gather known facts and report them. It is unsurprising that students find such exercises uninteresting and unimaginative. It is no wonder they seek the path of least effort to accomplish these tasks. It is no surprise that students complain of boredom in school. In the 2009 High School Survey of Student Engagement (HSSSE), two of three respondents reported being bored every day in class in high school (Yazzie-Mintz, 2010). In that survey, about one-third of students reported they were bored because the work was not challenging enough. Only 28% reported that their classes emphasized in-depth analysis. Yet, HSSSE data also indicated that students like to be intellectually challenged. A majority of the independent school students (71%) surveyed strongly agreed that they enjoy assignments that demand a lot of thinking and mental effort. Similarly, public high school students (58%) indicated liking this type of schoolwork (Torres, 2014). Learning in the library should present opportunities to enrich student learning activities to address concerns of interest and cognitive complexity, but these must be tasks that call for in-depth analysis—not merely gathering facts. Library learning experiences need to demand enough of students to be interesting, and then need to be accompanied by the supportive expertise of the school librarian. Because the students must integrate facts to arrive at implications for economic development, they have a more challenging task.

Another example might be the concept of ecosystem. Let's say that students begin their inquiry by studying the behavior of a migrating species. They might wonder where the species migrates to and from. When do they migrate? What prompts their migration? Now, if we impose the conceptual lens of ecosystem, students can begin to wonder about the effect of migrating species on an ecosystem and wonder, for example, "What if migrating geese stop migrating southward because of climate change and remain in more northerly habitats—how would their stay affect the geese? How would the change affect the new permanent habitat? How would it affect the place they used to travel to?" By exploring these questions, students are investigating the concept of an ecosystem and the interrelationships of its parts. This takes them beyond studying only the migratory species to a bigger idea. Moreover, their findings may inform them about other ecosystems and the relationships that exist within them and may help them understand how interventions can upset systems as well. These insights take student learning well beyond facts.

We can reframe low-level fact-finding into conceptual frames to raise the level of inquiry. The result will be tasks that pique curiosity and urge students to more analytical thinking. If high school students are indeed as bored as some studies suggest, then librarians working with teachers can engage students in learning that will be interesting, challenging, and relevant by shifting the frame to conceptual inquiry.

Note

Portions of this chapter were previously published in "Deep Learning through Concept-based Inquiry," by Jean Donham. *School Library Monthly*, Vol. XXVII, Number 1 (September–October 2010).

References

Erickson, H. L. (2008). *Stirring the Head, Heart, and Soul.* Corwin Press.

Gordon, C. (1999). "Students as Authentic Researchers: A New Prescription for the High School Research Assignment." *School Library Media Research 2.* American Library Association. Retrieved from http://www.ala.org/ala/mgrps/divs/aasl/aaslpubsandjournals/slmrb/slmrcontents/volume21999/vol2gordon.cfm

Harrison, P. (2004). "Unleashing Deep Learning Through Questioning." *Education in a Changing Environment Conference,* University of Safford, UK.

Kuhlthau, C., L. Maniotes, and A. Caspari. (2012). *Guided Inquiry Design: A Framework for Inquiry in Your School.* Santa Barbara, CA: Libraries Unlimited.

Loertscher, D., C. Koechlin, and S. Zwaan. (2005). *Ban Those Bird Units: 15 Models for Teaching and Learning in Information-rich and Technology-rich Environments.* Salt Lake City, UT: Hi Willow Press.

Nahl, D. (2005). "Affective Load." In *Theories of Information Behavior,* edited by Karen E. Fisher, Sanda Erdelez, and Lynne McKechnie, pp. 39-43. Medford, NJ: Information Today.

Taba, H. (1962). *Curriculum Development: Theory and Practice.* San Diego, CA: Harcourt, Brace, and World.

Torres, A. (2014, Spring). "Assessing Student Engagement: HSSSE Pilot Study with Independent Schools." *Independent School Magazine.* Retrieved from http://www.nais.org/Magazines -Newsletters/ISMagazine/Pages/Assessing-Student-Engagement.aspx

Yazzie-Mintz, E. (2010). *Charting the Path from Engagement to Achievement: A Report on the 2009 High School Survey of Student Engagement.* Bloomington, IN: Indiana University. Retrieved from http://ceep.indiana.edu/hssse/images/HSSSE_2010_Report.pdf

Using Inquiry Tools to Activate Reflection and Assess Student Learning

Anita Cellucci
with figures from Leslie Maniotes

At the high school level, educators must be ready to understand the challenges involving motivation for learning, diverse emotional competencies, as well as habits and attitudes that are already firmly in place when a student steps foot into the school. This understanding helps to create a solid foundation in order to guide students through the learning journey of Guided Inquiry Design®.

As illustrated in *Guided Inquiry: Learning in the 21st Century* (2015) by Kuhlthau, Maniotes, and Caspari, inquiry provides a way of teaching and learning that benefits all students because an inquiry approach develops skills that are essential for college and career as well as personal growth. The basis of the approach allows students to learn how to learn and is most effective when a Learning Team works together to develop an inquiry unit. The students are then presented with meaningful content in an authentic way that connects students to their world (p. 7). The library teacher proves integral to this learning while embedding information literacy and technology skills throughout the process.

Throughout the Guided Inquiry Design process, Inquiry Tools help to guide students through their research as well as present a platform for assessment by educators. Teachers are able to check in with students and view where students currently are in the critical thinking process. The tools work to engage students in the process, and at the same time, they offer a window into student thinking and engagement and allow the Learning Team to facilitate learning. Within this context, teachers are able to remain flexible about student learning of the process and content. Students of all abilities are able to participate and become knowledgeable about their topic while digging through the research at their individual pace. The Inquiry Tools and integrated technology provide a vehicle for students to become experts within their own learning. We have found that a collaborative teaching approach including the content teacher, library teacher, and technology integration specialist through Guided Inquiry Design increases the depth of learning through research in contrast to typical compilation-based projects that tend to give shallow results.

The specific Inquiry Tools are the following: Inquiry Community for collaboration, Inquiry Circle for conversing, Inquiry Journal for composing, Inquiry Log for choosing, Inquiry Charts for charting understanding and decision making, as well as the use of inquiry technology tools for learning (Kuhlthau, Maniotes, and Caspari, 2015). Information literacy is embedded throughout the process with the use of the tools, technology, and instruction. Integrated technology includes the use of TRAILS (Tool for Real-time Assessment of Information Literacy Skills), the

NoodleTools research platform, Google Classroom or Edmodo for classroom management, and LibGuides or research guides.

A Guided Inquiry designed unit has the essential elements for learning and requires collaboration within a Learning Team to provide the best learning environment possible for the students. Guided Inquiry can look differently depending on the discipline, teacher, and students involved. Inquiry is a fluid process. This should be considered when planning with the Learning Team. Flexibility is of utmost importance when reflecting on the learning outcomes as well as planning for future units. A unit may be, and in most cases is, different each year. For our teams the use of tools has evolved over several years to support student learning and has grown with our use of the available technology to support our management of all these moving parts.

Inquiry Community

The Inquiry Community for collaboration is an essential component for the learning process in Guided Inquiry. Students quickly discover, with routine and clear instruction, that their peers and the Learning Team are their community for learning. In the instances when more than one class is meeting in the library during the same block, students are in a community of learners with different skill sets, learning styles, and learning levels. The teachers in this community also become co-teachers, and in the case of the physical science inquiry grade nine unit (see Chapter 7), science teachers are effectively teaching information literacy skills to their students as well. Teachers have had the opportunity to learn the skills by observing the modeling of the librarian during whole group instruction. Over time they become comfortable with viewing the library as a true learning lab or learning commons (Loertscher and Koechlin, 2012).

An Inquiry Community is a vibrant space where all members feel able to show their growth openly as well as share their process and ideas around content that support their learning. Creating this type of space is one of the goals of our library. Allowing for differences in the way students learn, what and when they are learning, and when they are learning is part of planting this seed to grow an Inquiry Community. Inquiry Community in Guided Inquiry Design is important to the process and is an Inquiry Tool for collaborating for learning. There are some effective ways of infusing community into the process for students.

One way to create a community of learners is to have the classes who are working on the same assignment sign up for library time together. Teachers can co-teach the same lessons, allowing students to benefit from different teaching styles. Classes of all levels can be together to learn the process as it is naturally differentiated. Students benefit from hearing directions and instruction in more than one style. When setting up the classes in this way, the librarian can work with more than one class at a time. This atmosphere creates the tone of a team. Students can have inquiry conversations with more than one teacher and students, as well as observe how other students are working through their inquiry research.

The library space is also set up to create a community of learners. In our library three classes can fit in the space at the same time with division of the library shelves. One section has a large wall where anchor charts, posters, and the lists of the student inquiry questions are hung for all students to view. One team member used sketch notes to create anchor charts of the Guided Inquiry Design process (see Figure 4.1). We also created charts that listed the inquiry questions from every member of our Inquiry Community and posted them for all to see the variety of perspectives and ideas represented (see Figure 4.2).

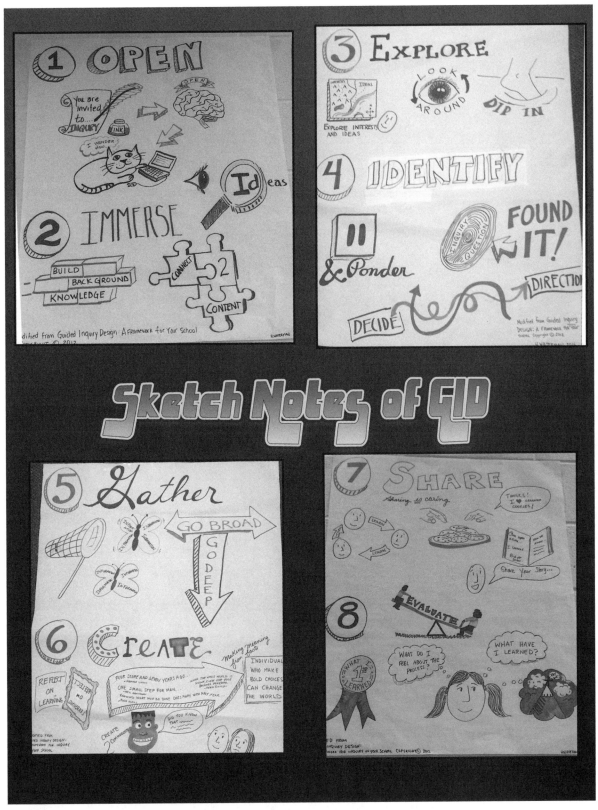

Figure 4.1 Anchor Charts

Figure 4.2 Questions in the Inquiry Community

Inquiry Journal—Reflecting throughout the Process

As the act of reflecting is an integral part of the Guided Inquiry Design process. Allowing time for students to reflect on their learning gives the space necessary for students to think, ask questions, and ultimately synthesize their information and understanding of the content within the inquiry research. Many times in education, students are not given this time to reflect. Teachers are also unfamiliar with viewing reflection as a valid learning process. Accepting reflection as a valid assessment and strategy may be a needed shift in the community philosophy. Collaboration plays a subtle role in shifting the perception for reflection. When a collaborative team has trust, it is easier to infuse the reflection aspects into the projects as the educators engage in collegial discourse throughout project planning and implementing.

When working with students of all levels, it is important to instruct on the art of reflecting. This can be done through whole group instruction, handouts, assignments, short conferences, and written feedback. As students gain experience and receive feedback, they become adept at reflecting on their learning and the Guided Inquiry process. It is often observed that the reflection process allows students to connect with their personal reasons, or Third Space, for learning about their topic within the inquiry question (Kuhlthau, Maniotes, and Caspari, 2015). This connection is often the motivator to sustain students through the process.

Students are asked to reflect daily and immediate feedback is offered in a variety of ways (see Figure 4.3). Teachers and the librarian offer feedback to students on their reflections. One way to keep track of all of the reflections is through Google Classroom. Within Google Classroom, an assignment entitled *Inquiry Journal* is created and students upload their Google Doc to this assignment. This can be completed in one assignment or in a daily assignment, depending on teacher preference. There are times when it's important to have students handwrite the reflection and meet with the teacher and/or librarian during the next class. This strategy may be used for a student who has been struggling with keeping up with assignments, using the Inquiry Tools, or a variety of other issues. Students will then receive face-to-face feedback as well as just in time instruction for a skill that they may be still grasping. NoodleTools is another way for teachers to assess student reflection on resources. The "My Ideas" section can be used to jot down connections or for synthesizing information and allowing students to reflect on their learning about the content (see Figure 4.4).

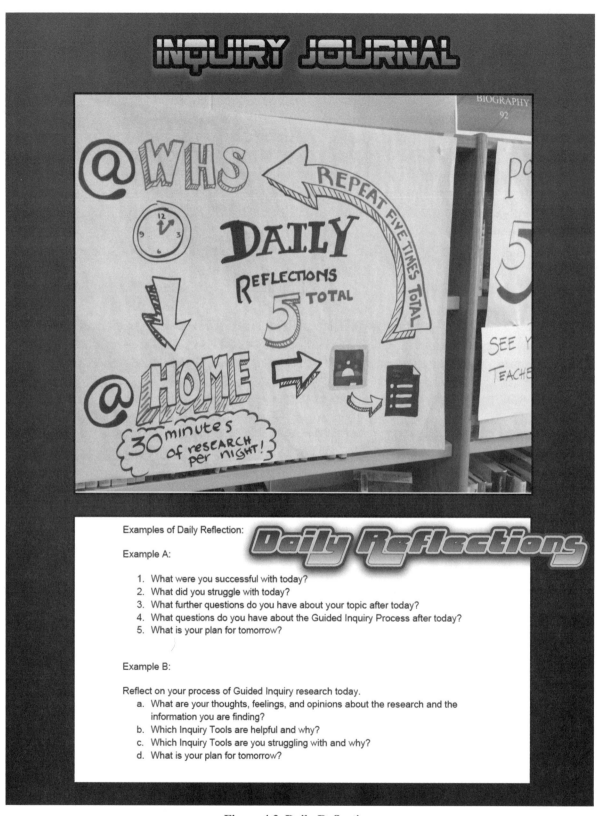

Figure 4.3 Daily Reflection

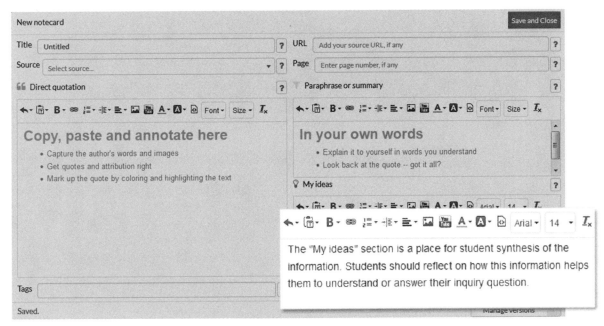

Figure 4.4 My Ideas in NoodleTools
© NoodleTools, Inc. http://my.noodletools.com

Inquiry Log

The Inquiry Log serves to keep students organized with the many resources they are using as well as a way to make a note of why the resource may be useful to them in their research. Students are asked to enter every source that they look at in their Inquiry Log. By entering every source, students are able to review sources later in their research. Reviewing resources at various points during the process helps students to determine when a source may be valuable to them as their topic knowledge increases. The students keep track of the sources they have been using for their background research in the Inquiry Log and can easily transfer the most meaningful ones into NoodleTools.

During the **Explore** phase, the students use the Stop and Jot strategy to capture ideas alongside the log (Kuhlthau, Maniotes, and Caspari, 2012). They use the Stop and Jot strategy in **Gather** as well, as they begin to gather notes on their question (see Figure 4.5). The log is made available to students in digital format as well as print. Because we are also a Google for Education school, students are able to save articles from the databases directly into their Google Drive and can make a note of this on their Inquiry Log as well. Students comment that the log is a helpful tool for organization and thinking through whether a source is useful or not.

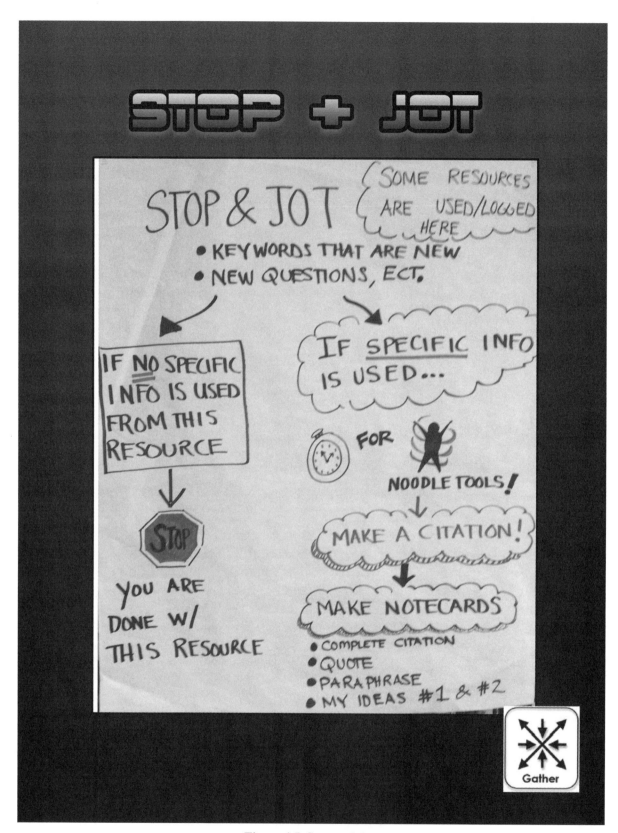

Figure 4.5 Stop and Jot

Inquiry Charts

Inquiry Charts are also helpful for students to facilitate the thinking process throughout inquiry research. Anchor charts are used within the Inquiry Community as continuous reminders of the Guided Inquiry Design process, the Inquiry Tools, and resources. Inquiry Charts provide a vehicle for scaffolding learning for students and quick assessment measures for teachers while students are engaged in the process. For example, as students are preparing for Inquiry Circles or conferring with a teacher, their Inquiry Charts provide a review of the phases as well as struggles and successes that the students have encountered for the students and teacher.

Together, Inquiry Tools support students' thinking process necessary in choosing and creating inquiry questions to allow students to gain clarity on their topic of choice. In the **Identify** phase Inquiry Circles meet with the librarian to develop their individual inquiry questions. Students are given a model of what a good inquiry question looks like and then are able to work through the process of generating their own questions with the assistance of their Inquiry Community (their peers and teachers) to solidify their question. Students use the *Chart to Decide Protocol* to help them to think critically about their interests and to choose a question that is important to them. (See Figure 4.6.) In some instances, the chart is modified for students to think about their topic ideas, how to narrow their topic, what is interesting about their topic, and also to reflect on their background knowledge search that has already been completed. They can ask questions such as: What is my background research telling me? What interesting things have come out of my background searching? How does this help me to narrow my topic?

Inquiry Circles

At the high school level, Inquiry Circles are a powerful means to continue building the Inquiry Community. Inquiry Circles offer a way to add a social component to engage students in their own learning. Conversations demonstrate that other students are following their personal interests as well. The versatility of using Inquiry Circles in many ways is helpful as a teaching strategy. Students come together to help each other through challenge in the research as well as to normalize the feelings that are often associated with struggle in the **Explore** phase (Kuhlthau, 2004).

Preparing students to participate in an Inquiry Circle can also take many forms. Often, when teachers need a "temperature gauge" of the students in the room, it is helpful to quickly meet in Inquiry Circles, focusing the conversation only on the struggles and how the students were able to overcome them. This type of Inquiry Circle needs very little preparation as students typically are able to talk about the challenging aspects of their projects on the spot. This also helps teachers to determine what type of help the students may need next and if it will be a whole group activity or a one-on-one interaction. This can be done in small groups of 3 or 4 or slightly larger, depending on the size of the class. The teacher can walk around facilitating and observing while noting which students may need a check-in later.

Other times there is more preparation before the Inquiry Circles. For homework, nightly reflection in the Inquiry Journal is a helpful strategy that keeps students focused on the information

Identify Chart to Decide

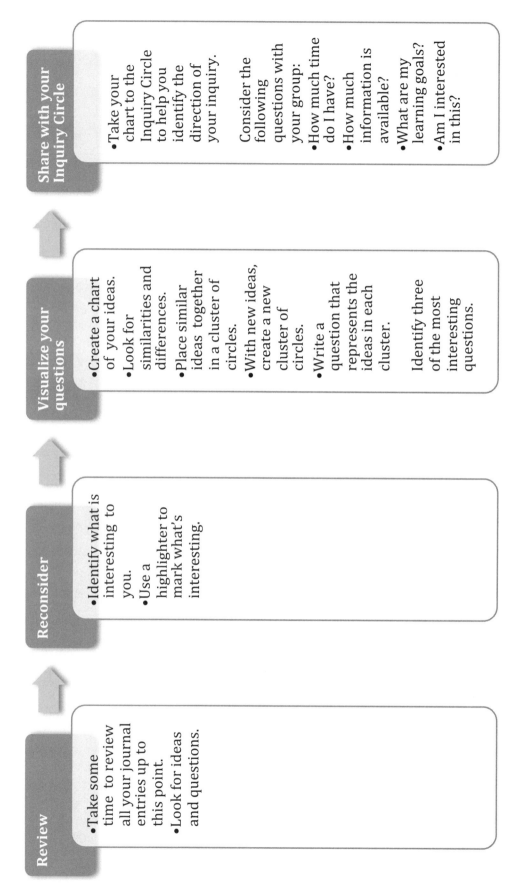

Review
- Take some time to review all your journal entries up to this point.
- Look for ideas and questions.

Reconsider
- Identify what is interesting to you.
- Use a highlighter to mark what's interesting.

Visualize your questions
- Create a chart of your ideas.
- Look for similarities and differences.
- Place similar ideas together in a cluster of circles.
- With new ideas, create a new cluster of circles.
- Write a question that represents the ideas in each cluster.

  Identify three of the most interesting questions.

Share with your Inquiry Circle
- Take your chart to the Inquiry Circle to help you identify the direction of your inquiry.

  Consider the following questions with your group:
- How much time do I have?
- How much information is available?
- What are my learning goals?
- Am I interested in this?

Guided Inquiry Design: A Framework for Inquiry in Your School (2012) by Carol C. Kuhlthau, Leslie K. Maniotes & Ann K. Caspari, Santa Barbara, CA: Libraries Unlimited, Copyright © 2012.

Figure 4.6 Chart to Decide Protocol

that they are finding as well as keeping them embedded in the specific vocabulary of their topic. Daily reflections are a positive way to help students prepare for Inquiry Circles, as well. Often, a handout or reflection form helps students to synthesize the information they are finding and hone their ability to talk about their topic, research struggles, research successes, and prepare for the group conversation. (See Figure 4.7.) This handout allows students to have a guide through the Inquiry Circle but also gives them a place to make notes within an Inquiry Circle if they notice a positive strategy that a classmate is using or a teacher mentions. The Inquiry Circle time becomes a forum for sharing ideas, asking questions, and creating motivation and excitement about the research.

In one unit, Inquiry Circles even began with the **Open** phase. Here the **Open** took place in the science classroom where the content teachers provided an invitation to inquiry—opening students' minds through curiosity about the content. For **Immerse** the teachers provided provoking background knowledge on the topic in the form of text sets including articles, podcasts, and videos. Students then had the opportunity to reflect on these resources and the information provided. (See Figure 4.8.) An opportunity to share in Inquiry Circles deepened their thinking and offered multiple perspectives on the ideas presented. So, Inquiry Circles can be woven through any phase of Guided Inquiry as a means to get students talking about ideas together.

Managing the Learning—Tools for the Learning Team

As students progress through their research, the Learning Team is available for individual conferences to guide student learning or for just in time instruction. Students learn that any member of the Learning Team can assist in their learning due to the easy access to all their work in Google Classroom and NoodleTools.

Google Classroom

Managing 220 high school students in an entire grade moving through an inquiry at one time can be a logistical headache. At our school, we found that Google Classroom is a major support to our Learning Teams as we work with large groups of students through the Guided Inquiry process. We use it to provide students with resources, to give teachers access to student work, and to monitor progress and guide student learning along the way. For example, text sets are provided to the students through a classroom management tool, in this case, Google Classroom. Students are able to reflect on their learning within the Inquiry Journal online.

When a Guided Inquiry unit is designed with an entire grade as we did, a Google Classroom facilitates easy access for all teachers to all student work through the inquiry. Google Classroom is a digital learning management system that provides all teachers equal access to student journals to track engagement and progress. This allows each member of the Learning Team to see all student work and to offer support when necessary. All assignments and Inquiry Tools are made available to students in the Google Classroom. Students turn in their assignments through the use of their Google Drive and teachers grade students' entries. Throughout the process, all teachers troubleshoot with student conferences.

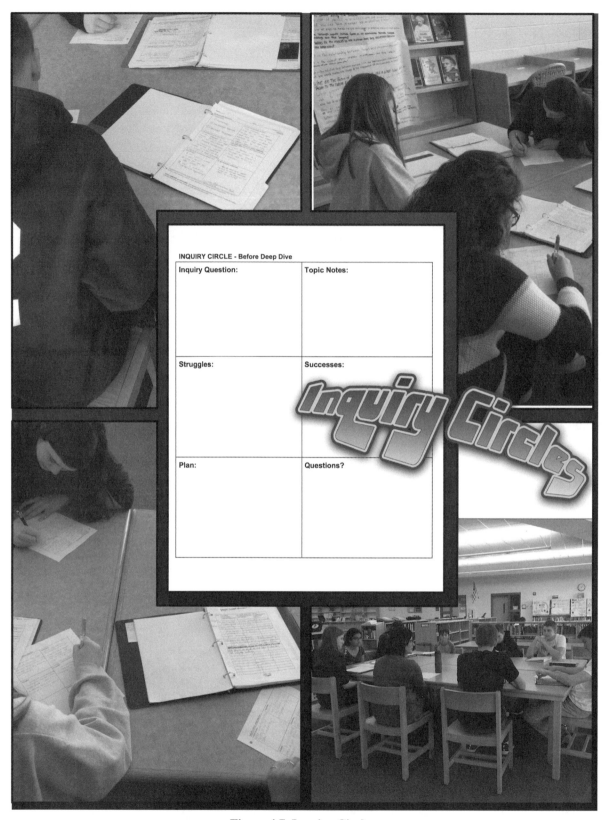

Figure 4.7 Inquiry Circles

Immerse

Build background knowledge

Connect to content

Discover interesting ideas

Reflection

			Immerse

Name: _____ Date: _____ Period: _____

REFLECTION

Identify 3 topics that REALLY INTEREST you.	Identify what you ALREADY KNOW about these topics: your prior knowledge.	What *more* would you like to know about these topics?	Write at least 3 questions per topic based on what you would like to know.
1.			1. 2. 3.
2			1. 2. 3.
3			1. 2. 3.

(If you need more space, continue on the back of this page, but clearly label your topics!)

STUDENT PAGE

Figure 4.8 Reflection from Immerse Inquiry Circle

In conjunction with the asynchronous space of Google Classroom, the library serves as a physical help space after school. We work as a team to support students in every way through the process. The content area teachers rotate through a schedule to be available to students in the library along with the school librarian and the tech integration specialist.   -

Google Classroom (or another learning management system) is essential in assessing the learning. For us, Google Classroom allowed for a contained asynchronous space for all students to turn in classwork, homework, and other assignments that related to the process and also provided a collaborative space for the Learning Team. All teachers in the Learning Team had access to all students and their assignments. Students were able to access all links, assignments, and instructions in one place. This is essential for students to stay organized and also essential for teacher organization for data, evidence, and grading as well as planning future lessons.

NoodleTools

NoodleTools is an integrated technology tool that can be used to help students reflect on sources in the **Explore** phase and manage their research and resources for the **Gather** phase. In **Gather** our students not only use NoodleTools to create a citation for their works cited, but also to take notes on notecards (see Figure 4.9). The notecards in NoodleTools are divided into three sections that allow the students to systematically organize the information from their resources. In part one of the card, students can add direct text from their resource. Directly next to this section is the summary section that allows students to write about the information in their own words. The third section is the "My Ideas" section. The students are instructed to use this section for their inquiry synthesis. They are asked to think about questions such as: *How does this*

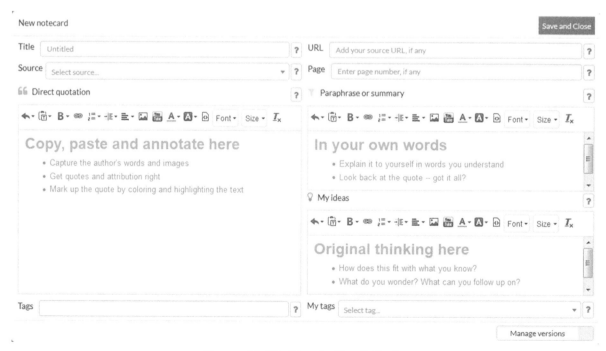

Figure 4.9 My Ideas in NoodleTools
© NoodleTools, Inc. http://my.noodletools.com

information help me to answer my inquiry question? Why is this information important to my inquiry question? How does this information help me to understand the content?

By using notecards in NoodleTools in a very intentional way, teachers are able to assess student learning throughout the process and examine students' use of resources in their research. What's more, students synthesize the information that they have located while creating the "My Ideas" section that is used during their **Create** and **Share** phases. Each notecard is linked to a citation and the citation is linked to the source. This allows the teacher to easily view individual student sources throughout the inquiry process. Teachers can then confer with students as necessary to help further students' understanding of their topic and inquiry.

NoodleTools used as a collaborative assessment tool is helpful to the Learning Team as all students share their work with the team. Teachers can view the student citations, notecards, and "My Ideas" sections as students are synthesizing their resources. Students are able to view the direct text in direct alignment with their own summarizing and paraphrasing of the resource, which allows them to think about the direct text in relation to their inquiry question. Using the "My Ideas" section is a self-assessment of how well students are close reading their resources and if they are checking for understanding of the content.

At our school, students in grade nine take part in one inquiry unit each semester. The first semester is more structured and heavy with instruction about the tools and process. Google Classroom is the management space for the students to identify their focus. The librarian also uses the LibGuide to instruct students to use search strategies; tips, tools, and suggestions for databases; and keyword creation. Students learn the strategy of how to record their keywords and how to show growth in their learning through the use of keywords. (See Figure 4.10.)

Inquiry Tools are extremely important throughout the Guided Inquiry Design process. Students are most likely using all of the tools provided by the **Gather** phase. This can be overwhelming for some students. For our incoming ninth-grade students, we frontload learning about tools in use. These steps taken at the beginning of the process are essential to creating the foundation for students to be able to own their individual learning process through this and subsequent units. This is how students will learn how they learn. The tools are helpful for students to visualize their learning and also helpful for teachers to provide the data and evidence of the learning.

Inquiry Tools as Evidence of Student Learning

Assessment in inquiry can be looked at comprehensively through the use of all the Inquiry Tools. These tools offer ways to view student growth in quantitative and qualitative measurements. TRAILS offers a quantitative measurement of information literacy, and the use of Google Classroom or Edmodo, as well as NoodleTools, offers a way to measure qualitatively. Both types of measurement enable teachers to gather a full understanding of student learning.

TRAILS (Tool for Real-time Assessment of Information Literacy Skills) is a useful pre- and postassessment of information literacy skills that we use with all freshman students and senior students. Our goal is to have all ninth graders leaving ninth grade with a solid understanding of the available tools for research and information needs as well as foundational skills in ethical use of information. Students should be able to inquire, think critically, and make meaning from digital and print resources. By using the TRAILS assessment, the Learning Team is provided with a baseline of information literacy skills of the incoming ninth-grade students. The students

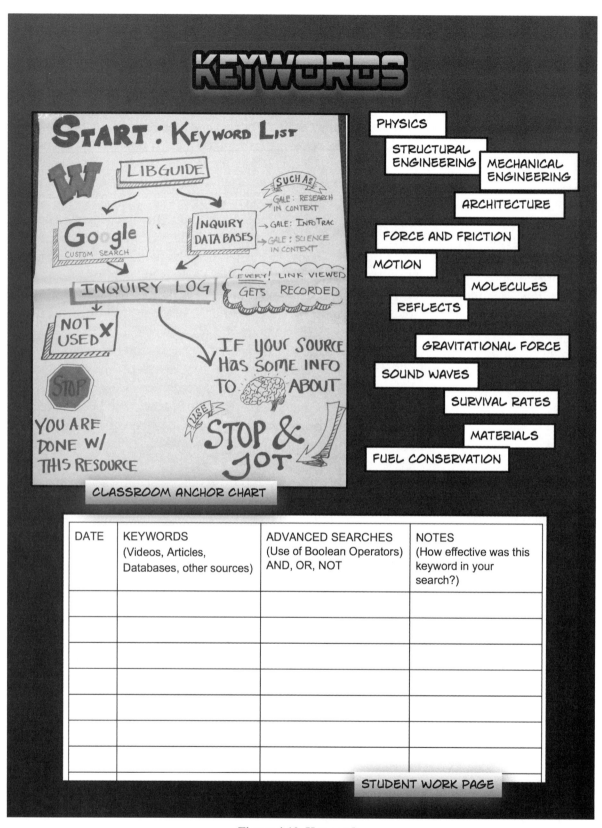

Figure 4.10 Keywords

also use this data to know which information skills they do not yet solidly understand, so they can do some personal goal setting.

Using Inquiry Tools to assist in assessment and to motivate students for learning allows the Learning Team to effectively evaluate each learner and his or her level of engagement with the research and content. Students are motivated to learn each day as they dig deeper into their interest and as they tap into deeper levels of intrinsic motivation. Student choice in the focus of their research through the creation of inquiry questions about content, and through the Guided Inquiry process, ensures that students effectively become confident with information literacy, content, and learning how to learn. The result of using Guided Inquiry as a whole including the embedded tools with a Learning Team ensures a dynamic library learning space and a collaborative learning environment for teachers and students alike.

References

Kuhlthau, C. (2004). *Seeking Meaning.* Santa Barbara, CA: Libraries Unlimited.

Kuhlthau, C., L. Maniotes, and A. Caspari. (2012). *Guided Inquiry Design: A Framework for Inquiry in Your School.* Santa Barbara, CA: Libraries Unlimited.

Kuhlthau, C., L. Maniotes, and A. Caspari. (2015). *Guided Inquiry: Learning in the 21st Century* (2nd ed.). Santa Barbara, CA: Libraries Unlimited.

Loertscher, D. V., and C. Koechlin. (2012). "Theory and Research as the Foundational Elements of a Learning Commons." *TeacherLibrarian, 39*(3), 48–51.

Maniotes, L. K., L. Harrington, and P. Lambusta. (2015). *Guided Inquiry Design in Action: Middle School.* Santa Barbara, CA: Libraries Unlimited.

McKenzie, J., and H. B. Davis. (1986). "Filling the Toolbox: Classroom Strategies to Engender Student Questioning." Retrieved February 20, 2016, from FNO: From Now On website: http://questioning.org/

Emotions in the Inquiry Process

Carol Collier Kuhlthau

Most high school students consider inquiry learning to be solely an intellectual process. They expect simply to investigate a question and report on what they find without feeling anxious or frustrated or even excited. They assume that all they need to do is take some action toward getting information and give it a little thought. It turns out that inquiry learning is a much more complex and holistic process that engages emotions as well as thoughts and actions in profound and dynamic ways. High school students, in particular, are affected by their emotions in inquiry learning, which can be daunting if misunderstood. Feeling confused and uncertain can seem as if something is wrong rather than being an integral part of the learning process.

What Research Tells Us About Emotions

My research on students' experience in the process of learning from a variety of sources of information provides insight into the changes in students' emotions during the inquiry process. These studies showed that no matter how well students were oriented to the library and to the relevant resources or how capable they seemed, there was a common emotional pattern when they pursued an extended research project. Students became increasingly confused and uncertain in the early stages of research. Their confusion was found to increase with more information rather than steadily decreasing, as one might expect. Students reported feeling uncertain and anxious until they formed a focused research question or central theme, somewhere around midpoint in their inquiry. After forming their focus, students reported an emotional shift to feeling more confident and less anxious. They also had increased engagement and interest (Kuhlthau, 2004).

George Kelly's Personal Construct Theory (Kelly, 1963) offers some clues as to what this is about. Kelly explains the experience of constructing meaning from new information in this way. Information is assimilated in a series of phases, beginning with confusion. Confusion increases as inconsistencies and incompatibilities are confronted between new information and the constructs the person already holds. Confusion mounts, frequently causing increasing doubt. The disruption caused by new ideas may become so threatening that the information is discarded and the task of constructing new meaning is abandoned as the person falls back on more familiar

41

ground. At this point, Kelly proposes an alternative that moves the process of construction along. The person instead may form a "tentative hypothesis" to move toward incorporating new constructs into an existing system of personally held constructs.

I found that when high school students are engaged in extensive inquiry projects, they do indeed experience the process of construction described by Kelly. If we think of inquiry learning as involving students in constructing their own deep understanding, we can expect them to experience an emotional process. Without guidance, they can misinterpret their confusion in the early stages as something going wrong rather than a natural part of the learning process. They can become impatient and frustrated with their inability to move on quickly. At this point they often expressed annoyance at the assignment, the resources, and themselves. They assumed that they were "procrastinating" rather than needing time to work through the new, often conflicting and disconnected information to form a focus or, according to Kelly, a "tentative hypothesis" to move toward incorporating new constructs into their personal construct system.

My research revealed that when students' information seeking requires extensive construction for learning, they experience similar changes in their feelings as they strive to accomplish their task. As their thoughts shift from vague to clearer, their feelings change from anxious to confident. These are the stages of learning from a variety of sources of information that are described in the model of the Information Search Process (ISP). Guided Inquiry is designed to help students learn by supporting them emotionally and intellectually throughout the process of inquiry learning (Kuhlthau, Maniotes, and Caspari, 2015).

Information Search Process and Guided Inquiry's Response

The Information Search Process (ISP) describes six stages in the process of constructing deep understanding and learning from a variety of sources. One of my data collection methods is a timeline on which students describe their thoughts, feelings, and actions at several points during an inquiry project. The timeline has been applied to the ISP model to capture the sense of process over a period of time and to display the three layers of experience in each stage of the process. The stages are named for the main task to be undertaken to move on to the next stage: **Initiation, Selection, Exploration, Formulation, Collection,** and **Presentation** (Kuhlthau, 2004). In the first three stages students are preparing to form a focus. Formulation is the turning point of the process when students formulate a focus or theme for their work. In the last two stages students are building their understanding of their focused question. **Assessment** is a time of reflection that follows the close of the ISP. (See Chapter 2 for the ISP and Guided Inquiry Design® framework.)

The next sections of this chapter describe students' emotional experience in each stage in the ISP with a brief explanation of the comparable phase in Guided Inquiry Design that supports students through their learning process. Guided Inquiry is designed to respond to students' need for the help indicated by the ISP studies. Guided Inquiry Design is a framework for supporting students' emotional as well as intellectual processes by providing strategic actions for each phase of learning (Kuhlthau, Maniotes, and Caspari, 2012). The icons for each phase represent the task to be undertaken to move along in the inquiry process. The next sections discuss students' emotions in preparing to form an inquiry question, formulating an inquiry question, and building deep learning.

Preparing for an Inquiry Question

The first three stages of the ISP describe students' emotions at the beginning when they are preparing to form an inquiry question. The first stage is **Initiation** when the teacher first announces a research assignment. Most students reported that they immediately felt uncertain and apprehensive. One student explained, "When I first hear about an assignment, personally I just get upset." Another described feeling "a spontaneous kind of fear." This was found to be a common experience among students. "In the real beginning I guess I was like everyone else. I didn't know what I wanted to do. . . . I felt anxious" (Kuhlthau, 2004, p. 38).

Guided Inquiry Design responds to these feelings in the **Open** phase with an invitation to inquiry. Rather than announcing the research assignment, the teacher opens with something to open minds and stimulate curiosity. A picture, object, or short video might be used to capture attention and get students thinking about what is going on here. The opening is brief, dwelling on ideas rather than the detailed requirements of the assignment. The whole class engages in the opening together as an Inquiry Community.

The second ISP stage is **Selection** when students select a topic. Once a general topic is selected, they begin to feel less anxious and are ready to get started with the investigation. Students described feeling optimistic when they can get the project going. "Once I have my topic I usually feel a great deal better and the idea of a research paper doesn't seem so cumbersome." However, if a topic is not chosen quickly, students explained that their apprehension increases. "I felt anxious when I didn't have a topic. I was upset because even though I knew that the paper was due a long way off, everybody else seemed to be working and I wasn't" (Kuhlthau, 2004, p. 39). At this point many students didn't know enough about the area of study to select a topic for their research and certainly not enough to settle on a clear research question.

Guided Inquiry Design provides an **Immerse** phase at this point that is designed to build sufficient background knowledge and make connections to the content so that each student can discover interesting ideas to pursue. These studies show that this is not a time to leave students on their own. An experience, such as a visit to a field site, a presentation by an expert, extensive discussion with the teacher, reading a lively account, or some combination of these immerses and orients the class to the content of the unit of study. Each student is guided through the **Immerse** phase to find interesting ideas and preliminary questions to begin the investigation.

The third ISP stage is **Exploration** when students investigate information on their topic to gain a focus. For many students this was the most difficult stage of the process. As they began to find information on their topics, they frequently became confused by the inconsistency and incompatibility they encountered, which is the reaction Kelly's theory of construction predicts as a natural phase of learning. The following comments describe typical feelings during this stage. A student described feeling "so confused up until the 25th, I had no idea what direction I was going in." Another recalled, "I felt kind of blind because I didn't know what I was looking for." A third described feeling increasingly anxious: "It seemed there was so much to do, it really scared me" (Kuhlthau, 2004, p. 39). They frequently used the negative term "procrastination" to describe their sense of inaction during these early stages. Their difficulty was compounded by attempting to move along too quickly to collect information and complete the assignment without giving enough time and attention to forming a central focus or question.

For some students the confusion became so threatening that they wanted to drop their topic altogether. "I went to look for a total change because I was really sick of it. . . . I had trouble with it. . . . I didn't want to do it anymore" (Kuhlthau, 2004, p. 39). The inclination to turn back and to abandon the quest at this point is also a common reaction, according to the constructivist theory of learning. This stage is characterized by feelings of confusion, uncertainty, and doubt, which frequently increase during this time. Information rarely fits smoothly with previously held constructs, and information from different sources seems inconsistent and incompatible. Students may find the situation quite discouraging and even threatening, causing a sense of personal inadequacy as well as frustration.

The Guided Inquiry Design phase of **Explore** is a critical time in inquiry learning when students' emotions can lead them astray. The ISP shows that as they begin to investigate their interests, they can become overwhelmed with all of the information and confused by ideas that don't fit together. Guided Inquiry is designed to help them understand and manage their emotional reactions. Purposeful guidance helps students to slow down and give themselves time to think about new facts and ideas. They learn strategies for working through an overwhelming amount of confusing information. They are guided to explore interesting ideas by browsing to look around to get a sense of what is out there. They learn that dipping into a few sources that seem relevant helps to prepare them to formulate a clear inquiry question to pursue. In this phase, although they may be investigating on their own, they are organized in Inquiry Circles to try out their ideas and clarify their thinking. Guided Inquiry Design provides students with a range of strategies for these early phases of inquiry learning that incorporate using Inquiry Circles, Inquiry Journals, and Inquiry Logs. They are not left on their own to muddle through what can be unnecessarily discouraging and frustrating. However, they will need to learn that constructing deep understanding takes time, patience, and persistence.

Forming an Inquiry Question

Forming a focused theme or question is the central, pivotal task of the ISP that prompts a change in students' emotions. **Formulation** is the fourth stage when a focus is formed that gives direction to the search. Students feel more confidence once they have formed a clear focus for their research. "I felt relieved. It makes things a lot easier once you have a basis for where you are going" (Kuhlthau, 2004, p. 39). This was the turning point of the search process for those students who formed a clearly focused theme or question from the information they had explored. With their increased sense of clarity and purpose, their feelings of confusion and uncertainty began to diminish.

However, when students did not form a focus at this point in the search process, they experienced difficulty throughout the remainder of the project. One student elaborated on the difficulty that she had experienced. "I had a general idea not a specific focus, but an idea. As I was writing, I didn't know what my focus was. My teacher says she doesn't know what my focus was. I don't think I ever acquired a focus. It was an impossible paper to write. I would just sit there and say, 'I'm stuck.' . . . If I learned anything from that paper it is, you have to have a focus. You have to have something to center on. You can't just have a topic. You should have an idea when you start. I had a topic but I didn't know what to do with it. I figured that when I did my research it would focus in. But I didn't let it. I kept saying, this is interesting and this is interesting and I'll just 'smush' it all together. . . . It didn't work out" (Kuhlthau, 2004, p. 40). This student was well intentioned but needed help in working through this stage of the search process.

Many high school students do not find a focus for their research. They just copy some information on a topic without much thinking or learning and consider their work done. Today's technology has made it easy to take a "copy and paste" approach that results in little real learning.

Although teachers are troubled by this "plagiarism," the way an assignment is presented may be at fault as much as the student's intent and the capability of technology. Students need to understand that their pivotal task at this point is to form a clearly focused question to pursue their own deep learning.

The first three phases of Guided Inquiry Design, **Open, Immerse** and **Explore,** have prepared students for **Identify** when they formulate their inquiry question. Some may still feel confused and realize that they are not quite ready to form a focused question. Their sense of confusion may indicate a need to explore further. At this midpoint in the inquiry process, it is important to stop and not move forward until they have their inquiry question. Kelly refers to forming a "tentative hypothesis" to move toward incorporating new information into one's existing system of personally held constructs. Their inquiry question need not be thought to be "written in stone." However, this is the time to pause to reflect on what they have already learned, to decide on the direction they want to pursue, and to articulate that decision as an inquiry question. The question may be somewhat tentative and perhaps may change as they gather more information, but identifying a clear question is essential at this point.

Identify is the central phase when students pause and ponder to identify a clearly focused inquiry question. They stop to consider what they have already learned and decide on the direction of their inquiry. An Inquiry Chart is a strategy for organizing their ideas to visualize possible ways to take their inquiry. Guided Inquiry is designed to make students aware of the changes in their emotions throughout the phases of inquiry learning and to recognize that they can expect their emotions to change to being more positive in the next phases of constructing deep learning.

Understanding an Inquiry Question

The last three stages of the ISP describe students' emotions when they are gaining deeper understanding of their question and getting ready to present their learning. The fifth stage is **Collection** when information is gathered on the focused research question. Students describe a sense of direction and rising feelings of confidence. As one student explained, "On the 9th I got my main focus. Before this, I did basic research. After I got my focus, I got all my sources to support the focus I had found." Another described, "After you know exactly what you are going to do it on, the research is easy." Many reported that their interest increased at this stage. As one student noted, "I sat down . . . and became totally interested in what I was reading." Another student added, "I didn't find this boring. I have senioritis and really didn't feel like doing it but it was interesting what I found." The topic becomes more personalized at this stage and feelings of confidence increase as uncertainty subsides and interest in the project deepens. "I was very excited about the topic. When I had a hard time finding information I didn't want to change it. There was nothing else I wanted to do. It turned out to be a really fun paper to write. I got some pictures and sketches. I had to get materials on interlibrary loan" (Kuhlthau, 2004, p. 40).

The Guided Inquiry Design phase of **Gather** is a time for gathering important information to address the inquiry question. It is the time to concentrate on information that specifically addresses their focused question. Unrelated interesting ideas may be noted and set aside for a future project. Now they will need to keep focused on the work at hand. Students develop strategies to "go broad" to find a wide range of sources of information for learning about their question. They also are guided to choose a core of what they consider the most useful sources and to "go deep" to make meaningful connections and gain personal understanding. Inquiry Journals are used to make thoughtful notes from their sources with detailed citations recorded in their Inquiry Logs. Emotions continue to be important for tracking the progress of their learning. They may hit some rough patches, but they should feel much more comfortable and engaged in their work. As students choose what is personally meaningful and compelling about their inquiry question in their information sources, they should feel an increasing sense of purpose and interest. Getting into the flow of ideas is what you are aiming for in Guided Inquiry Design.

The last ISP stage is **Presentation** at the conclusion of the search process and the "starting phase" of the writing process. Students experienced a sense of satisfaction if the search had gone well or disappointment if it hadn't. They were found to have different reasons for closing a search. Some ended when they encountered diminishing relevance. "You get what you want and then afterward start getting off the topic a little." Another consideration is redundancy or encountering information that you have already collected. "In the end you are just looking for extra things so you're sure you have everything. But it's a lot of repetition." Others concluded when they felt they had put forth sufficient effort. "After digging and digging . . . I said this is good enough. I've done a good enough job. The material I've gotten is sufficient" (Kuhlthau, 2004, p. 40). At this point students become very aware of time constraints and the necessity of closing the search as they near the date the assignment is due. Time was an important consideration throughout the search process but became a predominant factor in the later stages. Students often miscalculated the amount of time needed to accomplish their work in each stage of the process and underestimated the time required. Some felt quite anxious about the stress to finish in time.

Two phases of Guided Inquiry Design, **Create** and **Share,** are designed to guide students through the work of preparing and presenting their inquiry learning. In **Create** students reflect on what they have learned, go beyond the facts they have gathered to make meaning, and create a way to communicate their learning. Analyzing and synthesizing what they have gathered is not an easy task. All students will benefit from guidance at this point, some more than others. An Inquiry Chart is a useful tool for synthesizing what they have recorded in their Inquiry Journals. Organizing the many facts and ideas that they have gathered into an Inquiry Chart prepares them to create a meaningful, well-thought-out presentation for sharing. Students who have formed a focused direction in the **Identify** phase rarely feel frustrated and "stuck" at this point. **Create** incorporates two related tasks: one is to create a synthesis of what they have learned about their inquiry question, and the other is to create a way to share their learning in a meaningful, engaging way. Pulling things together should be exciting and engaging. They should feel pleased that they now have insights that they want to share. Creating an interesting way to share their learning at first may seem daunting, but once they get some ideas about how that sharing might look, their creativity builds confidence and competence.

In the **Share** phase students share what they have learned about their inquiry question and learn from one another. They should be considered experts on their question for the other students in their Inquiry Community. Many students feel intimidated and fearful about presenting their work before classmates. They need guidance to help develop a way to communicate their ideas in an interesting, informative way. A sense of pride in their accomplishment increases when they can tell their story well. Students' inquiry products will need to demonstrate what they have learned about their inquiry question in a way that benefits the whole Inquiry Community. This is the culminating phase of the inquiry process when personal engagement in productive and worthwhile learning is most evident. A sense of ownership in their ideas and pride in their work is what you are aiming for in Guided Inquiry Design.

Assessing and Evaluating the Learning

Assessment is a time for reflection at the close of the ISP after the project is completed. As students reflected on their search process, they often were surprised to discover phases in their learning. One student explained, "Well I guess there are three phases. . . . I never realized I did this. . . . I never realized that I did all the work in three phases. I just thought I did all of the work the last minute and did my report" (Kuhlthau, 2004, p. 51). Students reflected on what had taken place during the process and their expectations of the next time they encounter a similar task revealed their new sense of process.

At this point some students felt they had done something important and wanted to share what they had learned more broadly. A student explained the commitment she felt to her work in this way. "I didn't want to just put it in a drawer and forget about it. I wanted to show it to someone who could do something . . . send it to the Governor" (Kuhlthau, 2004, p 50). The impact of inquiry learning was evident in longitudinal studies of these same students after college. Many students built on questions in their college work that they had raised in high school, some even leading to specialization and careers, as in the case of one student quoted here who became a lawyer.

Although **Assessment** is ongoing throughout the phases of inquiry learning in Guided Inquiry Design, the **Evaluate** phase is essential at the close of every inquiry unit. This is the time to evaluate the achievement of learning goals by reflecting on both content and process. As students reflected on the entire process they had experienced, they began to become aware of the difference in their emotions between the **Explore** and **Gather** phases and the role **Identify** plays in moving from one phase to the other. A check on their feelings about the project at this point gives an indication of the depth of their learning. Do they feel a sense of accomplishment in what they have learned? Do they feel disappointed in how it turned out? Carefully reviewing their content learning helps students to become aware of how well they have achieved their learning goal and how they feel about it.

Emotions Indicate Zones of Intervention

Emotions indicate Zones of Intervention in inquiry learning for the Learning Team. A Zone of Intervention is that area in which a student can do with advice and assistance what he or she cannot do alone or can do only with great difficulty (Kuhlthau, 2004, p. 129). By tracking students' emotions, you can tell when they are in particular need of guidance. An important Zone of Intervention is in **Explore** when feelings of uncertainty and confusion can lead students to think something is going wrong. However, there is a Zone of Intervention in each phase of inquiry learning.

The Guided Inquiry Design framework is built on an understanding of emotions in the process of learning that indicates the kind of guidance required in each phase of inquiry. The icons represent the main learning task of each phase, and the shape of the model depicts the flow of emotions that students experience as they seek to accomplish each task. Students begin inquiry in **Open** and **Immerse** with moderate confidence and initial interest. The dip in confidence in the **Explore** phase is often unexpected by students. They will need help and support to work through the overwhelming and often confusing facts to purposefully **Identify** a focused inquiry question. Once they have formed their inquiry question, feelings of interest and confidence increase in **Gather, Create,** and **Share**.

Studies found that students who experienced this sequence of changes in feelings in the ISP were constructing their own understanding and deep learning. Students that merely cut and pasted information did not experience the stages in the ISP and did not achieve deep learning. Guided Inquiry is designed around Zones of Intervention for each phase of inquiry learning that leads to deep understanding.

Inquiry Tools for Strategic Guidance

The ISP studies gave some hints as to what strategies might help students construct their own understandings in a complex inquiry project. There were certain strategies that helped students construct understandings that they applied to some extent throughout the process. Students talked to each other about what they were thinking about. Trying to articulate their ideas seemed to help clarify their thinking. They worked alongside each other sometimes, sharing sources that they thought others might find useful. All students were required to keep journals noting sources they were using, interesting facts they were finding, questions they were raising, and ideas they were developing. As the inquiry progressed, their entries in the journals changed from noting interesting facts to detailed notebooks for gathering information about their inquiry question. They had to choose what sources to use and find a way to keep track of their sources. Some students used a chart or outline to organize their ideas and decide what was most important, what could be left out, what was the central idea, how to begin, and how to conclude.

These strategies were reported as the 6 Cs of construction: collaborate, converse, compose, choose, chart, and continue (Kuhlthau, 2004, pp. 134–141). In Guided Inquiry Design these construction strategies are applied in inquiry tools: Inquiry Community, Inquiry Circles, Inquiry Journals, Inquiry Logs, and Inquiry Charts (Kuhlthau, Maniotes, and Caspari, 2012). These inquiry tools are systematically employed for learning throughout the inquiry process.

Gradual Release of Responsibility for College and Career

Schools organized around inquiry learning prepare students for an adult life of work, citizenship, and personal living. By secondary school, students are ready to employ the full inquiry process with a gradual release of responsibility. As they become aware of their emotions in the process of learning, they become more comfortable, confident, and in control of their own learning. As one college student explained, "I used to be very anxious. But now I know how to go about it. I don't get upset anymore. I know it will take x amount of time to do the research, to narrow down my topic and to begin writing. I know how I work" (Kuhlthau, 2004, p. 77). Inquiry is hard work but well worth the effort. It involves not merely narrowing a topic but formulating a topic. The participants in these studies referred to this as forming an angle or strategy, a perspective or point of view, something that someone else might not have thought of in this way, a new way of looking at something (Kuhlthau, 2004, p. 81). As we have seen, this is driven by a well-formulated inquiry question that is identified somewhere toward the middle of the inquiry process.

As students mature and take on more complex inquiry tasks, they may experience the cycle of this process repeatedly in one project. In higher education students confront new ways of thinking about a written argument, combining theories and multiple disciplinary perspectives with their own insights. An academic librarian reports, "The ISP model precisely describes what I see, except that, of course, in college there needs to be several iterations of the exploration/formulation/collection trio. I try to explain that anxiety should/will lessen with each spiral toward insight, but they rarely believe me" (Kuhlthau, Maniotes, and Caspari, 2015, p. 93). Guided Inquiry Design prepares high school students to take on the challenges of the academic work of college.

As one college student reflected, "I had more exposure to research papers than most high school students. I had a lot of friends in college who were panicked at doing a research paper. . . . By working with you I learned not to panic if it doesn't fall in together the first day. . . . I'll worry about a paper because things don't fall into place but it's not the kind of thing I loose [*sic*] sleep over. I've learned to accept that this is the way it works. Tomorrow I'll read this over and some parts will fall into place and some still won't. If not, I'll talk to the professor. The mind doesn't take everything and put it into order automatically and that's it. Understanding that is the biggest help" (Kuhlthau, 2004, p. 132).

Many of the college students studied revealed a commitment to their inquiry projects as they became more engaged in learning in this way. An economics major explained that he chose topics that "weren't even on the list of one hundred possible topics that the professor gave out. Those were ideas that I had in the back of my mind that I had researched to a lesser degree and had touched on in other classes. Both dealt with the economic development of Mexico. Actually one was a continuation of the other" (Kuhlthau, 2004, p. 77).

Studies of students as they moved into their careers revealed the importance of inquiry learning for success in the expansive information workplace. A case study subject acknowledged, "I do research papers for a living." This type of learning was found to have lasting meaning and impact on their lives. One participant described feeling uncertain in preparing extensive reports that involved a dynamic change in his thinking. But he now expected to feel unsure and somewhat confused in the beginning phases and recognized that these were the projects in which he learned the most. He referred to these as "the really good ones that you loose [*sic*] sleep over." These projects took an extended period of time. "Those are the ones that are really time consuming because you are changing your entire thinking. . . . You feel anxiety because you are changing your whole view of the world. . . . So you wonder is this right? Is this wrong? Is this going to work out? Is this not going to work out? Am I going against the grain here?" He went on to explain that some projects take him into "new territory" and that it is "very unsettling to have to move out of your element and ramp up on something entirely new" (Kuhlthau, 2004, p. 168). He also lamented that this process is rarely taught. "Many courses in writing for business don't address the issue of the thought process and the emotional process that one goes through in getting out a research paper or getting out written material or getting out a report and how to deal with it" (Kuhlthau, 2004, p. 173). Guided Inquiry Design prepares high school students for career success by extensive experience in the thought process and emotional process of inquiry, which opens up their own way of learning.

Dynamic Deep Learning for Life

Using the Guided Inquiry Design framework assures that students are guided and supported through the emotional as well as the intellectual phases of the inquiry process revealed in the ISP studies. Forming a well-thought-through inquiry question involves an intellectual and emotional struggle that is an essential component of deep learning. If students are not forming their own inquiry questions, it is not true inquiry learning and certainly not Guided Inquiry. The inquiry question is formed in the middle of the inquiry process. Carefully designed guidance through the first three phases of Guided Inquiry Design, **Open, Immerse,** and **Explore,** prepares students to **Identify** a well-formulated inquiry question.

We have seen that this is an emotional process as well as an intellectual one. Along with the students, you may feel impatient to push the process along. It is all too easy to fall back into old practices of pressuring students to "pick" a question too early or actually giving them a question. We need to respect the mystery of the human ability to learn and to have a strong sense of responsibility and privilege in guiding students in pursuit of their own understanding. It is inspiring to observe emotions lift through the **Gather, Create,** and **Share** phases of Guided Inquiry Design as students experience dynamic, deep learning.

Inquiry learning prepares students for all aspects of the technological information culture of the postindustrial era. Understanding the emotional process as well as the intellectual process enables students to acquire inquiry as their personal way of learning. Guided Inquiry Design provides a framework for designing learning that prepares all students for dynamic deep learning for life.

References

Kelly, G. (1963). *A Theory of Personality: The Psychology of Personal Constructs.* New York: Norton.

Kuhlthau, C. (2004). *Seeking Meaning: A Process Approach to Library and Information Services.* 2nd ed. Westport, CT: Libraries Unlimited.

Kuhlthau, C., L. Maniotes, and A. Caspari. (2012). *Guided Inquiry Design: A Framework for Inquiry in Your School.* Santa Barbara, CA: Libraries Unlimited.

Kuhlthau, C., L. Maniotes, and A. Caspari. (2015). *Guided Inquiry: Learning in the 21st Century.* 2nd ed. Santa Barbara, CA: Libraries Unlimited.

Meeting Students Where They Are Through In-Depth Conferences

6

Heather Hersey

In-depth conferences allow us to meet students where they are. As a result, they involve a lot of deep questioning and investigating on the librarian's end—like a doctor's visit—to determine where a student is not only in terms of skill and process but also in terms of feelings (see Chapter 5 for more information about student emotions during the inquiry process). In my current school, we do conferences that are embedded in the history curriculum, most specifically in the sophomore year when students are working on their Model United Nations project and often during junior year when students are working on that year's National History Day theme. This chapter follows the process that my colleagues and I have developed over the years as we practiced the art of conferring and collaborated with colleagues to improve our craft. It walks through how to set up conferences for success, the process throughout the meeting with the students, and the reflection process after the meeting is over.

For papers with very open topics, we will usually have feedback from the teacher regarding the direction that the students are proposing; however, we also add a preconference requirement as a means of getting to know where students are prior to the meeting. This can be collected through many mechanisms, including a Google survey or on paper. Currently, we use a preconference email. The preconference email gives us a sense of where students are in many ways, so we can better prepare for their visit. It's like the paperwork you have to do prior to meeting with your doctor the first time. Through carefully worded questions, we can learn much about students' actions until now, their thoughts, and their feelings. Because this is not a series of conferences like those teachers often hold in the classroom, the preconference email is vital, putting more focus on our need to get as much information before the conference and our question-asking during it. My initial preconference prompts were these:

- Tell me about your topic, including how it has developed/changed since you wrote your proposal.
- Then tell me a bit about the information you have found so far, which sources have been most helpful, and what types of information you still need to look for or have been unable to find.

Our current preconference requirements are similar, but they are written as questions, which seem to work better since they are a more direct request for information. The information

51

sought in the second bullet point above is also parsed out in separate questions so students can focus better on what we're asking. Each question serves a different purpose, of course, and may vary depending upon the topic and grade level.

Preconference Email: Four Questions

Question One

The first question is usually a probe about their topic. Since the librarians prepare beforehand by doing some presearching, we need to know what the student's topic is, and we need to know what their understanding of it is. For our Model United Nations (MUN) research with our sophomores, the initial question is "What is your country, committee, and issue?" For our junior classes participating in National History Day (NHD), it is slightly different and contains two parts: "What is your research topic?" and "How does your topic relate to the National History Day (NHD) theme of _____?" If teachers are giving students the option of not doing the theme, the second part of the question would also ask if they plan to use the current NHD theme.

Narrowing Topics During Research Conferences

Most of the answers to this first question are pretty standard for the MUN project; however, this question is especially important for broad inquiries like that of NHD. While some students come to us with a clearly focused inquiry, other students still need help narrowing their topics to something interesting and manageable. Seeing answers like these ahead of time gives me the opportunity to investigate the topic a bit and be able to walk students through a few strategies for narrowing a topic while also asking questions to make sure their interests are represented in the final outcome.

Librarians are in a unique position: they may not be content-area experts, which helps them approach information tasks in a similar way as students who are novices in the subject; however, librarians are experts in the Information Search Process—curious-by-nature questioners who can follow trails of information in a genuine way. They can help students learn how to use their prior knowledge and sources to initiate and later focus a topic. As research has shown, this is one of the most difficult parts of the research process (Kuhlthau, 2004).

For example, during the **Immerse** phase, a student had settled on writing about states' rights. When we first began talking during his conference, he didn't realize that he would need to narrow his topic and wasn't sure how to hone in on something interesting and manageable, a common point of intervention in the **Explore** phase. Many history teachers, with those beautiful, encyclopedic brains of theirs, could rattle off lots of possible topics for him. As a librarian and former English teacher, I couldn't. Instead, I explained to him that using a reference article is a great way to get a handle on a topic. After I showed him an article about states' rights, he saw for himself the depth and breadth of the topic and how many subtopics and time periods were within it. As a result, he made the decision to narrow it down. Afterwards, we talked a bit about what aspect of states' rights interested him the most. For example, was there a certain time period or topic that he would like to learn more about? Though he had no certain time period, he was really interested in economics. Since the focus of the essay was rights and responsibilities, we used a states' rights article in *West's Encyclopedia of American Law* to search for the term "economics." Using CTRL+F, we found a few options, including his favorite, "The Commerce Clause." The student learned an excellent technique for connecting the assignment to his interests while narrowing down his topic to a manageable size.

Question Two

The second question is always "Where are you in your research process?" This is such an important question because it allows us to meet them where they are, and it enables us to check their understanding of the research process. As I mentioned previously, we meet with students over a three- to four-week period. While this is not ideal because some students will not meet with us at the best time for them, it is what we can do given the number of students. As a result, some answers to this question are "I've barely started gathering resources" or "I don't even have a single notecard." To make this even more specific, during our current round of conferences, we have included descriptions of each phase, so they have to think through where they are, where they have been, and where they are going. We hope that adding these descriptions and having them name the phase will improve our understanding and theirs.

For many students, the answer to this question becomes an important opportunity to discuss the assignment itself. Although I have never done an official count, the number of students who have not read through the assignment or looked at the project calendar always surprises me; however, in the Guided Inquiry Design® process, this is normal since the focus in the early stages is on wondering, questioning, and connecting the assignment to topics of interest (Kuhlthau, Maniotes, and Caspari, 2012). Many of the answers to this question prompt me to ask, "Have you read your assignment sheet yet?" which leads to the opportunity to discuss the goals of the assignment and the timeline. When students are ready to **Identify**, becoming more familiar with the specifics of the assignment is timely and relevant at this point and works to move students into future phases. These specifics will help them decide their direction. This discussion also sets most students at ease because they see how scaffolded the process is and get a better understanding of the assignment.

Using Inquiry Charts During a Conference

Initially, I thought the conferences would be all about sources and search strategies, but as I do more of them, I see that some students need to learn how to approach the assignment. As discussed by other researchers, conferences are excellent places to work on mental models and habits of mind. During the conference, I make sure to do several think-alouds, and one of the most frequent ones is to review the assignment itself. For example, my colleague, Sue Belcher, devised a graphic for discussing the goal of the NHD topic of turning points.

This simple graphic (Inquiry Chart), found in Figure 6.1, helped students to actually see what they were working toward as well as the structure of their paper. After gaining their initial background context, it helped them to decide what was important—what they should take notes on. For example, many students are overwhelmed by the amount of information available. Using this graphic, we can ask students if a piece of information helps their reader to understand any of the following: (1) what led up to the turning point, (2) what happened immediately after, or (3) what was the ripple effect of the event later. If it doesn't fit one of these aspects, they likely won't need it. We want students to think about what they *need* instead of just what they happen

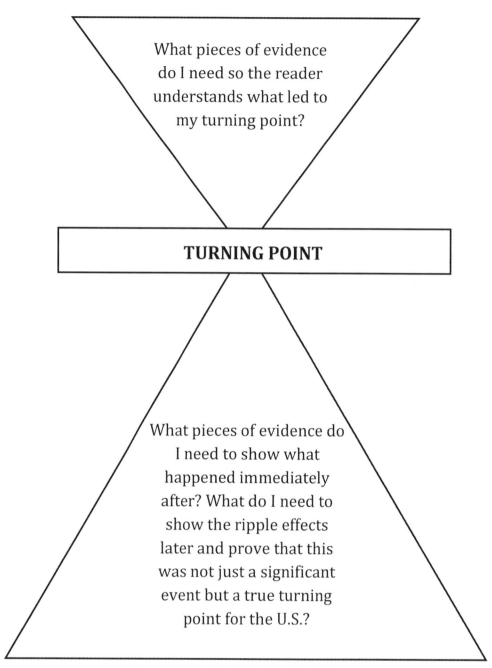

Figure 6.1 Turning Point Inquiry Chart

to find. Students need to hear messages like this so they can better control the amount of information they have. Also, if we are having a discussion like this, it lets me know whether or not the student has enough background information. If students can't answer questions of this nature, it usually indicates that they are in an earlier phase than they assumed. I am then able to bring our discussion back to the **Immerse** phase to help them continue to build the knowledge necessary for answering these questions.

The Guided Inquiry process encourages the use of Inquiry Charts, similar to the one developed by my colleague above, "to help students visualize ideas, issues, questions, conflicts, and connections that emerge during the inquiry process" (Kuhlthau, Maniotes, and Caspari, 2012, p. 46). These charts can take any form and should arise naturally from the goals of the assignment. For example, I devised a similar way to chart the goals of the Model UN project. Since each student is on a particular United Nations committee and is studying a country and an issue, I chose to use a Venn diagram because students need knowledge of each "circle" prior to being able to overlap them. They also need overlaps of just two circles at a time in order to be successful. This could be an overwhelming project, but seeing this diagram usually sets students at ease because they can see where they are headed, how they will use the information, and that they don't need to know "everything" about their country, committee, or issue. For students who really didn't understand the project, which includes a paper and a full day of "UN meetings" within their committees, this provides a visual guide map for not only gathering but also using information. Lastly, I discuss with them how helpful it is to use charts like these for other projects as they read through assignments, and that if they ever need help talking it through, they only need to ask.

Question Three

Question three is generally "Where are the gaps in your research?" We want students to do work ahead of time. I still have a tendency to procrastinate myself, but a question like this pushes me to at least start something. This is a difficult question early in the process; as some students say, "my gaps are everything." Later in the process, the gaps become more specific. If they aren't, this gives us an indication that students might be behind a bit. For the sophomore MUN project, students are given specific prompts found within their assignment sheet, such as "finding connections between data/issue/country" or "finding sources published in your country." The junior class working on the NHD project is not given prompts. The question is left open due to the unrestricted nature of the project and the greater sophistication of the students.

Modeling an Inquiry Stance

The fact that we are asking about gaps really models to the students the inquiry stance we would like them to have. A lack of thoughtful answers here might indicate being behind, but when it's combined with definitive language in their other answers, it might be a sign that a student is entering the inquiry with a closed mind. For some students their answers to these questions are full of questions, but others may already have statements that resemble a thesis. We'd prefer students to use questions or say "I'd like to investigate . . . explore . . . or look into." When I read definitive statements like, "I will prove . . . argue against . . . or argue for," I check in with these students to make sure they are doing a true inquiry and not proving what they think they know. This is a point where referring to the Information Search Process or Guided Inquiry process can be helpful to remind students that they are currently in an early stage. By asking them to keep in mind what expert researchers do, we hope to focus their efforts on an open inquiry and true learning.

Question Four

We always ask students, "What would you specifically like to focus on during our research conference?" These answers can range from precise needs like "finding primary sources" or "finding data on my country" to larger needs like "figuring out exactly what I'm doing." We make sure not to phrase it as what would you like to find or what do you need, because then this becomes only a question of sources, and that is not what the conferences are for.

Moving Beyond Location

Focusing on charts that synthesize and organize information isn't the only way that these conferences move beyond locating sources. Students often have tunnel vision when it comes to research, so we model approaches to various research skills that students may not traditionally take. We may focus on strategies for narrowing topics, why you would use different types of sources, or connecting ideas to their interests. These conferences are also becoming ways to teach basic skills that a student might not necessarily apply when researching. For example, when students are at the beginning of their Model UN project, we show them a variety of resources, including the database *Country Watch*. While working with a student, I breezily said, "So you can just skim the article since it's really long at over 500 pages." Quietly she said, "But how do I skim it?" I had never thought about how much students compartmentalize what they do in school. Skills that they learn in one class may not be applied in other classes unless we tell them explicitly to do so. If she hadn't asked me this question, her prior knowledge of skimming, a skill that she knew from other history assignments, would have been wasted, and I wouldn't have been able to show her another skimming technique that was helpful for this article (and future ones). I asked what she already knew about skimming, and she told me about the idea of reading the first sentence of each paragraph, not very helpful in a 500-page document. I shared with her something that I had been doing automatically as an experienced researcher—scanning for capitalized or italicized words since they indicated importance to the topic. I'm so glad she felt comfortable enough to ask her question about skimming, but not all students are. As a result, I am hoping to incorporate this as a whole-class activity in our instruction for next year.

Conference Strategies for Best Practice

Building Rapport

One of the most difficult parts of the conference is starting. I'm nervous; they're nervous and likely under other deadlines, so my first course of action is to put them at ease. Opening is easy if I already know the students; I start by asking them about something other than research. School play, sports, previous research projects . . . I use anything to make a connection to the student that doesn't jump directly into the current project. For students I don't know well, a simple "Hey, how's it going?" is enough to set the tone and open up a conversation that can be about the project or not. The opening will be different for everyone. You have to decide what works for you when setting a comfortable atmosphere. Regardless, the most important thing is to be yourself.

Ways to Listen

Though the answers in the preconference email give me a lot of information, I try not to cut off any other avenues that might come out during the conference, helping me to keep and model an inquiry stance, too. To that end, I will often begin by paraphrasing their answers to the questions, so they know I have processed them and they can correct any misperceptions. I also ask if there is anything else they would like to add to the information in their preconference email. Then I use the same technique that I use in shorter conferences—beginning with an open-ended prompt that elicits a starting point. Paraphrasing and asking an open-ended question usually gives us plenty of talking points and places to begin. Depending upon what the student needs and how big the list of needs is, we may have to do some prioritizing as well. This is also an excellent time to dig into any emotions that might present themselves.

Emotions During Research

As mentioned previously, the conference allows us to see how students are feeling as well as what they are doing and thinking. Gauging the emotions of students is very difficult to do during full-class instruction, though I have attempted to do so with a raising of hands or an anonymous exit ticket or survey. After introducing students to the roller coaster that is research by showing them the emotions they experience throughout the Information Search Process and Guided Inquiry Design, conferring with students is one of the best ways to discover how they are feeling.

To that end, I keep a copy of the Information Search Process (or Guided Inquiry Design framework) by my side during conferences. Students will have been introduced to it already during full-class instruction, but it bears repeating in conferences so they can see confusion and frustration as a normal part of the learning process. I even jokingly mention that the couch in our office is always open for research therapy. One of the most powerful ideas for some of my students is hearing that Kuhlthau's (2004) research was not limited to students. To hear that people who make a living doing research go through the same process seems to be comforting and enlightening at the same time. I acknowledge to students that inquiry has become less uncomfortable for me as I have grown as a researcher, or maybe that I just enjoy the discomfort now. Knowing that this roller coaster of emotions is normal and not based simply on being students or novice researchers can provide motivation and help them push through difficulty since they now know it is simply part of the process. (See also Kuhlthau's Chapter 5 in this text on emotions in inquiry.)

Don't Be a Superhero

I have to admit that sometimes I get caught up in being a "source superhero" instead of ensuring that the conferences are as much about skills and strategies that can transfer to other projects. Particularly when a conference doesn't seem to be going well, I become too focused on speedily providing cool sources and content because, you know, I've found some pretty awesome stuff while presearching. Instead I use this presearching to model various ways to meet each student's needs. The tension between giving students great sources for a project and providing them with skills and strategies is a dilemma we will always have, especially with our time-stretched teens. As a result, I have to constantly remind myself to make sure students do the majority of the searching, to keep my question-asking stance, and to be explicit about the skills and strategies we are learning, not just the current research task.

Just Have Them Do It

When I first started doing extended conferences, I focused on sources and mostly on how good I was at finding them. I was new at my school and wanted students and their teachers to like me. Did students come away with some great sources and maybe a couple new tricks? You betcha! Would they be able to replicate what I had done? Were they aware of the skills and habits of mind I was using? Not likely. As a result, I now make sure that each student brings his or her laptop to the conference, opens it up, and works with me. One of my favorite results of this change is that we can do two different searches and compare the results, which is much more powerful than simply seeing me do it. In fact, I have even stopped sharing all of the source links that we find and instead opt to save a screenshot of the search we did to find it. If we find a seminal source, we will often add it directly to NoodleTools or I will send the link; however, it serves our students much better to, as the saying goes, teach them how to fish.

Questioning

I make sure to ask students what they have tried already so I don't repeat what they have done. It validates their prior knowledge and keeps the tone of collaboration in the conference. Referring back to the student with follow-up questions also keeps the collaborative nature of the conference in sight while developing skills and habits of mind for future inquiry projects. During conferences, it is especially difficult to know when to answer a question and when to put it back on the student. Likewise, I struggle with when to pose a question instead of just giving students a direction. Michael W. Smith, one of my professors, always cautioned against playing "guess what's in my head?" with students because it leads to frustration and you wind up giving the answer anyway. Instead, I try to ask broad questions, or if I do ask something more specific, I provide a few options as answers from which students can choose. Furthermore, when asked a question, instead of parroting it back to the student, which can sound off-putting, a simple rephrasing can do the trick. If a student asks, "How do I find primary sources?", try to rephrase it to emphasize your curiosity about their process.

For example, when we work with sophomores and juniors, we know that prior curricular requirements have necessitated a search for primary sources, so I might ask, "What have you tried with prior projects that worked to find primary sources?" If this is a different type of project (for example, the Model United Nations assignment differs significantly from the historical investigations that students do in freshman year), ask students whether the same would work for this project, and if not, why. Though this conversation will ultimately lead me to giving the students a few places to start looking (during the conference, of course), by choosing not to immediately answer the question, I am preparing the student for future inquiry projects. This section must end with a word of caution, however. During conferences, my main stance is one of questioning, but there are times when students, and even teachers, just need an answer, not to be taught how to find it, and we must be sensitive to those times.

Be Explicit

In the example above and in most cases of encouraging collaboration and critical thinking, we need to be explicit with the students about what we are doing, like wrapping up the conversation with "Next time you need primary sources, you'll be able to consider how the type of project affects where you search." If we don't, students may not see the conference as a learning opportunity and instead view it as a way to get some sources or, even worse, just one more process hurdle to jump through. This focus on the learning of skills and habits of mind is something that I have worked on throughout my years of doing conferences, and it is one of the most difficult parts for me to keep in focus, particularly for students who are struggling. I simply want to help get them back on track, but I have to remember that our purpose is twofold. Being explicit is important in our expectations, too. Figure 6.2 is a snippet of the current version of the email we send to all students. Being explicit in our expectations is so important, especially if conferencing is not something that the student has done before.

To Grade or Not? That Was the Question

Talk of expectations usually leads to assessment and grades. Initially, we had considered using a rubric. Students are aware that attending the conference, as well as sending the pre-conference and postconference emails, is part of their process grade, but we wanted to make sure that our expectations were clear and that students were taking the conferences seriously, so we began working on a rubric. However, one of my colleagues, Julie Nanavati, made a clear and compelling case against using it. She went back to our survey data from last year and showed how much of our focus was on making students comfortable and building rapport. We are often asked questions that students are reluctant to ask their teachers because we are not grading them. Also, if students felt that they were being assessed on their performance, questions that might be seen as weak or representing a lack of knowledge (like the young woman who asked how to skim) would likely go unasked. So we decided to be intentional about assessing during conferences, and all of our feedback is formative; the only penalty given is for not showing up. On the whole, we were concerned that a rubric would send the wrong message and build up a wall that would prevent a successful conference, so instead of using a rubric, we used the "advanced level" in the "rock star researcher" criteria found in the email to students in Figure 6.2.

Late-Stage and Follow-Up Conferences

Though we try to catch students during the **Explore** phase prior to their creating a focus, we have to spread out our conferences, so some of them occur later in the process. Similarly, we often have students requesting follow-up conferences. Librarian conferences are quite helpful later in the process as students begin to fill in gaps in their research and restructure arguments after receiving feedback from their teachers. For instance, a junior student was told in her feedback that she would have to do some extensive research to make her idea work. In its current form, her paper was not delivering what was promised in the introduction, which was an analysis

Setting Clear, Explicit Expectations

What you can expect from me:

- An Outlook meeting request for the time that you signed up for.
- An email reminder for that meeting.
- I will spend some time researching your topic in advance of our meeting.
- After our conference, I will send you the list of sources that we discussed.

What I expect from you:

(Only spend about 15 minutes preparing the answers to these questions.)

A **PRECONFERENCE EMAIL** at least 24 hours in advance of our meeting, which addresses the following questions:

1. What is your country, committee, and issue?
2. Where are you in your research process?
3. Where are the gaps in your research?
4. What would you specifically like to focus on during our research conference?

A **POSTCONFERENCE EMAIL** within 48 hours after our meeting, which outlines the following:

1. Reflect on and explain your key takeaways from the research conference.
2. What do you think will be the most challenging part of this project/process and how do you plan to tackle it?
3. What are your next steps?

* NOTE: Send this email to me and CC your teacher.

Included in this email are our expectations for rock star researchers:

Rock Star Researchers	
Preconference Preparation	Student thoughtfully and fully answers each question. Reponses show initiative and genuine engagement with country, committee, and issue.
Conference Engagement	Student is actively engaged in learning. Student is curious; asks relevant, thoughtful questions; and takes risks when necessary.
Postconference Reflection	Student articulates clear takeaways from the conference. Student uses feedback to develop understanding and move his or her research process forward with clear, relevant next steps.

Figure 6.2 Setting Clear, Explicit Expectations

of rights and responsibilities during the creation of the Federal Communications Commission's (FCC) "Fairness Doctrine." I asked her if she wanted to do more research, and she admitted that she has already done so much and wasn't finding enough about the creation of the doctrine. I asked her if there were any points in the timeline of the Fairness Doctrine that had more primary and secondary sources available. As she looked at her sources and notecards, she realized that much of what was written about her topic was about its demise in the 1980s. My next question, again, revolved around her interest in this aspect of the topic, which was strong. So I wondered aloud if she could simply shift her focus to how the doctrine fell out of favor, making its creation a necessary part of the background. We talked through how putting the crux of her argument into the abolishment of the doctrine in 1987 would strengthen not only the number of sources she could use but also her connection to rights and responsibilities since the FCC believed that the Fairness Doctrine violated the First Amendment. Through our conversation, she realized that a change of focus would give her more opportunity for analysis and investigation, allowing her to continue with a topic she loved, without more researching.

Capturing the Conference

As mentioned above, I send students links and screenshots of the work we do during our conference. Thanks to my colleague, Janelle Hagen, we were introduced to Microsoft OneNote as a method for capturing all of the vital information about the conferences. I have a section in my notebook for each student with a page for my preconference notes that I use to capture ideas, searches, and pieces of text that I'd like to remember. Since we are regularly doing four to five conferences a day and sometimes more, these preconference notes are vital for me in my preparation as long as I don't use them to dictate the conference. When the conference begins, I use a blank page with only the student's preconference email information at the top, so we can keep our focus. This allows me to paste in specific things we learned or found. We tell students to capture the information on their own computers, too. Usually this involves keeping their tabs open, putting sources in NoodleTools, or downloading documents. OneNote enables us to email a page to the students so they have a record, copying in the teacher so he or she has a record and can see the progress of each student. We have begun sharing the notebooks with some teachers, so they can peek in anytime. Lastly, we add text at the top of the email, which allows us to encapsulate the main points of the conference and clarify ideas if needed.

Conference Conclusions

Clearly, conferencing is an integral part of the Guided Inquiry process and allows us to do some of our most focused and in-depth guiding. Sitting side-by-side with a student uncovers thoughts, feelings, and challenges that don't always get through to teachers and librarians in other ways. Furthermore, when two people put their heads together and simply talk about a topic, magical things happen. In fact, when we ask for feedback from students, this sentiment is shared frequently. Of course, they appreciate the sources we find together and the new strategies that they learn, but we also see the relief that comes as a result of simply having a person to talk to who is interested in their learning and excited to help them move forward. We want our students to see the value of working with librarians, of talking through ideas, and of asking for help when they need it. This is not something that comes naturally to some of our students, but through conferences that are simply part of the research process, they can, we hope, change their perspective.

Note

Portions of this chapter were previously published on the author's blog, "Two Heads Are Better Than One: Librarian as Co-Teacher," blog posting, February 17, 2004, https://letgotolearn .com/2014/02/17/two-heads-are-better-than-one-librarian-as-co-teacher/?

References

Kuhlthau, C. (2004). *Seeking Meaning.* Santa Barbara, CA: Libraries Unlimited.

Kuhlthau, C., L. Maniotes, and A. Caspari. (2012). *Guided Inquiry Design: A Framework for Inquiry in Your School.* Santa Barbara, CA: Libraries Unlimited.

Model United Nations, http://www.unausa.org/global-classrooms-model-un.

National History Day, http://nhd.org.

"Minds on Science": Creating an Inquiry Community in Ninth Grade

Marci D'Onofrio

Guided Inquiry Design® within science courses provides a vehicle for students to become experts on a science topic of their choosing. The science topics in this unit are based on the physical science curriculum. A collaborative teaching approach of the ninth-grade science teachers, librarian, and tech integration specialist provided depth of learning through research that exceeds typical compilation projects.

Westborough High School in Westborough, Massachusetts, is a suburban high school with more than 1,000 students. The student demographic is constantly changing, and the needs of the students are continually evolving. This Guided Inquiry Design project meets students at their own ability level and provides them with skills to increase their level of understanding and analysis in the physical sciences.

Academic rigor is important to this community; it is important for students to have multiple opportunities to analyze and research information. Furthermore, within this inquiry-based learning context, students develop the essential skills of synthesizing new knowledge and sharing this knowledge with peers and educators. We are proud of the mission statement of our school as it clearly illustrates the focus on instruction and learning:

Effective teaching and learning balances content and skills, encouraging critical and creative thinking. This requires expectations that challenge all community members to work hard to achieve their greatest potential. We need to communicate effectively and encourage the use of appropriate tools and technologies to share ideas and solve problems. By keeping an open mind while engaging and collaborating with our diverse population, we foster acceptance, appreciation and ultimately empathy. We strive to be responsible, informed citizens who make ethical decisions and honor our commitments. Every member of this community can achieve the greatest academic, civic and social growth by following these beliefs.

This project has enhanced our science curriculum. Through it, students became engaged in learning about a physical science topic of their choice. The project allowed students to become part of a science Inquiry Community. Students were given opportunities to work with several adults in this rich learning environment. As an educator, I found that Guided Inquiry Design provided me with an essential opportunity to learn about the process of learning. I truly enjoy the continual collaborative effort of the ninth-grade science team and librarian.

The Evolution of a Guided Inquiry Design® Unit

In order to sufficiently introduce this unit, it is necessary to recognize the process of how this unit of Guided Inquiry Design within the freshman physical science course came to be. Several years ago, ninth-grade physical science students were participating in a Science Forum. This forum consisted of each student choosing and reading an article from the previous six months about any current event in science. The class followed a framework for sharing that reading with the class. "Science Forum Days" occurred once a month with three to five students presenting a PowerPoint on the article explaining the article and how it relates to science. Both the presenter and audience wrote a reflection about that presentation. The strength of this activity resided in the student connecting with the real world and presenting the class with science in action. The weakness was students' lack of ability to choose articles with depth of scientific content, which produced weak presentations.

As a science teacher, I approached our new (at the time) librarian, Anita Cellucci, and asked for some guidance about getting a stronger, deeper, and more meaningful product. Anita asked questions about the specific goals of the project. I explored my reasons for doing the project and the expected outcomes. I was confident that I wanted students to explore a science topic of interest and that I wanted students to read, learn, and share information about that topic. The intended audience of the project was my Honors Physical Science students. I had flexibility in their schedule because I was the only one teaching that particular level. Guidance and instruction expanded from paper products to both paper and online instruction.

Anita applied her expertise in information literacy and inquiry and created a project that modeled the Guided Inquiry Design process. As we collaborated, I could go through the Guided Inquiry Design process and work one on one with Anita, learning as I went. I added my expertise in science content where needed. In the spirit of true collaboration, we each had our own areas of expertise. I did not need to know about research techniques and information literacy in order to participate in this project. However, it was daunting not knowing what the final product would look like. In our first round, Anita implemented the process of the project as I was introduced to Guided Inquiry Design. After year one, with this process in place, it seemed that the projects had more depth and meaning.

The newly designed project targeted a few objectives:

1. Deep learning of physical science content
2. Development of information literacy and research skills for use across any curriculum
3. Students' exposure to the inquiry-based process rather than compilation research

In year two, the incoming grade nine Honors Physical Science students again participated in the project. Through reflecting on the outcomes of our project, Anita and I made changes to the instruction and implementation of the unit. We added Guided Inquiry Tools documentation such as the Inquiry Log, Stop and Jot, and Inquiry Journal prompts. (For more on the use of these tools see also Chapter 4.) At this time, we also formally implemented a keyword list in students' Inquiry Journals. We increased the use of Inquiry Circles to better support students' collaboration throughout the process. Anita continued to curate resources for the LibGuide. Although specific conference times were set aside for students before presentations were due, time management for students continued to be an issue. Unfortunately, several students were caught in the assumption that this was simply a compilation project, and they did not have sufficient support (nor the time) to complete their project well. A paradigm shift in understanding the philosophy for inquiry learning was still in progress.

During year two, Anita identified an opportunity for applying to and participating in a Guided Inquiry Design Institute held at Rutgers University in the summer of 2014. Our team, consisting of the librarian, science teacher, English teacher, and assistant principal, was accepted into the institute. While there, I extended my understanding of the Guided Inquiry Design process. The team worked on further developing the ninth-grade science unit as well as a Psychology in Literature unit. Both Guided Inquiry Design units continue to be utilized in our school today.

Each year, students were creating deep, meaningful projects. In doing so, they were gaining research skills and critical thinking skills that could be applied to any future course. During the Rutgers Guided Inquiry Design Institute, our learning team discussed how helpful it would be if all freshmen had a similar learning experience. As the current administration/principal at the time was in favor of creating a library orientation, this project would allow the librarian to offer a way to bring all the grade nine students into the library to learn about resources and acquire information literacy skills while engaged in meaningful content learning. This would also sustain the equity of the library space and resources for other grade levels. Our administrative representative concurred. The other ninth-grade physical science teachers were approached and asked to participate in the Guided Inquiry Process. This is a huge challenge for an educator who has other classes to prepare for with different content while learning about the Guided Inquiry Design process.

What a change going from sixty students and two educators to more than two hundred students and five educators. This created so many new concerns and issues while students worked on the project. Collaboration among teachers, explaining what we were doing and why we were doing it, was essential.

From the beginning, the librarian had used an electronic forum in Edmodo.com as a central location for communication to all teachers and students involved in the project. A bonus is that we were able to include the administration, who were evaluating us, and they could follow our lesson plans as we proceeded through the project. It was also a major asset that our assistant principal was aware of the positive effect of using the Guided Inquiry Design process. The outcomes that were obtained through this approach and the potential for further growth for educators and students was clear to the administration since they had gone to the summer institute with us.

Throughout the project in the past, some learning time was in the classroom and some learning time was in the library. At this time, all class time spent on the inquiry project was moved to the school library regardless of whether the activities were led by science teachers or the librarian or tech integration specialist. The reasons for this were amount of available space, access to technology, as well as allowing the librarian to be available for this project and to other students and teachers. There were now anywhere from one to three classes of physical science students participating in the inquiry project at any given time. The library had space and computers for the larger class sizes. Bringing classes together in the library in this way also created the sense of an Inquiry Community. Students were able to work beside other grade nine students not in their assigned class who were also experiencing Guided Inquiry Design. Because the location for all the activities was now the library, the educators responsible for the class activities are listed under the Team prompt in the introduction to the Guided Inquiry Design phase.

Now that the unit included all ninth-grade science students, the new project served multiple objectives: (1) deep learning of physical science content, (2) integrating the library information literacy orientation for incoming freshmen into content, (3) developing information literacy and research skills for use across any curriculum, and finally, (4) exposing all students to inquiry-based rather than compilation research.

Along with more students in this third year, we added a component that the science content needed to relate specifically to the physical sciences. As a science teacher, I am aware that this encompassed most students' interests in some way even if loosely based. Here is where another issue arose: it is very difficult to have students identify a science-specific topic when they have not been exposed to much of the scientific content. What became evident from this year's projects is that students were having difficulty understanding and explaining the science content. Students did make some science connections, but from the science perspective, there were gaps. Within the projects, students continued to make connections with their research and were able to analyze information in a meaningful way. For the next year, we expanded the **Immerse** section of the project, where students build background and connect to content.

In year four of this process, we have expanded the **Immerse** section of the project so that students are exposed to a wide variety of physical science topics. As we became a Google for Education school, our classroom management tool shifted to Google Classroom. The final research reflection evolved to be a small-group Inquiry Circle. Students who miss this opportunity due to absence or different pace of learning are invited to create a Screencastify video as their research reflection. To further include differentiated instruction, the final product now includes more student choice. Students are required to create a visual element that demonstrates their knowledge gained from their inquiry research. Student choices include, but are not limited to, Prezi, Glogster, and Google Slides. The presentation may be prerecorded using a screencast tool that is shown to the class. Students may also choose to do a live presentation.

Throughout the process and transformation of the Guided Inquiry learning, technology has played an important role. As technology devices shifted in our school, we modified as necessary. It was a goal from the start that students were able to access content for the Guided Inquiry project on a consistent platform as well as having unlimited access to tools and resources.

Use of a classroom management system, Edmodo and later Google Classroom, allows students to ask questions when they have them while also giving teachers the time to respond. Teachers and the librarian are able to monitor and assess student progress. (See more in Chapter 4.) TRAILS (Tool for Real-time Assessment of Information Literacy Skills) provides an assessment measure regarding incoming information literacy skills as well as a demonstration of growth in this area of learning. NoodleTools provides the same collaborative opportunities between teacher, librarian, and students. The librarian-curated resources in a LibGuide allowed for immediate addition or subtraction of resources as well as 24/7 access to these resources. An additional goal for the LibGuide is to provide a vehicle for information literacy instruction and learning. For presentation tools, the goal has consistently been to provide students with transferable skills regarding the technology as well as differentiation for student preference and learning.

Successful Guided Inquiry requires educators willing to step outside the comfort zone of the traditional classroom environment and give up the autonomy of their class. Along with Anita Cellucci and myself, the following ninth-grade science teachers contributed to the success of the Guided Inquiry Design project: Alisa Hilfinger, Michael Holmes, and Heather Waterman. This highly collaborative environment allowed us to co-teach the curriculum, benefiting the students by playing to the strengths of individual educators. One example of the benefits of the collaborative effort is being able to recognize and adapt the curriculum to meet the diverse needs of our students at different levels of instruction, thus ensuring project success for all learners.

Guided Inquiry Design®
Unit Overview
"Minds on Science"

The Team: 9th grade (Physical) Science Teachers, Librarian, Technology Integration Specialist

Concept: *Physical science in our daily lives*

Guiding Questions:
What is physical science?
How does science actualize in the real world and our daily lives in the areas of physics and chemistry?
What are the connections between the physical sciences?

Unit Learning Goals:
Students will be able to speak expertly about a topic in physical science.
Students will transfer their understandings of larger scientific concepts of chemistry such as isotopes and properties of physics into their area of interest through research.
Students will recognize the phases of the research process as they self-reflect.
Students will analyze and synthesize information to discover deeper meaning using science content.
Students will have autonomy in their individual learning process.
Students will demonstrate information literacy as a foundation for high school careers.

 **Open**	At this point in their academic careers, students have limited knowledge of the physical sciences. This <u>Open</u> creates an opportunity for students to view science from a few interesting perspectives. During <u>Open</u>, students read about, reflect on, and share unique, real-world issues in science. This activity serves to raise students' awareness about the wide variety and applications of science.
Immerse	<u>Immerse</u> provides multiple opportunities for students to be exposed to a large variety of broad physical science topics while relating these topics to previous class content and personal experiences through a blended learning approach. Students are immersed in a wide variety of physical science content through videos, articles, websites, and online simulations.
 **Explore**	Based on <u>Open</u> and <u>Immerse</u>, students identify three areas of physical science they may be interested in. After exploring three areas of content through the curated sources on our LibGuide, students narrow their topics to one broad physical science topic. Students reflect on what is interesting to them about their topic in preparation for writing their inquiry question.

Figure 7.1 Unit Overview

	Students take time to reflect and meet with the librarian in small groups to confer about HOW to build a good inquiry question. When they are ready to do so, students then work to finalize questions. Both the content teachers and librarian approve of the inquiry question.
	Inquiry Week—Students spend time in the library gathering articles and information on their question itself and then the application of that topic. Students use the resources from the LibGuide to analyze resources through reading, take notes, and synthesize in NoodleTools. Students go deep by keeping track of keywords and a path of breadcrumbs in their Inquiry Log and by using the Stop and Jot format. Students complete a daily reflection on their progress and participate in timely Inquiry Circles.
	During Create, students will create an oral presentation that uses visual components.
	Inquiry Day–Students present their findings. This happens once in a 7-day cycle with 3-4 presenters in each class period. Audience members complete reflections based on the presentations seen that day. At the end of the presentation, presenters reflect on their inquiry presentation and process.
	The inquiry project involves evaluations by students about student work AND teacher evaluation of student work. Student evaluation—Among other evaluations mentioned throughout the project through the use of Inquiry Tools, students complete a self-evaluation reflection about the inquiry process. Students also retake the TRAILS assessment, exploring their growth in information literacy knowledge and skills. Further, audience members during Share reflect on the presentations they saw that day. Teacher Evaluation—Throughout the GID process, teachers evaluate using a variety of methods. Reflections are evaluated for completion and depth of thoughtful responses, NoodleTool citations and notecards are evaluated for completion and accuracy based on the example given, and the final oral presentation is evaluated using a comprehensive rubric. Teachers also meet to reflect on the process used in the current year identifying successes and areas for improvement and revision.

Figure 7.1 Unit Overview (*Continued*)

Open

Minds on Science

Learning Goals

Process: Invitation to inquiry, open minds, stimulate curiosity about physical science.

Content: Students will understand how chemistry and physics appear in the real world.

Location: Library

Team Members: 9th grade Science Teachers, Librarian

Starter Time: 10 minutes See Figure 7.40 for links to articles	*"Today you will be reading some quirky articles about interesting science topics. What do you think we mean by quirky?"* Class defines quirky. (Refer to thesaurus or dictionary) *"What might be some reasons that we might give you 'quirky' articles to read?"* Listen to students' ideas. (Get ideas from 5–6 students) *"We are using these articles to open your minds to the possibilities of physical science in the real world. We have carefully chosen four articles here."* Teacher and librarian give a quick introduction for each one. *"The first one is about natural antifreeze in arctic fish. The second one is about forensic techniques related to images in eyes. The third tells the story of a London skyscraper that melts cars and fries eggs. And, finally, there is one that tells how software can detect forged photographs. Sound interesting?"*
Worktime Time: 25 minutes Inquiry Journal	Divide the students into groups of 4 and place one of the articles at each table. *"As you read, think about what makes this interesting to you. What is new about this for you, and how do you connect the article contents to what you understand about physical science?"* *"At the end of the period, you'll reflect in your journal about those connections."* Once students have completed reading and summarizing, have them review and highlight the important physical science concepts in the article.
Reflection Time: 5 minutes	*"Take 5 minutes to reflect in your journals on the following prompts."* Inquiry Journal prompts: (post prompts) *"How does this relate to science? Write this as an opinion statement. What about the article is interesting to you?"*
Notes:	In advance, the learning team curated these articles related to the science of chemistry and physics using databases and other library resources.

Figure 7.2 Open Day 1

Open

Minds on Science – Day 2

Learning Goals
Process: Invitation to inquiry, open minds, stimulate curiosity in physical science.

Content: Students will broaden their understanding of and ideas about physical science as they share information and listen to others.
Location: Library or classroom
Team Members: 9th grade Science Teachers, Librarian

Starter Time: 5 minutes	"So, yesterday you read and reflected on some quirky articles about physical science. Today, you are going to work in groups to expand your thinking even further. Everyone probably was interested in these articles for a variety of personal reasons, based on your own background and experiences. We want to give you a chance to share your ideas with one another to potentially spark some new thinking about science."
Worktime Time: 30 minutes ***Save the Last Word for Me*** protocol* Inquiry Journals Inquiry Circles Inquiry Community	Save the Last Word for Me (Protocol): Chime a bell to indicate the close of one round and beginning of the next so each person has a turn. Divide the students into groups of four, labeling one student A, one B, one C, and the other D. Invite the A students to read their opinion statement from their Inquiry Journal (from previous Open session, Figure 7.2). Then students B, C, and D each have 45 seconds to respond using any of their thoughts from their own journal or current thinking. "What is interesting about this?" "What connections to science are we noticing?" After several minutes, give the A students 1 minute to summarize others' ideas and discuss their statement, thus having "the last word." This process continues with the B students sharing and then students C and D. The round will go quickly. The turns are timed so everyone has a turn having "the last word." Teachers chime a bell after each 7 minutes have passed to indicate the beginning of a new round. Alternatively, you could have each group rotate one member as the timekeeper and listeners for each round.
Reflection Time: 10 minutes	Share as an Inquiry Community 1. Reflect on process: "What did that protocol, Save the Last Word for Me, help you to do? What worked for you in that protocol?" 2. Reflect on content: Students share their article and discuss how their group believes that the article relates to science in general and specifically to chemistry or physics.
Notes:	The written work is graded for completion. All Inquiry Journal reflections are used as a stepping-stone for conversation for the development of the individual Science Inquiry question when students meet with the librarian in Identify.

*Adapted from: http://www.nsrfharmony.org/system/files/protocols/save_last_word_0.pdf

Figure 7.3 Open Day 2

Immerse

Minds on Science

Learning Goals

Process: Students will build background knowledge, connect to content, and discover interesting ideas in the area of chemistry.

Content: Students will integrate knowledge and organize concepts and information about isotopes to understand this part of chemistry as a component of physical science in the world.

Location: Science Classroom or Library (depends upon available technology)

Team Members: 9th grade Science Teachers

Starter Time: 3 minutes	"Now that you've read and heard about this quirky part of chemistry called isotopes, we are going to help you understand them a little more by viewing some videos about how they work in the real world. Using notecatchers as you watch will help you to remember some important information and concepts about isotopes. Why isotopes? Isotopes are a basic component of chemistry with a wide and vast variety of world-wide scientific applications. "Keep thinking about what is interesting as you view and respond to these videos."

Worktime
 	
Time: 45 minutes
 	
Over 2 class periods and 2 night's homework.
	Introduce video.
	Students watch each of the videos on isotopes and their possible uses in the world. As they watch the videos, they complete the "Isotopes and You!" notecatchers highlighting important science concepts in the videos. Students have the class period to complete the assignment and finish any portion of the videos and sheets for homework. (See Figures 7.5-7.9)
	
	Topics include:
	   Nuclear Chemistry
	   Archaeology
	   Forensics
	   Geology
	   Medicine
	
	Links for the videos are embedded in the Isotopes and You for our work in Google; for text they are on the forms and in the resources section of this chapter (Figure 7.40).

Reflection Time: 5 minutes	At the end of the videos, students complete an online survey in Google Classroom (Google form) that serves as a brief reflection (see Figure 7.10).
Notes:	

Figure 7.4 Immerse

Isotopes & You!

Name: _____   Period: _____   Date: _____

Keyword: You

SC120/130/140

Directions: Watch the following video and use this notecatcher to help you recall information as you connect to content and build understanding about isotopes for the Inquiry Project.

Video: http://v.gd/isotopescrashcourse (10 Min)

Crash Course Chemistry 38

Keyword: Nuclear Chemistry

1. Which releases more energy? (circle one)

   When electrons in elements interact   When proton and neutron numbers change in the nucleus

2. Changing (circle one) electrons, neutrons, or protons will change the **identity** of an element. (Pb → Au)

3. _____ Atoms of the same element (i.e., same number of protons) that have different numbers of neutrons

4. _____ Changing one element to another or one isotope to another

5. Can you transmute Pb → Au? Would you do it? Why or why not?

6. Why would a nucleus change its number of subatomic particles?

7. _____ Decomposition of an (unstable) nucleus to form a different (stable) nucleus

8. _____ The time it takes for exactly one-half (½) of a radioactive sample to decay

9. Do all isotopes have the same half-life? Give some examples.

10. What is one origin of these unstable elements? _____

Figure 7.5 Isotopes & You

11. The release of energy that allows an unstable nucleus to attain a more stable form. You typically call this_____.

12. _____ is the "most famous" radioactive element; _____-238 is the most abundant with _____% of all naturally occurring _____ being in this form.

13. _____-238 decays into _____-234, releasing a(n) _____ particle, which is essentially the same as a(n) _____ nucleus_____.

$$\,^{238}_{92}U \quad \rightarrow \quad \,^{234}_{90}Th \quad + \quad \,^{4}_{2}He^{2+}$$

14. Alpha (α) particles can be stopped by _____.

15. _____ decay emits _____(subatomic particle) that can be stopped by a(n) _____ or your _____ _____.

16. What is the nuclear notation for an electron?

17. _____ decay is different from _____ or _____ decay because it doesn't emit a(n) _____, just _____, and is highly dangerous.

18. _____ energy level of an electron that is higher and less stable than other levels

19. _____ lowest, most stable energy level of an electron

20. _____ is when an atom breaks into two smaller atoms, but doesn't happen at a very fast rate.

Figure 7.5 Isotopes & You (*Continued*)

Isotopes & You!

Name: _____   Period: _____   Date: _____

SC120/130/140

Directions: Watch the following video and use this guided notecatcher to help you recall information as you connect to content and build understanding about isotopes for the Inquiry Project.

Video: http://v.gd/xtombs (5 Min)

Who's Buried in the X Tombs

Keyword: Archaeology

Learn how isotopic analysis of elements, such as oxygen and carbon, provides clues about ancient human remains in this video from NOVA: Roman Catacomb Mystery. In 2003, an interconnected set of tombs, called the X Tombs, were discovered under the city of Rome. Analyses of the bones and teeth found in the X Tombs indicate that the people buried there were wealthy and mobile; they ate a diet rich in meat and fish (unlike average Romans) and may have come from northern Europe and northern Africa. Scientists are still searching for clues to better understand who the people of the X Tombs were and why they were buried in mass burials.

1. What parts of remains do archaeologists study using isotopic analysis to find out where ancient remains came from?

2. What are some elements' isotopes that are studied by archaeologists?

3. What does matching teeth and bones vs. nonmatching teeth and bones tell us about a person's life?

4. Other than location, what else can be determined by isotopic analysis? What is an example from this tomb?

5. Where were the people from the X Tombs from? Were they all from Rome?

6. From what the archaeologists discovered, what is the best hypothesis about the X Tombs' occupants' demise?

Figure 7.6 Isotopes & You

From *Guided Inquiry Design in Action: High School*. Leslie K. Maniotes, Editor. Santa Barbara, CA: Libraries Unlimited. Copyright © 2017.

Isotopes & You!

Name: _____   Period: _____   Date: _____

SC120/130/140

Directions: Watch the following video and use this guided notecatcher to help you recall information as you connect to content and build understanding about isotopes for the Inquiry Project.

Video: http://v.gd/forensics (3 Min)

Forensics Identification

Keyword: Forensics

Learn how Chelsey Juarez developed a new technique to identify the remains of migrant workers; how teeth are prepared and examined to provide information about where we come from; and the important role forensic anthropologists play in forensic science.

1. _____ _____ A person educated in physical anthropology (particularly skeletal biology), archaeology, anatomy, and allied sciences, who applies that knowledge in the courts or public discussion and debate

2. What is Chelsey Juarez's goal in her work?

3. What elements is Juarez studying in particular? Are they in the hard or soft tissues of the body?

4. Which element does she focus on, and why?

5. What part of the anatomy does Juarez study?

6. Is Juarez able to tell with 100% certainty where a person is from? Why?

Figure 7.7 Isotopes & You

Isotopes & You!

Name: _____   Period: _____   Date: _____

Keyword: You

SC120/130/140

Directions: Watch the following video and use this guided notecatcher to help you recall information as you connect to content and build understanding about isotopes for the Inquiry Project.

Video: http://v.gd/radiometric (1.5 Min)

Radiometric Dating

Keyword: Geology

Geologist Ralph Harvey and historian Mott Greene explain the principles of radiometric dating and its application in determining the age of Earth in this video segment from A Science Odyssey. As the uranium in rocks decays, it emits subatomic particles and turns into lead at a constant rate. Measuring the uranium-to-lead ratios in the oldest rocks on Earth gave scientists an estimated age of the planet of 4.6 billion years.

1. What did the uranium-enriched rock enable scientists to do?

2. Describe radioactive decay (Use U → Pb as an example) as a tool for geologists.

3. How old is the age of the Earth? How did studying radioactive rock samples determine this?

Figure 7.8 Isotopes & You

Isotopes & You!

Name: _____   Period: _____   Date: _____

Keyword: You

SC120/130/140

Directions: Watch the following video and use this guided notecatcher to help you recall information as you connect to content and build understanding about isotopes for the Inquiry Project.

Video: http://v.gd/dragontail (8.25 Min)

Half-life | Uranium: Twisting the Dragon's Tail

Keyword: Medicine

Learn about half-life in this clip from Uranium: Twisting the Dragon's Tail. *Half-life is the rate at which radioactive atoms decay and change. The rate of decay varies, which is why some radioactive substances can remain dangerous for a very long time. In 1986, after the Chernobyl nuclear accident, the damaged reactor was encased in a concrete sarcophagus, but now the sarcophagus is cracking and needs to be replaced. Watch Derek show a new confinement structure being built to last one hundred years. In 5 billion years, only half of that leftover uranium will be decayed. Hear how scientists developed a way to use the half-life of the radioactive atoms for medicinal purposes in cancer patients with the medicine Technetium 99m.*

1. What is the half-life of Cesium-137? _____ years
   a. A 500-gram rock sample of Cesium-137 would have _____ grams of Cesium-137 after 120 years.

2. The Chernobyl meltdown occurred in _____ so _____ of the Cesium-137 is still emitting radiation.

3. Chernobyl is still dangerous because the half-life of uranium-238 is _____ years.

4. Is all radioactive material bad? _____

5. _____ is a medicine created in an nuclear reactor with a half-life of _____. It is used to detect _____.

6. _____ is a tool used to measure radiation. _____ rays are the form in this video detected from the patient, which helps doctors make a _____ because _____ gathers at the site of _____ _____ _____, allowing doctors to find _____ in a patient.

7. Is the patient in danger by using the medicine Technetium 99m? Why or why not?

Figure 7.9 Isotopes & You

Isotope Video Reflection—Google Form

Who is your Physical Science teacher? * (Multiple Choice—Names of teachers)

What period is your Physical Science class? * (Multiple Choice—Periods 1–7)

Of the topics that were introduced, rank your interest from (5) Greatest to (1) Least *

	5	4	3	2	1
Geology	◯	◯	◯	◯	◯
Nuclear Medicine	◯	◯	◯	◯	◯
Forensics	◯	◯	◯	◯	◯
Nuclear Chemistry	◯	◯	◯	◯	◯
Archaeology	◯	◯	◯	◯	◯

What are three new things that you learned? Be specific about the video and knowledge gained. * (Short Answer)

What are two things that are clearer to you, but you are interested in exploring further? * (Short Answer)

What questions do you have after viewing the introductory videos? (Short Answer)

* Required questions

Figure 7.10 Isotope Video Reflection

Immerse

Minds on Science

Learning Goals
Process: Students will build background knowledge, connect to content, and discover interesting ideas.

Content: Students will organize and understand some basic properties of physics.
Location: Library or classroom
Team Members: 9th grade Science Teachers

Starter Time: 2 minutes	In this Immerse session, continue with informational science topics. Now, students will use an online resource to learn about a wide variety of physics topics including, but not limited to motion, Newton's laws, electricity, and the three types of wave energy: www.physicsclassroom.com (see Figure 7.12).
Worktime Time: 2 class periods, 2 nights of homework	Students access www.physicsclassroom.com through a webquest found in Google Classroom. The links are embedded into each of the lessons, and students type answers directly into the webquest below the question.
Reflection Time: 10 minutes	A content reflection and a teacher check for completion of work: Content Reflection: What are three new things that you learned? Be specific about the knowledge gained. What are two things that are clearer to you, but you want to explore further? What questions do you have after completing the physics webquest? Webquest Assessment: Open Note Multiple Choice Check-In (30 questions)
Notes:	This session occurred in the library for access to computers. If your school has laptops or other technology, it could happen in the science classroom.

Figure 7.11 Immerse

Directions: Follow the links (found in Figure 7.39) and read each of these pieces from the website http://www.physicsclassroom.com

Teacher Notes: This document was created and used in Google docs, so students could easily click the link and answer the questions right on this page. Teachers would review and comment online as well as monitor student progress.

Understanding Motion

Lesson #	Student questions/response
Lesson 1: **Describing Motion with Words**	Lesson 1—Describing Motion with Words 1. What is a scalar? Give three examples. What is a vector? Give three examples. What is the difference between distance and displacement? Can distance and displacement be the same? Give an example. Can distance and displacement be different? Give an example. What is the difference between speed and velocity? Can speed and velocity be the same? Give an example. Can speed and velocity be different? Give an example.
Lesson 5: **Free Fall and the Acceleration of Gravity**	Lesson 5—Free Fall and the Acceleration of Gravity 1. What is the acceleration of gravity on Earth? Is it a scalar or a vector? 2. What are the <u>SI</u> units used to create the unit for acceleration? 3. What is free fall? 4. What is the "big misconception" about free fall? (International System of Units SI link to Wikipedia in question 2 https://en.wikipedia.org/wiki/SI_base_unit)

Electricity

Lesson 2: **Electric Current**	Lesson 2—Electric Current 1. What is electric current? 2. What are the requirements for a circuit? 3. What is power? How does it differ from current? 4. What are some common misconceptions about electric circuits?

Waves

Lesson 3: **The Nature of a Wave**	Lesson 3—The Nature of a Wave 1. What is a basic definition of a wave? 2. What are the categories of waves? How are they similar and different? 3. How do waves affect your daily life?

Figure 7.12 Understanding Motion

Lesson 4: **Properties of a Wave**	Lesson 4—Properties of a Wave 1. What is the anatomy of a wave? Draw a picture and save it. Upload this picture to your Google drive and insert it here (you can delete these instructional pictures when you are done). *w* Insert Format Tools Table Add 🖼 Image... Insert image Upload Take a snapshot By URL Your albums Google Drive Search Drag an image here 2. What is the frequency of a wave? How does it relate to the period of a wave? 3. What is transported by waves?
	Sound
Lesson 5: **The Nature of a Sound Wave**	Lesson 5—The Nature of a Sound Wave 1. Describe sound in terms of pressure, mechanical wave, and longitudinal wave. 2. Why can't we hear sound in space?
Lesson 6: **Sound Properties and Their Perception**	Lesson 6—Sound Properties and Their Perception 1. What is pitch? How does it relate to the frequency of sound? 2. How do we measure how loud (intense) a sound wave is? 3. What is the speed of sound? Can it change, and if so, how? 4. How does the ear help us "hear" sounds?
	Light Waves
Lesson 8: **How Do We Know Light Is a Wave?**	Lesson 8—How Do We Know Light Is a Wave? 1. How does light behave like a wave?
Lesson 9: **Color and Vision**	Lesson 9—Color and Vision 2. What is the electromagnetic spectrum (EMS)? 3. What parts of the EMS do humans see? What parts do/can we feel? 4. Where are the light-sensing cells in the eye (rods and cones)? What do each of these cell types do to help us see? 5. What causes the sky to appear blue? What causes the atmosphere to appear to change at sunset?

Figure 7.12 Understanding Motion (*Continued*)

Minds on Science

Learning Goals
Process: Students will build background knowledge, connect to content, and discover interesting ideas.

Content: Students will conduct a Personal Interest Inventory.
Location: Library
Team Members: 9th grade Science Teachers

Starter Time: 10 minutes	"For the past week, you have spent time building background knowledge in some broad topics in physics and chemistry. "When you are doing a project over a long period of time, it is important that you have an interest in that topic. We want you to have a personal investment in your Inquiry Question. So today we want to you take an inventory of your interests." (Think, Pair, Share) "Talk to your elbow partner about: What is inventory? Where have you heard that term before? Who do you know that has to take inventory? You'll be sharing ideas with the class after 3 minutes." (Give three minutes of talking time.) Share ideas—Class discusses other places where people have to take inventory. Summarize the ideas: "So we think an inventory is . . . " "We want to encourage you to eventually identify a topic that connects to you personally. For that reason, in this inventory, we ask about some personal things like what you like to do and so on. These questions are meant to activate your thinking and make connections between this science content and your real life. We also want to help you think about what arose out of watching these videos and experiences from the last few days."
Worktime Time: 30 minutes	Students and teachers review the variety of questions that pertain to their personal interests, fun facts, and possible science careers. Students are given about 30 minutes of in-class worktime to complete the inventory. (See Figure 7.14) "Share your inventory highlights with a partner. What is most interesting and exciting to you about this?"
Reflection Time: 5 minutes	"Summarize your interests as you stand today. Take into account ALL of your learning in the <u>Open</u> and <u>Immerse</u> phases as well as the inventory you took today. Put your ideas into a reflection: Reflection: My interests are in____ because_____."

Figure 7.13 Immerse

Immerse Personal Interest Inventory

Part 1: Interest Inventory Answer the following questions with as much detail as possible.
What are your hobbies?
What technology/social media or other do you use on a regular basis?
Is there any technology that you don't use but you want to learn how to use?
How does physics or chemistry affect your life?
If there were two or three questions that you could ask about *anything* that you have always wanted to know, what would they be?
What is your favorite thing to learn about in history?
What is your favorite thing to learn about in science?
What is your favorite thing to learn about in math?
Are there any current events (in the news) that you are paying attention to and/or curious about?
Is there anything (in general) that you are really interested in? Something you love to learn about?
What problem(s) do you want to help solve now and in the future?
If you were a superhero, what would you want your superpower to be?

Part 2: Investigate Possibilities
Now, read the following lists of careers. They all require knowledge of physics!
Click the link to investigate the careers that might interest you.
http://www.physics.org/careers.asp?contentid=381
http://www.physics.org/careerprofiles.asp?SectorId=0&Degree=0

What interests you? *Complete the table below.*

	Career Title	Why does this interest you?
1.		
2.		
3.		
4.		
5.		

Figure 7.14 Immerse Personal Interest Inventory

Minds on Science

Information Literacy Deep Dive

Learning Goals
Content: Students will become familiar with the Guided Inquiry Design process, learn about the LibGuide Resource, and choose from a list of a variety of resources exposing them to a variety of science concepts.

Location: Library

Team Members: Librarian
Introduction of the LibGuide—a Web-based resource accessible to students in and out of school. (See Figure 7.16.) A LibGuide is used as a curated set of resources to help students navigate through the process of Guided Inquiry Design. This LibGuide acts as a portal to databases, websites, and library catalogs as well as tutorials and lessons that students can use to refresh their memory while working independently. In order to help the students become familiar with the extensive resources found in the LibGuide, students are asked to complete a webquest that familiarizes them with all aspects of the LibGuide as a resource and research tool.

Starter Time: 15 minutes	Librarian introduces the phases of the Guided Inquiry Design process to students in a slide presentation, discussing the thoughts, feelings, and actions associated with the process. Librarian indicates where students currently are (in the <u>Immerse</u> phase). Introduce the LibGuide to students: Students use a Chromebook while the librarian demonstrates how to use the tabs and resources. "This LibGuide webquest will help you to understand how LibGuide works, become familiar with the resources that will be available for this project, and see how it will help you to do research."
Worktime Time: 35 minutes	Students participate in the webquest. Students work during class in the library and complete at home if necessary. (See more at this award-winning LibGuide site, http://whs.westborough.libguides.com.) Students work on this at their own pace and complete at various times. To help students continue to Immerse and Explore some ideas on their own, the teachers created a document called <u>Online Science Simulations—More interesting Ideas in Science.</u> (See Figures 7.19 and 7.20) This document allows students to use online physics simulations whenever they have extra time. These activities offer students differentiated support to continue immersing and exploring in various topics of chemistry and physics that may interest them or spark new ideas. There is no reflection or grading piece to this.

Figure 7.15 Information Literacy Deep Dive

Reflection Time: 5 minutes	Students are asked to reflect within the webquest: "In what ways could this LibGuide support your Inquiry Research? Identify at least 3 ways and explain your answers completely." The webquest also provides a way for the librarian and students to check for understanding of use of the LibGuide as a tool.
Notes:	**Because this is introduced to all students in 9th grade, these sessions serve doubly as the library orientation and introduction to the available resources for research that they will use throughout their high school career. Students learn information literacy searching skills such as use of OPAC (online library catalog), database searches, Boolean operators, as well as keyword searching. These information literacy skills build confidence in students' ability to search for information independently. This time spent with the librarian ensures that students view the library and librarian as resources for this project and any future information needs.

Figure 7.15 Information Literacy Deep Dive (*Continued*)

Figure 7.16 Westborough High School LibGuide

WHS LibGuide Webquest
http://whs.westborough.libguides.com

Your Inquiry Question:
Find the Research Guide Home.
A. Use Destiny OPAC
   1. Search for your topic. What did you search for?
   2. Explain the steps of using OPAC to search.
   3. What are your results? Please list at least one resource: title, author, call number
   4. If you were unable to find a resource in your initial search, what should you do next? List the steps.
B. Use Britannica Encyclopedia
   1. Search for your topic. What did you search for?
   2. What are your results? Please list 2 different resources.
   3. Find an image for your topic. Add it to your document.
C. Use the database: Research in Context
   1. Search for your topic. What were your keywords?
   2. Did you use a Boolean operator? If so, which one?
   3. What are the different types of resources that you found? List them.
   4. Choose a resource. List what type of resource it is.
   5. What are some subjects related to the topic you searched for? Use the database side panel for help.
   6. What are some tools that you can use in an article? List them.
   7. Email the article to your school email.
   8. Copy the Bookmark URL and add it here.
D. What is an inquiry question?
   1. Name 5 things that are important to a "good" inquiry question.
E. Find the RSS FEED for articles.
   1. What is an RSS Feed?
   2. Choose an article from 2 of the 4 RSS Feeds.
   3. Write the title, author, and a short description of the article.
   4. Were you able to find something on your topic?
F. Visit the Avoiding Plagiarism page.
   1. List 5 things you learned from this page.
G. Find the page: Massachusetts State Databases @ WHS
   1. What can you find on this page?
     i. Name 3 databases (different from the databases listed on the Research Guide Home).
     ii. List 2 other resources from this page.
H. Use the database: Science in Context
   1. Sign in with your Google account.
   2. Search for your topic. What were your keywords?
   3. Choose a resource (article, audio, video, podcast).
   4. Save the resource to your Google Drive.
I. Find the Works Cited page.
   1. Find the NoodleTools YouTube channel link.
   What types of tutorials can you find on the YouTube channel for NoodleTools?
   1. List 3 titles.
J. Where can you find information about research skills?
   1. List the name of the page.
   2. What else can you find on this page?
   3. Write 5 things you learned from this page.

Reflection: In what ways could this LibGuide support your inquiry research? Identify at least 3 ways and explain your answers completely.

Figure 7.17 WHS LibGuide Webquest

From *Guided Inquiry Design in Action: High School*. Leslie K. Maniotes, Editor. Santa Barbara, CA: Libraries Unlimited. Copyright © 2017.

WHS LibGuide Checkpoint Rubric

Item	Points	Item	Points
Inquiry Question	__/ 1	Visit the Avoiding Plagiarism page • List 5 things you learned from this page. -5	__/ 5
Use Destiny OPAC • Search for your topic. What did you search for? -1 • Explain the steps of using OPAC to search. -1 • What are your results? Please list at least one resource: title, author, call number. -3 • If you were unable to find a resource with your initial search, what should you do next? List the steps. -2	__/ 7	Find the page: Massachusetts State Databases @ WHS • What can you find on this page? • Name 3 databases (different from the databases listed on the Research Guide Home). -3 • List 2 other resources from this page. -2	__/ 5
Use Britannica Encyclopedia • Search for your topic. What did you search for? -1 • What are your results? Please list 2 different resources. -2 • Find an image for your topic. Add it to your document. -1	__/ 4	Use the database: Science in Context • Sign in with your Google account • Search for your topic. What were your keywords? -1 • Choose a resource (article, audio, video, podcast). • Save the resource to your Google Drive.	__/ 1
Use the database: Research in Context • Search for your topic. What were your keywords? -1 • Did you use a Boolean operator? If so, which one? -1 • What are the different types of resources that you found? List them. -2 • Choose a resource. List what type of resource it is. -1 • What are some subjects related to the topic you searched for? Use the database side panel for help. -2 • What are some tools that you can use in an article? List them.-2 • Email the article to your school email. • Copy the Bookmark URL and add it here. -1	__/ 10	Find the Works Cited page • Find the NoodleTools YouTube channel link. • What types of tutorials can you find on the YouTube channel for NoodleTools? - 1 • List 3 titles. -3	__/4
What is an inquiry question? • Name 5 things that are important to a "good" inquiry question.	__/ 5	Where can you find information about research skills? • List the name of the page. -1 • What else can you find on this page? -1 • Write 5 things you learned from this page. - 5	__/ 7
Find the RSS FEED for articles. • What is an RSS Feed? -1 • Choose an article from 2 of the 4 RSS Feeds. -1 • Write the title, author, and a short description of the article. -2 • Were you able to find something on your topic? -1	__/ 5	Conclusion: • In what ways could this LibGuide support your inquiry research? Identify at least 3 ways and explain your answers completely. (-3/way)	__/ 9
Subtotal column 1		Subtotal column 2	
Comments:			
		Total	/63

Figure 7.18 WHS LibGuide Checkpoint Rubric

From *Guided Inquiry Design in Action: High School.* Leslie K. Maniotes, Editor. Santa Barbara, CA: Libraries Unlimited. Copyright © 2017.

Online Science Simulations

Discover more interesting ideas in science

Once you are done with your webquest, please look at these options for further investigation:

PhET—Simulation

These are science simulations from the University of Colorado at Boulder. You can explore them like a game. While you do, think about what is happening and what makes it work. Consider the elements the designer has included in the game. Enjoy!

Skate Park

https://phet.colorado.edu/en/simulation/energy-skate-park-basics
- Play with the simulation and determine what conditions are needed to make a good skate park.
- What is energy? What types of energy do you see here?
- What similarities do you see in this simulation and what they are <u>constructing</u> in Fenway? <u>http://www.usatoday.com/story/sports/olympics/2015/09/22/big-air-fenway-park-ty-walker-joss-christensen/72621822/</u> http://boston.redsox.mlb.com/bos/ticketing/big_air.jsp

The team worked hard to help students connect to their interests. Embedded in some of the resources were links to local articles related to the content. Connecting to local content encourages the "Third Space" (Maniotes, 2005; see Figure 7.39).

Static Electricity

https://phet.colorado.edu/en/simulation/balloons-and-static-electricity
- Play with the simulation and determine what conditions are needed to make things be attracted by static electricity.
- Play with the simulation and determine what conditions are needed to make things be repelled by static electricity.
- How is this force similar to gravity? How is it different?

Waves on a String

https://phet.colorado.edu/en/simulation/wave-on-a-string
- Play with the simulation. How do you make the amplitude (how tall the crests are or how deep the troughs are) larger? Smaller?

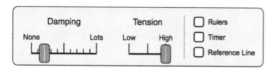

- Play with the simulation. How do you make the wavelength (distance between crests or troughs) larger? Smaller?
- When a wave is on a string, what is the difference when it is bound on both ends vs. free to move on one end? What do you see happen when the wave "hits" the far point?

What happens to the speed of the wave on a string when the tension is higher? When it is lower?

Figure 7.19 Science Simulations

Online Science Simulations

Discover more interesting ideas in science

Fluids https://phet.colorado.edu/en/simulation/under-pressure 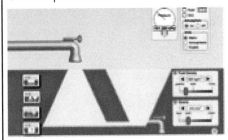	Using this portion of the simulator, does the shape of the vessel matter to the height of the fluid? 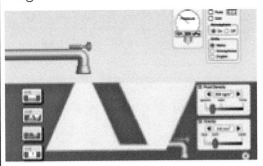
Using this portion of the simulator, what happens with the right side fluid level when the weights are put on the left side? https://phet.colorado.edu/sims/html/under-pressure/latest/under-pressure_en.html	
Color Vision https://phet.colorado.edu/en/simulation/color-vision Write the "color recipe" of what light needs to be absorbed by the eye to see the following color: Red = Orange = Yellow = Green = Blue = Violet = White =	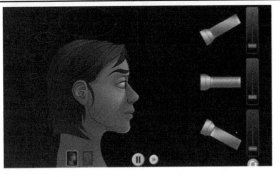

Other Videos:
Interested in learning more about astronomy? http://bit.ly/1Lk3J01 (Yes, astronomy is a part of physics!)
Interested in learning more about chemistry? http://bit.ly/1qzrpDN (Chemistry is also part of physics!)

Figure 7.20 Science Simulations

Explore

Minds on Science

Learning Goals
Process: Students will explore interesting ideas, look around, and dip in.

Content: Students will develop some ideas about their topic and what it is that they find interesting about it.
Location: Library
Team Members: Science Teachers, Librarian

Starter Time: 2 minutes	"In the Information Literacy Deep Dive, you were introduced to search strategies using keywords, Boolean operators, and databases from the LibGuide."
Worktime Time: 35 minutes	"Today you will have a chance to Explore your topic. During this worktime: 1. Read about your interests using the LibGuide resources to find some information. 2. Start to develop some ideas about your topic and what it is that you find interesting."
Reflection Time: 10 minutes Inquiry Journal	"Inquiry Journal Prompts—Answer questions about today's session and what you learned today."

Prompt	Ideas to Explore
Write three things you learned in today's session.	I learned that . . .
Write about something that surprised you or was new to you.	I was surprised that . . .
Write something that you already knew about. Tell how you know.	I knew that ...
List some ideas that seem interesting to you.	Interesting ideas I have are ...
List ideas that you want to know more about.	I would like to know more about ...

Notes:	Journal prompts with permission from *Guided Inquiry Design: A Framework for Inquiry in Your School*, Figure 5.1 by Carol C. Kuhlthau, Leslie K. Maniotes, and Ann K. Caspari. Santa Barbara, CA: Libraries Unlimited. Copyright © 2012.

Figure 7.21 Explore

Minds on Science

Information Literacy Deep Dive
Overview of NoodleTools for Proper Citation and Schoolwide Plagiarism Policy

Learning Goals
Content: Students will learn how to use NoodleTools to create authentic citations for their research while synthesizing the information found within a citation.

Location: Library
Team Members: Librarian

Starter Time: 10 minutes	The librarian embeds instruction on search strategies and how to access articles. Students learn how to use NoodleTools while researching. NoodleTools is a digital research platform where students analyze and synthesize information while sharing their work with the teachers. A brief review of schoolwide plagiarism guidelines is followed by an introduction of NoodleTools. Through the mini-lesson, students understand that NoodleTools will help them to create proper citations and not plagiarize.
Worktime Time: 35 minutes	Each student will set up his or her NoodleTools student account and share the account with the teacher(s). Then students complete the following: 1. A tutorial showing students how to create a citation linked to a source and how to create a notecard linked to a citation. 2. A sample notecard to help guide students in creating their notecards. Assignment: Students create a citation of a source used for the Narrowing Your Topic activity. Each citation will include a sample notecard in the correct format using all 3 sections of the notecard: • Direct text, • Summarize in own words, and • My Ideas about how the information relates to the Inquiry topic/question.
Reflection	The "My Ideas" section of the notecard (based on a citation) is the reflection for each and every direct text quote that students create.
Notes:	Each notecard (after the practice notecard) will be graded. Students are given the rubric during the training session on NoodleTools. (See Figure 7.23)

Figure 7.22 Information Literacy Deep Dive

Name: _____ **Phase: GATHER**

NoodleTools Notecard Rubric

The following rubric identifies the expectations and scoring guide for each and every notecard.

Quotation:

Topic	Possible Points	Points Earned
Direct Text from Source	1	
Appropriate Length based on article (1–6 paragraphs)	1	
Edited Quote • cross out • highlight • evidence of active reading	2	

Paraphrase:

Topic	Possible Points	Points Earned
Main Idea	1	
Supporting Ideas • bulleted information • no sentences • relate to main idea	2	

My Ideas:

Topic	Possible Points	Points Earned
Reflection • Clearly state if this notecard is a background note-card or application notecard. • With specific detail explain the way(s) the quotation and synthesis from the paraphrase apply to answering your question. (3–5 sentences)	4	
Application Rephrase your reflection for use in your final project.	4	
Total Points Total Points Possible/Earned	15	

Figure 7.23 NoodleTools Notecard Rubric

Minds on Science

Learning Goals
Process: Students will pause and ponder to identify their inquiry question.

Content: Students will reflect on their inquiry question and consider a rationale for its viability as a research topic.
Location: Library
Team Members: 9th grade Science Teachers, Librarian

Starter Time: 5 minutes	Students work at their own pace through Explore. In the Identify phase students meet in small groups with the librarian and teacher. Meetings are on a first come, first served basis, so students may continue to work at their own pace until they are ready. At the beginning of the Identify sessions the teacher and librarian review the order of documents to be completed prior to the small group meetings. "It's time to stop and think about the direction of your inquiry. Today you will be working on a sheet to help you do that. In class we worked together to build inquiry questions. Attached are the handouts that we used. You are to do the following: 1. Complete the worksheet Science Inquiry Project—Building Inquiry Questions 2. and hand it in to your teacher. "In small groups, meet with the librarian to learn how to develop inquiry questions. 3. Create a question based on the small group lesson. 4. Obtain librarian and science teacher approval of your question. 5. Enter your question into the Google Doc set up by your teacher."
Worktime Time: 40 minutes	Students individually complete a-e of the Build Your Own Inquiry Question document. (See Figures 7.25 and 7.26) In small groups, students meet with the librarian. The librarian begins a discussion. Describe a "good" inquiry question. Students follow along with their copy of the worksheets (What is a "Good" Inquiry Question?, 10 Questions for Inquiry: The Bigger the Better!, Research Question Help) while the librarian explains the aspects of an inquiry question. At this point, students are given an opportunity to write an inquiry question.

Figure 7.24 Identify

From *Guided Inquiry Design in Action: High School*. Leslie K. Maniotes, Editor. Santa Barbara, CA: Libraries Unlimited. Copyright © 2017.

	Librarian approves question using the rationale presented by the student from the Building Inquiry Questions sheet.

As inquiry question building is a process, some students need some time to identify a question that works for them. In that case, students are moved to a small group session run by a teacher so that they may have an opportunity to discuss and explain their topic. Students continue working until they come up with a new question and then revisit with the librarian to get approval or suggestions on continuing to build their question. This process continues until each student has a correctly formatted inquiry question.

Next, the science teacher approves the question by considering the science content alongside the Building Inquiry Questions worksheet.

The librarian reviews the inquiry question one final time, checking to see if the fusing of inquiry and science content still meets the requirements of a good research question. |
| **Reflection**
Time: 5 minutes | Research Question: What's next?

At this point, students are directed to pull out the main science ideas from their question so that they can begin researching science content. The content teacher reviews the initial list with each student. |
| **Notes:** | This blog was very helpful to us as another scaffold for students who needed more support in identifying great questions: https://k12.thoughtfullearning.com/blogpost/10-questions-inquiry-bigger-better, and this one helped us think about what we wanted to see in the questions: http://cll.mcmaster.ca/resources/misc/good_inquiry_question.html |

Figure 7.24 Identify (*Continued*)

Building Inquiry Questions

a) TOPIC IDEAS:	b) What are the questions that I already have about this topic?
c) What about this is interesting to me?	d) What have I learned from **OPEN, IMMERSE, and EXPLORE*** that I can use to help me focus my research? Consider everything you have done so far while addressing this prompt.
e) How am I narrowing my topic?	f) My inquiry question: Library Teacher: _____ Science Teacher: _____ Library Teacher (2nd): _____

Adapted from Figure 7.5 Chart to Identify from *Guided Inquiry Design: A Framework for Inquiry in Your School* by Carol C. Kuhlthau, Leslie K. Maniotes, and Ann K. Caspari. Santa Barbara, CA: Libraries Unlimited. Copyright © 2012.

Figure 7.25 Inquiry Chart—Building Inquiry Questions

Name: _____

Phase: **GATHER**

Researching Your Question: What's Next?

Record approved question:

Look at your question. What are the major science topics in your question? List them here:

What science applications does your question have embedded within it? What relationships are mentioned in the question? (Think Boolean operators)

Keywords! You have now started your keyword list. Use these keywords to begin building your keyword list and breadcrumbs.

Figure 7.26 Researching Your Question: What's Next?

Minds on Science

Learning Goals

Process: Gather important information, go broad, go deep.

Content: Students will articulate and synthesize their research to date and discuss what to do next, linking complex science content with their inquiry question.
Location: Library
Team Members: Librarian, Physical Science Teacher(s)

Starter Time: 5 minutes Inquiry Circles	"Today we will check in with each Inquiry Circle as you continue to gather information and take notes. We are looking to see that you are connecting the science content to your inquiry question. We are here to help you if you are stuck or having problems at this point."
Worktime Time: 45 minutes Inquiry Circle	Students meet in Inquiry Circles to summarize their thinking and articulate their synthesis of ideas to one another. As they articulate their ideas, gaps become evident, and students in Inquiry Circles help one another recognize where they are not clear or need more information. Students will be able to provide the teachers with an update on their progress and address difficulties with technology, research techniques, and documentation.
Reflection Time: 10 minutes	Journal entry: INQUIRY JOURNAL PROMPT 1. What are your successes thus far? 2. Write three things that you learned in today's lesson. 3. What is something that surprised you or was new to you? 4. What questions or concerns about the project did you have before the meeting? In what way(s) were these questions answered? 5. What questions/concerns are still unanswered? 6. Describe a connection that you are making between your background science research and the application of the research.
Notes:	During Phase 1 of Gather, students are given more detailed materials to support their organization specific to this process.

Figure 7.27 Gather 1

Gather

Minds on Science

Learning Goals
Process: Gather important information, go broad, go deep.

Content: Students analyze information, determine its importance, and keep track of keywords and new vocabulary.
Location: Library
Team Members: Science Teachers, Librarian

Starter Time: Continuous	During Gather, students continue to research, record, and analyze resources that provide information relating to answering the inquiry question as it applies to the science topics.
Worktime Time: 5–7 class periods (and/or Homework) Inquiry Circle Inquiry Log	Using resources to answer the question, students analyze resources through reading, note taking, and synthesizing. Students will use a keyword list (Figure 7.29) and keep track of their resources through the Inquiry Log (Figure 7.30) and Stop and Jot (Figure 7.31) or an electronic version. At the end of this time period and before creating the final inquiry project, students will participate in another Inquiry Circle, allowing them to reflect on the work they have created thus far.
Reflection Time: Continuous throughout the sessions	Continue daily reflections on the research in NoodleTools and in Google (See Figure 7.32).

Figure 7.28 Gather 2

KEYWORD LIST AND "BREADCRUMBS"

DATE	KEYWORDS	ADVANCED SEARCHES	NOTES
	Videos, Articles, Databases, other sources	Use of Boolean Operators AND, OR, NOT	How effective was this keyword in your search?

Figure 7.29 Keyword List and "Breadcrumbs"

INQUIRY LOG

Use this inquiry log from the Explore stage through the Create stage.

	Explore	Gather
Track your choices through the inquiry.	As you explore, check the box if you might use the source for your inquiry. ✔ "Maybe"	As you gather, check the box if you will use the source for your inquiry. ✔ "Use it"
Track the reading strategies you use.	As you explore, place an x after the sources you dipped in to.	As you gather, mark an * after the core sources you read deeply.

Cite all your sources.

ANY ARTICLE OPENED MUST BE DOCUMENTED, ALL SOURCES MUST BE CITED

	Date	Source Citation (URL)	Not used ✗ / Notecard started ✔	In Google Drive? ✗	Notes: What makes this useful	Notecard Completed ★
1						
2						
3						
4						
5						
6						
7						
8						
9						
10						

Adapted with permission from Guided Inquiry Design: A Framework for Inquiry in Your School by Carol C. Kuhlthau, Leslie K. Maniotes, and Ann K. Caspari. Santa Barbara, CA: Libraries Unlimited. Copyright © 2012.

Figure 7.30 Inquiry Log

STOP AND JOT
with Source and Citation

When you come across a good idea or a question occurs to you, get in the habit of stopping to jot it down in your Inquiry Journal. Use this form or make two columns in your journal with the page number in the margin and jotted notes beside it.

This is important for keeping track of where you found the idea so that you can find it again when you want to. In addition, you will record the citation in your Inquiry Log so that later, when you are further along in your inquiry, you can cite the source that you used.

Source:	
Keywords	Ideas & Questions
Citation created? Circle one: Yes or No	

Adapted from *Guided Inquiry Design: A Framework for Inquiry in Your School* by Carol C. Kuhlthau, Leslie K. Maniotes, and Ann K. Caspari. Santa Barbara, CA: Libraries Unlimited. Copyright © 2012.

Figure 7.31 Stop and Jot with Source and Citation

Physical Science—Daily Inquiry Reflection

Answer the following questions each day you work on the inquiry project. Send yourself a copy of your responses each day to create a record of your work and thinking. Your username will be recorded when you submit this form. * Required

Today's date * Your class/teacher *

What did you do/find that was successful today? *

What did you do/find that you struggled with today? *

What further questions do you have about Physical Science after today? *

What further questions do you have about the inquiry process after today? *

What is your plan for tomorrow? *

Send me a copy of my responses.

Figure 7.32 Physical Science—Daily Inquiry Reflection

Create

Minds on Science

Learning Goals
Process: Reflect on learning, go beyond facts to make meaning, create to communicate.

Content: Students will create a visual representation of their findings. In addition, students will present a summary and analysis of their inquiry question and the research process and resources.

Location: Library
Team Members: Tech Integration Specialist, 9ᵗʰ grade Science Teachers, Librarian

Starter Time: 10 minutes	*"Today the technology integration specialist will provide a brief summary of what makes a high-quality presentation called 'How to Create a Great Presentation No Matter the Tool,' located in our LibGuide of resources. The main concepts about presentation are focused on Poise, Voice, Life, Eye Contact, Gesture, and Speed. Slide content and use of visuals will also be discussed."* http://whs.westborough.libguides.com/physcienceinquiry
Worktime Time: 35 minutes	During the worktime students are engaged in creating to communicate their ideas with the class. Students use guiding questions to help create visual and oral components of their presentation. They also reflect on their process using a self-assessment and in interviews with the librarian.
Reflection Time: 5 minutes	Students synthesize their information through interviews with the librarian and teachers. Students self-assess their progress using a checklist.

Figure 7.33 Create

Share

Minds on Science

Learning Goals
Process: Learn from each other, share learning, tell your story.

Content: Students listen to learn new content from one another about the connections from real life to physics and chemistry that other students highlight.
Location: Library
Team Members: 9th grade Science Teachers, Librarian, Tech Integration Specialist

Starter Time: 5 minutes	"Today we are beginning (or continuing) the presentations from our peers. We are so proud of all the hard work that everyone has done on this project. Each of you has chosen a unique topic but all the work is related to the concept that physical science plays a role in our everyday world. "From these presentations, our hope is that you will learn unique and interesting information from one another. We hope that you will get information that might spark a new interest in you. "You will be required to choose two of the presentations to provide feedback to the presenter. Use the form provided to do so. Be sure to include positive comments and make any critique constructive. "A schedule for presentations has been prepared in advance so all students know when they are presenting."
Worktime Time: 45 minutes	Presentations occur weekly during one class period until all students have presented. 3–4 students present their project in a class period. The audience members must choose 2 of the presentations to reflect on. Each presenter presents while the audience listens. At the end of each presentation, the audience may ask questions.
Reflection Time: 5 minutes	Presenter Reflection is done at the end of class. Audience Reflection is completed during the presentation and finished for homework. (See also Figure 10.1, Student to Student Evaluation, from <u>Guided Inquiry Design: A Framework for Inquiry in Your School</u>)
Notes:	Presentations may be performed in front of individual classes or the group class that has been working together in the library; we have done both. Initially, willing students present in front of a large group and for time's sake, we move the presentations to the individual classrooms.

Figure 7.34 Share

Minds on Science

Learning Goals: Presentation Day Evaluations
Process: Evaluate the achievement of learning goals, reflect on the process, and reflect on content.

Content: Students will reflect on the construction of science knowledge through their research.
Location: Library
Team Members: 9th grade Science Teachers, Librarian

Starter Time: 5 minutes	Class comes back together once all students have presented to bring the unit full circle. Silent Chalk Walk: post 6 Charts (2 for each question) entitled • What? So What? Now What? Think about: • What—What did you learn from someone else about physical science in the real world? • So what—why does that matter? Why might this information be important to know? • Now what—what are you going to do with the information now that you know these things? How might it change how you think or interact in your life? Provide real examples when possible. Take a few minutes to think about what you will write for each poster.
Worktime Time: 20 minutes Inquiry Circles	Give students time to write on stickies (or directly onto the charts) and post their ideas. Complete the charts in silence, no talking this round. Next, in Inquiry Circles students go back to the charts, read the ideas, and discuss these questions for each chart: • What strikes you? What is interesting? • What hadn't you thought about? • What does this say about us as a learning community?
Reflection Time: 10 minutes Inquiry Community	As an Inquiry Community, come back together and discuss the question, "How has this experience changed our thinking about science?" Give specific details and examples.
Notes:	This activity can be done online using 3 padlets (padlet.com) where students post virtual stickies and then review the padlet boards in groups on computers to discuss. Using the computer requires less movement and more devices.

Figure 7.35 Evaluate

Minds on Science

Learning Team Evaluation Process for Student Learning

Evaluate

Progress Monitoring and Grading in GID	Throughout this process, teachers evaluate student progress, both formally and informally. We evaluate the five kinds of learning across the process. We also give grades for student work along the way, and for the end product.
Formal and Informal Evaluations Used	A summary of the variety of evaluation tools for this project follows. Reflections on Collaboration and Participation—Daily reflections (in Google forms) and Inquiry Circle notes are graded for thoroughness of response and participation. The daily reflections are graded on a ten-point scale. A student will receive full credit should all components of the reflection be filled in, complete sentences used, and depth of answers appropriate. WHS LibGuide Webquest—A rubric is used for the questions on finding information and using the tool. This was used as progress monitoring for information literacy in use. The LibGuide Webquest helped us to make sure that students knew how to navigate the LibGuide for use in the project and in other projects to follow. We checked the answers for complete sentences and that answers were correct. As this was an exploration, teachers used their discretion for giving credit for answers that were close to an answer. NoodleTools Notecard Evaluation—for every citation that students create, teachers complete the NoteCard Evaluation. As this can be time consuming to grade, this work is best broken up into smaller pieces. Our team arranged various deadlines for students to turn in their notecards. We identified the number of notecards due at each deadline and/or a specific breaking point for each deadline. For example, notecards are due once students are involved with inquiry week (when they have several class periods to work independently in Gather). Depending on the level of student, a different number of citations and/or notecards are due. Teachers graded these notecards while students continued to work on their research. In NoodleTools, all work carries a time stamp to help with the documentation of a timeline to note the student's workflow.

Figure 7.36 Learning Team Evaluation of the Process for Student Learning

	The TRAILS assessment—Completed as a preassessment in the beginning of the unit and as a postassessment at the end. TRAILS is an easily accessible and flexible tool for school librarians and teachers to identify strengths and weaknesses in the information-seeking skills of their students. In our unit, the Librarian compiles data regarding student growth for discussion with the teacher and student. Final Science Inquiry Assessment Rubric—This rubric is intended for the actual presentation combining the science content and the inquiry process into one rubric. Teachers discuss the rubric and agree on how to use the rubric in a similar manner so that grading is consistent throughout the 9th grade and, especially, throughout each level. (See Figure 7.37)
Team Reflection on Practice	As this project involved a larger team of teachers, the process of instruction constantly changed. Teachers met to reflect on practice throughout the entire process to discuss what was working and what needed improving. We kept track of our updates and truly worked as a team to meet the needs of the students. In developing the project, it was difficult to coordinate the teacher schedules and include daily check-ins with one another. Google Classroom has significantly improved the problem of time. We now use it as our platform for general communication to all students and with one another.

Figure 7.36 Learning Team Evaluation of the Process for Student Learning (*Continued*)

Name: _____ **Period:** _____

Guided Inquiry Assessment Rubric—Final Project Science Inquiry

Categories & Expectations	Criteria	1	2	3	4
KNOWLEDGE AND UNDERSTANDING Knowledge of content: Physical Science	The student demonstrates knowledge of physical science content (e.g., facts) identifying specific science topics that relate to answering the question.	The student demonstrates limited knowledge of physical science content.	The student demonstrates some knowledge of physical science content.	The student demonstrates good knowledge of physical science content.	The student demonstrates thorough knowledge of physical science content.
Knowledge of content: Application of Physical Science	The student demonstrates knowledge of content (e.g., facts) describing specific applications of physical science as related to the question.	The student demonstrates limited knowledge of physical science content.	The student demonstrates some knowledge of physical science content.	The student demonstrates good knowledge of physical science content.	The student demonstrates thorough knowledge of physical science content.
Understanding of content	The student demonstrates understanding of content by providing context to the physical science applications, and background knowledge on the topic to enhance understanding of the bigger topic.	The student shows limited understanding of the content.	The student shows some understanding of the content.	The student shows good understanding of the content.	The student shows insightful understanding of the content.
THINKING Use of creative/critical thinking processes Explanation of research process and synthesis	The student uses creative/critical thinking processes with effectiveness to create a new product and reflect on the learning. This includes answering questions 1–6, 9–11.	The student addresses very few (0–3) questions in reflecting on the inquiry process.	The student addresses some (4–5) questions in reflecting on the inquiry process.	The student addresses most (6–8) questions in reflecting on the inquiry process.	The student addresses all (9) questions in reflecting on the inquiry process.

Figure 7.37 Guided Inquiry Assessment Rubric—Final Project Science Inquiry

		# x 2.2	# x 2.8	# x 3.4	# x 4.0
THINKING Use of creative/critical thinking processes Explanation of research process and synthesis	*The student uses creative/critical thinking processes with effectiveness to create a product and reflect on the learning experience, demonstrating depth of answers that links the inquiry process with content.*	The student demonstrates a lack of creative/critical thinking processes to create a product with minimal to no reflection on learning. Audience is left not understanding how the project developed.	The student uses creative/critical thinking processes to create a product and to reflect on learning with some expression of knowledge, lacks specific detail about process, and leaves the audience with gaps in understanding how the project was developed.	The student uses creative/critical thinking processes to create a product and to reflect on learning with considerable expression of knowledge that allows the audience to understand how the project was developed; however, there is still room for growth.	The student uses creative/critical thinking processes to create a product and reflect on learning with a high degree of expression of knowledge that allows the audience to understand how the project was developed. Could be used as a model for future students' research.
COMMUNICATION Expression and organization of ideas and information in oral presentation, written, and visual forms	*The student expresses and organizes ideas and information with effectiveness.*	The student organizes ideas in presenting results of inquiry with limited effectiveness so that the listener has significant questions still left unanswered and/or the narrative is confusing and difficult to follow or vague.	The student organizes ideas in presenting results of inquiry with some effectiveness so that the listener has some questions still left unanswered and/or the narrative is, in parts, confusing and difficult to follow or vague.	The student organizes ideas in presenting results of inquiry with considerable effectiveness, which leaves the listener having very few or minor questions left unanswered. The narrative is clear and easy to follow.	The student organizes ideas in presenting results of inquiry with a high degree of effectiveness and can be used as a model for future students' research. The listener has no questions left unanswered and the narrative is clear and easy to follow.
Use of conventions, vocabulary, and terminology (Domain-Specific Vocabulary)	*The student uses conventions, vocabulary, and terminology related to inquiry.*	The student uses conventions, vocabulary, and terminology related to making and presenting products for inquiry with limited effectiveness.	The student uses conventions, vocabulary, and terminology related to making and presenting products for inquiry with some effectiveness.	The student uses conventions, vocabulary, and terminology related to making and presenting products for inquiry with considerable effectiveness.	The student uses conventions, vocabulary, and terminology related to making and presenting products for inquiry with a high degree of effectiveness.

TOTAL POINTS EARNED: _____ / 28 (x 100) = _____ %

Figure 7.37 Guided Inquiry Assessment Rubric—Final Project Science Inquiry (*Continued*)

Product Format: Audio and visual components of your final product.

The **visual** portion was created using (circle one):
Prezi   Glogster   Piktochart   Google Slides   Other _____

The **audio** portion was created using (circle one):
Screencastify   Oral Presentation   Other _____

Exit Interview—Process Reflection	Answered in Video
Introduction:	
1. What is your inquiry question?	__ Y or __ N
Body:	
2. Describe the process of how you developed a specific topic within the inquiry question.	__ Y or __ N
3. Which keywords did you find to be most effective for your search? In what way(s) were these words effective?	__ Y or __ N
4. Which part(s) of the LibGuide did you use? In what way(s) did the LibGuide help support your answer?	__ Y or __ N
5. Identify at least one difficulty you encountered during your inquiry.	__ Y or __ N
6. How did you overcome the difficulty?	__ Y or __ N
7. Identify and explain specific physical science topics related to answering your question. Be sure to identify supporting documents and where these documents were located.	__ Y or __ N
8. What scientific information answers your question? Be sure to identify supporting documents and where these documents were located.	__ Y or __ N
Conclusion:	
9. Identify what new question(s) you have about your topic; something that, if you had more time, you'd like to do more research on.	__ Y or __ N
10. Describe how you felt about working on this inquiry project (a) when you first started, (b) as you were gathering information, and (c) as you worked on the final product.	__ Y or __ N
11. What is the one piece of advice that you would give to a student doing this project next year?	__ Y or __ N

A final reflection on the process was captured in video form. The students used this form to create their videos.

Figure 7.38 Exit Interview—Process Reflection

"MINDS ON SCIENCE" UNIT RESOURCES

ARTICLES FOR OPEN

Lallanilla, M. "This London Skyscraper Can Melt Cars and Set Buildings on Fire." NBC News. 3 Sept. 2013. Retrieved February 8, 2016, from http://www.nbcnews.com/science/how-london-skyscraper-can-melt-cars-set-buildings-fire-8C11069092

Quenqua, D. "Software That Exposes Faked Photos." New York Times, 19 Aug. 2013. Retrieved February 8, 2016, from http://www.nytimes.com/2013/08/20/science/software-that-exposes-faked-photos.html

Ruhr-University Bochum. "Why Fish Don't Freeze in the Arctic Ocean: Chemists Unmask Natural Antifreeze." *ScienceDaily*, 26 Aug. 2010. Web. 8 Feb. 2016. https://www.science-daily.com/releases/2010/08/100825103832.htm

Spotts, P. "New Forensics Technique? Researchers Cull Images Reflected in People's Eyes." *Christian Science Monitor*. 27 Dec. 2013. http://www.csmonitor.com/Science/2013/1227/New-forensics-technique-Researchers-cull-images-reflected-in-people-s-eyes

VIDEOS FOR IMMERSE

Crash Course Chemistry 38:
http://www.pbslearningmedia.org/resource/520db484-0823-45ed-89b6-6db1da148d1a/nuclear-chemistry-crash-course-chemistry-38/

Who's Buried in the X Tombs:
http://www.pbslearningmedia.org/resource/nvrc-sci-whoxtombs/whos-buried-in-the-x-tombs/

Forensics Identification:
http://www.pbslearningmedia.org/resource/kqedq11.sci.forensicsidentifictication/forensics-identification/

Radiometric Dating:
http://www.pbslearningmedia.org/resource/tdc02.sci.phys.matter.radiodating/radiometric-dating/

Uranium: Twisting the Dragon's Tail:
http://www.pbslearningmedia.org/resource/2e4747f7-8bac-4b9a-b587-2fc7202c561f/half-life-uranium-twisting-the-dragons-tail/

PHYSICSCLASSROOM.COM IMMERSE PHASE

Describing Motion with Words
Introduction http://www.physicsclassroom.com/class/1DKin/Lesson-1/Introduction
Scalars and Vectors http://www.physicsclassroom.com/class/1DKin/Lesson-1/Scalars-and-Vectors
Distance and Displacement http://www.physicsclassroom.com/class/1DKin/Lesson-1/Distance-and-Displacement
Speed and Velocity http://www.physicsclassroom.com/class/1DKin/Lesson-1/Speed-and-Velocity
Acceleration http://www.physicsclassroom.com/class/1DKin/Lesson-1/Acceleration

Free Fall and the Acceleration of Gravity
Introduction
http://www.physicsclassroom.com/class/1DKin/Lesson-5/Introduction
Acceleration of Gravity
http://www.physicsclassroom.com/class/1DKin/Lesson-5/Acceleration-of-Gravity
Representing Free Fall by Graphs
http://www.physicsclassroom.com/class/1DKin/Lesson-5/Representing-Free-Fall-by-Graphs

Figure 7.39 Unit Resources

How Fast? and How Far?
   http://www.physicsclassroom.com/class/1DKin/Lesson-5/How-Fast-and-How-Far
The Big Misconception
   http://www.physicsclassroom.com/class/1DKin/Lesson-5/The-Big-Misconception

Electric Current
What is an Electric Circuit?
   http://www.physicsclassroom.com/class/circuits/Lesson-2/What-is-an-Electric-Circuit
Requirements of a Circuit
   http://www.physicsclassroom.com/class/circuits/Lesson-2/Requirements-of-a-Circuit
Electric Current
   http://www.physicsclassroom.com/class/circuits/Lesson-2/Electric-Current
Power: Putting Charges to Work
   http://www.physicsclassroom.com/class/circuits/Lesson-2/Power-Putting-Charges
   -to-Work
Common Misconceptions Regarding Electric Circuits
   http://www.physicsclassroom.com/class/circuits/Lesson-2/Common-Misconceptions
   -Regarding-Electric-Circuits

The Nature of a Wave
Waves and Wavelike Motion
   http://www.physicsclassroom.com/class/waves/Lesson-1/Waves-and-Wavelike-Motion
What is a Wave?
   http://www.physicsclassroom.com/class/waves/Lesson-1/What-is-a-Wave
Categories of Waves
   http://www.physicsclassroom.com/class/waves/Lesson-1/Categories-of-Waves

Properties of a Wave
The Anatomy of a Wave
   http://www.physicsclassroom.com/class/waves/Lesson-2/The-Anatomy-of-a-Wave
Frequency and Period of a Wave
   http://www.physicsclassroom.com/class/waves/Lesson-2/Frequency-and
   -Period-of-a-Wave
Energy Transport and the Amplitude of a Wave
   http://www.physicsclassroom.com/class/waves/Lesson-2/Energy-Transport-and-the
   -Amplitude-of-a-Wave

The Nature of a Sound Wave
Sound is a Mechanical Wave
   http://www.physicsclassroom.com/class/sound/Lesson-1/Sound-is-a-Mechanical-Wave
Sound as a Longitudinal Wave
   http://www.physicsclassroom.com/class/sound/Lesson-1/Sound-as-a
   -Longitudinal-Wave
Sound is a Pressure Wave
   http://www.physicsclassroom.com/class/sound/Lesson-1/Sound-is-a-Pressure-Wave

Sound Properties and Their Perception
Pitch and Frequency
   http://www.physicsclassroom.com/class/sound/Lesson-2/Pitch-and-Frequency
Intensity and the Decibel Scale
   http://www.physicsclassroom.com/class/sound/Lesson-2/Intensity-and-the
   -Decibel-Scale
The Speed of Sound
   http://www.physicsclassroom.com/class/sound/Lesson-2/The-Speed-of-Sound

Figure 7.39 Unit Resources (*Continued*)

The Human Ear
    http://www.physicsclassroom.com/class/sound/Lesson-2/The-Human-Ear

How Do We Know Light Is a Wave?
Wavelike Behaviors of Light
    http://www.physicsclassroom.com/class/light/Lesson-1/Wavelike-Behaviors-of-Light

Color and Vision
The Electromagnetic and Visible Spectra
    http://www.physicsclassroom.com/class/light/Lesson-2/The-Electromagnetic
    -and-Visible-Spectra
Visible Light and the Eye's Response
    http://www.physicsclassroom.com/class/light/Lesson-2/Visible-Light-and-the
    -Eye-s-Response
Blue Skies and Red Sunsets
    http://www.physicsclassroom.com/class/light/Lesson-2/Blue-Skies-and-Red-Sunsets

---

INFORMATION LITERACY RESOURCES

WHS LibGuide: http://whs.westborough.libguides.com/physcienceinquiry

TRAILS: http://www.trails-9.org

NoodleTools: http://www.noodletools.com/

RESOURCES FOR STUDENT QUESTIONING
10 Questions
    https://k12.thoughtfullearning.com/blogpost/10-questions-inquiry-bigger-better
Good Questions
    http://cll.mcmaster.ca/resources/misc/good_inquiry_question.html

---

SCIENTIFIC PHET SIMULATION RESOURCES
Skate Park
    https://phet.colorado.edu/en/simulation/energy-skate-park-basics

Static Electricity
    https://phet.colorado.edu/en/simulation/balloons-and-static-electricity

Waves on a String
    https://phet.colorado.edu/en/simulation/wave-on-a-string

Fluids
    https://phet.colorado.edu/en/simulation/under-pressure
    https://phet.colorado.edu/sims/html/under-pressure/latest/under-pressure_en.html

Color Vision
    https://phet.colorado.edu/en/simulation/color-vision

Introduction to Astronomy: Crash Course Astronomy #1
    https://www.youtube.com/watch?v=0rHUDWjR5gg&list=PL8dPuuaLjXtPAJr1ysd5y
    GlyiSFuh0mlL

The Nucleus: Crash Course Chemistry #1
    https://www.youtube.com/watch?v=FSyAehMdpyI&list=PL8dPuuaLjXtPHzzYuWy6fYEaX
    9mQQ8oGr

Chapter References:

Maniotes, L. (2005). "The Transformative Power of Literary Third Space." Ph.D. dissertation, School of Education, University of Colorado, Boulder.

Figure 7.39 Unit Resources (*Continued*)

Relationships Through *Romeo and Juliet*

8

Marc Crompton and Jennifer Torry

English teachers are always looking for ways of connecting high school students with Shakespeare, if for no other reason than that the language is foreign even to the English-speaking students, and those with English as their second (or third language) can struggle even more. · Jennifer Torry, an English teacher at St. George's School in Vancouver, British Columbia, was searching for a way to improve her class's study of *Romeo and Juliet* through looking at relationships. She had previously tried to explore the relationships in the play through a traditional project but found little success as the students struggled to personalize the topic. Because of this, she enlisted the help of Teacher Librarian Marc Crompton and Guided Inquiry Design® to make the learning and the play come to life.

St. George's is an independent boys' school whose mission is "Building fine young men, one boy at a time." Its student population is 1,150 in grades 1 through 12, and the vast majority of its graduates go on to universities around the world. One hundred twenty of our Senior School (grades 8–12) students live at the school in boarding facilities. Our students come from 26 different countries as far afield as China, Indonesia, Nigeria, Germany, and Chile.

This Guided Inquiry Design unit was experienced by students in a grade 10 English class and occurred during the second of three terms. Each class is typically 75 minutes long and there are 21 students in the class. The length of the unit may seem unusually long, starting in late November and ending in early March, but we felt that the students needed time to develop a strong understanding of *Romeo and Juliet* and build genuine connections with the topic of relationships in addition to dealing with a couple of other departmental requirements. A cross-grade exam occurs mid-year that was not related to the unit, and time was needed away from the unit to address it. There was also department involvement in a national poetry initiative, Poetry in Voice, that was woven into the study of relationships as an additional lens through which to view the topic. While the Poetry in Voice involvement wasn't key to the Guided Inquiry Design unit, it did add additional opportunities to reflect on the idea of relationships, find personal connections to the topic, and make comparisons to *Romeo and Juliet*.

There are a couple of ideas that play into this particular unit that may not be the norm in a Guided Inquiry Design unit and that are worth mentioning before the unit is laid out in detail. First, the line between **Immerse** and **Explore** is intentionally blurred. The sequence of classes alternates regularly between the emphasis on building the necessary understanding of integral concepts and examining different relationships in the play (**Immerse**) and allowing students

113

opportunities to connect, question, and play with ideas related to those concepts (**Explore**). The unit **Open** is prior to the reading of Shakespeare's *Romeo and Juliet* and supports the exploration of that text through both the **Immerse** and **Explore** phases. Our description of the unit here includes multiple **Immerse** and **Explore** classes presented in the order that they are encountered by the students. The reading of the play occurred primarily in class time and was done in a variety of ways, including performance readings of scenes where students take on specific roles, silent reading, and viewing of excerpts from the Franco Zeffirelli movie.

Second, the teacher and teacher librarian in this unit have undergone the National School Reform Faculty's (NSRF) protocol certification. These protocols that occur throughout this unit are included here and are described fairly fully where appropriate. Both teachers involved felt that the protocols used allowed students an opportunity to think through the ideas being addressed in different ways than they would normally while making that thinking more visible. These protocols tend to regulate contribution to discussion by providing opportunities for all students to participate. More information on these and more protocols from the National School Reform Faculty can be found at nsrfharmony.org.

The students who took full advantage of the way the unit was addressed really flourished and had an opportunity to delve into topics that they found engaging through the lens of relationships and the use of *Romeo and Juliet* as a springboard. Students' topics ranged from comparisons with other pieces of literature or pop culture to politics. One student drew parallels with relationships in *Star Wars*. Another looked at *Romeo and Juliet* as a potential allegory for the Cold War. Bill, another student in the class, found inspiration in Malcolm Gladwell: "My driving question was really interesting. . . . I read this book called *Outliers* that talked about opportunity and success and I wanted to figure out how to connect it to *Romeo and Juliet*." Whatever the personal interest was, the fact that the students had time to interact with Shakespeare and find relevance in their own lives was what made this unit particularly effective.

Guided Inquiry Design®
Unit Overview
"Relationships Through *Romeo and Juliet*"

Learning Goals:
Students will understand the relationships in their lives. They will do so by making connections between relationships present in *Romeo and Juliet* and relationships in their world.

Concept: Relationships
Guiding Question(s):

What relationships are important in your (student's) life?
How does society influence relationships?
How do your relationships relate to the relationships in Romeo and Juliet?
What does Shakespeare teach us about the nature of these relationships?

The Team: 10th Grade English Teacher, Teacher Librarian

This unit spanned an entire term, from November to March. It allowed for the study of *Romeo and Juliet* and the study of poetic structures as a way of thinking about relationships. There was significant time spent alternating between **Immerse** and **Explore** in an effort to give students multiple opportunities to draw personal connections and extend ideas in ways that fed and sparked their curiosity over time. The unit flows across the phases as indicated below.

 **Open**	In Inquiry Circles, the students are asked to brainstorm as many responses as possible to the prompt: "What relationships exist within our world?" After this step, they silently categorize the relationships, and then label the categories. The purpose of this exercise is, first, to have students expand their thinking about the relationships that exist in our world and, second, to kickstart a discussion about how we define relationships and what actually constitutes a relationship. After the protocol is completed, we debrief the activity and discuss some of the ideas that students found interesting or surprising to begin to push the boundaries of their definitions of relationships.
Immerse	We alternate between Immerse and Explore in this inquiry unit in order to develop critical understandings of relationships found in literature and how to analyze them from texts. In class, we read <u>Romeo and Juliet</u> to explore the different relationships present in the play. In each act, we focus on a different relationship. For example, Act 1 is friendship, Act 2 is romantic relationships versus lustful relationships, and Act 3 is mentorship. Following the reading or viewing of each act, there is either a discussion or a written piece that requires students to analyze the identified relationship type in a specific scene. Students document their understanding of relationships in each class in their Inquiry Journals during the Immerse stage.

Figure 8.1 Unit Overview

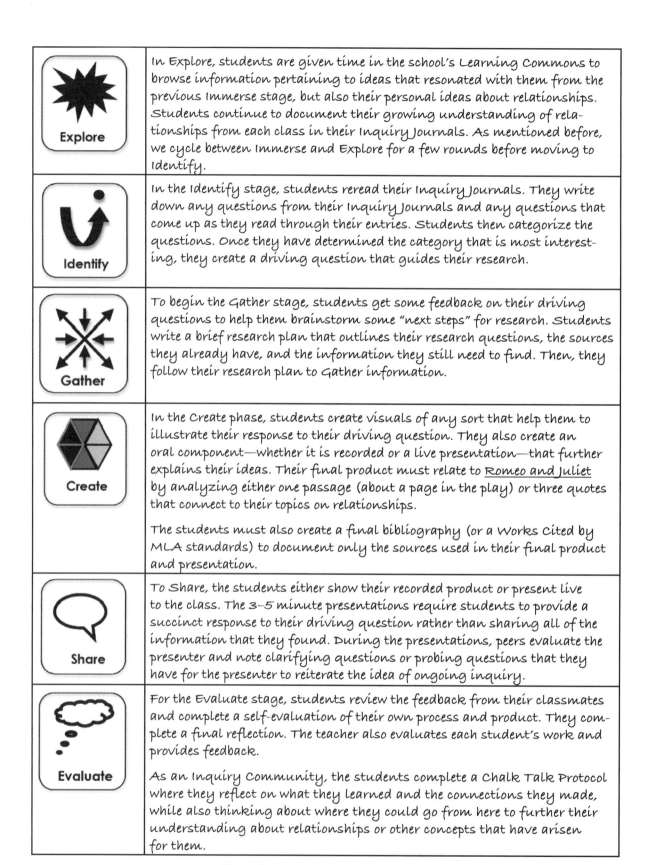

Explore	In Explore, students are given time in the school's Learning Commons to browse information pertaining to ideas that resonated with them from the previous Immerse stage, but also their personal ideas about relationships. Students continue to document their growing understanding of relationships from each class in their Inquiry Journals. As mentioned before, we cycle between Immerse and Explore for a few rounds before moving to Identify.
Identify	In the Identify stage, students reread their Inquiry Journals. They write down any questions from their Inquiry Journals and any questions that come up as they read through their entries. Students then categorize the questions. Once they have determined the category that is most interesting, they create a driving question that guides their research.
Gather	To begin the Gather stage, students get some feedback on their driving questions to help them brainstorm some "next steps" for research. Students write a brief research plan that outlines their research questions, the sources they already have, and the information they still need to find. Then, they follow their research plan to Gather information.
Create	In the Create phase, students create visuals of any sort that help them to illustrate their response to their driving question. They also create an oral component—whether it is recorded or a live presentation—that further explains their ideas. Their final product must relate to <u>Romeo and Juliet</u> by analyzing either one passage (about a page in the play) or three quotes that connect to their topics on relationships. The students must also create a final bibliography (or a Works Cited by MLA standards) to document only the sources used in their final product and presentation.
Share	To Share, the students either show their recorded product or present live to the class. The 3–5 minute presentations require students to provide a succinct response to their driving question rather than sharing all of the information that they found. During the presentations, peers evaluate the presenter and note clarifying questions or probing questions that they have for the presenter to reiterate the idea of ongoing inquiry.
Evaluate	For the Evaluate stage, students review the feedback from their classmates and complete a self-evaluation of their own process and product. They complete a final reflection. The teacher also evaluates each student's work and provides feedback. As an Inquiry Community, the students complete a Chalk Talk Protocol where they reflect on what they learned and the connections they made, while also thinking about where they could go from here to further their understanding about relationships or other concepts that have arisen for them.

Figure 8.1 Unit Overview (*Continued*)

Open

Relationships

Learning Goals
Process: Invitation to inquiry, open minds, stimulate curiosity.

Content: Students will be introduced to the broader idea of relationships.
Students will explore personal thoughts about relationships.
Location: Learning Commons
Team Members: English Teacher, Teacher Librarian

Starter Time: 8 minutes	The Affinity Mapping Protocol (See Figure 8.3) is used to help students explore the idea of relationships. The process involves each student spending 5 minutes silently brainstorming responses to the question we posed: "What relationships exist in our world?" Each response is written on a separate Post-It note.
Worktime Time: 42 minutes Inquiry Circles Affinity Mapping (NSRF)	Students, in Inquiry Circles of 4–6, place their responses on a larger piece of chart paper and silently organize those notes into categories. The essential aspect of this phase is that it remains silent. It can take 5–7 minutes, depending on the number of ideas the students have. Finally, the students are allowed to discuss the categories in their Inquiry Circles and come up with names for each category. The charts are each presented to the rest of the class and a large group debrief ensues. The debrief explores patterns, surprises, and similarities and differences between charts and opens students up to ideas about relationships that they may not have thought about.
Reflection Time: 20 minutes	The Inquiry Journal is introduced. For our Inquiry Journals, we used private discussions set up in our Learning Management System. We felt that this allowed us the convenience of a digital format, enabling us to keep in touch with students through their journals, but also allowed some privacy on a topic that might be sensitive for teenagers. The students are given 15 minutes to begin their journaling by reflecting on the ideas that they found interesting in the Affinity Mapping Protocol. They are asked to record insights and questions that they may want to follow up on later.

Figure 8.2 Open

Notes:	While the Affinity Mapping Protocol does a wonderful job of surfacing all sorts of ideas of what relationships are and the various kinds of relationships that exist, depending on the group, the teacher may need to probe to get students thinking less traditionally and more broadly about relationships. It is key that this thinking is imaginative so that there are opportunities for students to connect with the topic when they may be less comfortable addressing personal relationships. This Open phase could be extended, depending on how the teacher feels about the success of the initial exercise. During the debrief, the group could "fill in the blanks" as new ideas come up in the discussion. The group could come up with a definition of <u>relationship</u> that could be used going forward into the unit. The act of the class defining the word is far more productive than simply handing them the definition. It forces the students to wrestle with the actual meaning to be able to define it clearly.

Figure 8.2 Open (*Continued*)

National School Reform Faculty®
Harmony Education Center

Affinity Mapping Protocol

Sorting and Planning Protocol
NSRF,® Spring 2015

Facilitation Difficulty: 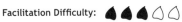   40 min.   Up to 15   📘 No preconference

Purpose — To define the elements of a larger topic or task, or to deepen a conversation around a question or topic that has many answers or perspectives. This protocol works best when begun with an open-ended analytic question such as, "What do we need to create and maintain inclusive and mutually rewarding relationships with parents in this school?" It can also be used for planning purposes.

Group size — Up to 15

Preparation — Bring pens and sufficient Post-it® notes (ideally the "super sticky" variety) for all participants. You'll also need a few markers. Hang 5-7 pieces of chart paper on the wall side-by-side, taping them together at the edges for one large working space. Ideally, write your question or topic in the center of the space but do not reveal it until after the setup.

Facilitation tips — Don't give people too many Post-it® notes or too much time to write ideas, or you'll have too many notes to sort! Ask people to write suggestions that are concrete as possible. Using the example of "What do we need to do to create and maintain an inclusive and mutually rewarding relationships with parents in this school?" Someone may write "Time to meet." This is not nearly as helpful as "Schedule a meeting on the first Tuesday of every month for an 'idea exchange' with parents."

Steps:

1. **Setup** — (2-4 min.) Explain that this protocol is to be done in silence, and that participants should write their ideas on the Post-it® notes, one idea per slip of paper. Read/reveal the question on the Affinity Map and set the timer for silent brainstorming.

2. **Place notes** — (1 min.) Instruct the participants to bring their notes to the chart paper, continuing in silence, and randomly place them on the Affinity Map.

3. **Categorize** — (5-7 min.) Directions for this step might sound like this: *"Which ideas go together? Continue to work in silence as you move notes near others that have an affinity, that seem to belong together. You can move your ideas and those of others, freely. Everyone's ideas became the group's ideas the moment they were placed on the chart paper. Do not be offended if someone moves your ideas to a place that you think they do not belong. Feel free to move a Post-it® again if you see a stronger affinity elsewhere. I will stop us when most of the notes are in groups."*

4. **Label** — (15 min.) Ask for a volunteer to read aloud an affinity group of notes. Ask the volunteer, *"Do you think all the notes here belong in this group? If not, please move them to the group where they belong."* Hand the volunteer a marker and ask, *"How would you title this group of ideas? Write down the title and draw a line enclosing the ideas within this group."* (The volunteer may get input from the group for titling.) Continue this process until all the groups have been labeled and all the post-its have found a home. At the end, there may wind up being a group of misfits at the end labeled, "Outliers" or "Potpourri."

5. **Discuss** — (5 min.) Have an open discussion using questions such as the following to help participants make connections between the categories:

   • *What themes emerged? Were there any surprises?*

Affinity Map Protocol page 1 of 2

Figure 8.3 NSRF Affinity Mapping Protocol

- *What is missing from our "affinity map"?*

6. **Next steps** — (8 min.) The group must now decide what their next steps will be. Commonly, participants will divide themselves into smaller groups, each one taking a "category" and developing:

   - Next steps

   - A time line to get these steps accomplished

   - Resources needed to accomplish these next steps

   - Who is responsible for what (All of the "who, what, when, where, and how" questions)

7. **Debrief and discuss** — (5 min.)

   - *How did this protocol expand your knowledge, or your perspective on the question?*

   - *Why did we do this activity in silence?*

   - *What did you think of the protocol? What worked for you, and what didn't?*

   - *How might you use this protocol in your work?*

Affinity Map Protocol page 2 of 2

Figure 8.3 NSRF Affinity Mapping Protocol (*Continued*)

From *Guided Inquiry Design in Action: High School*. Leslie K. Maniotes, Editor. Santa Barbara, CA: Libraries Unlimited. Copyright © 2017.

Immerse

Relationships

Immerse 1

Learning Goals
Process: Build background knowledge, connect to content, and discover interesting ideas.

Content: Students will begin to look at relationships as explored by poets and playwrights. Students will make inferences about relationships based on poetic texts. Students analyze and comprehend Shakespearean text. Students explore poems that connect with the theme of relationships.
Location: English Classroom
Team Members: English Teacher

Starter Time: 5 minutes	The students begin the class by spending 10 minutes journaling on the question "What relationships do we have with nonhuman objects?" The poem "The Author to Her Book" by Anne Bradstreet is then read aloud together.
Worktime Time: 50 minutes	Poetry analysis of "The Author to Her Book" by Anne Bradstreet: This process allows an efficient way of giving all students a chance to think about and discuss a topic. The students start this process by reading the poem silently. They are then put in groups of three (triads) and are given 2 minutes to read the first question (below) and reflect on how they might answer it. They are encouraged to write notes in preparation for their speaking time. At the end of their prep time, Round 1 begins and each person in the triad is given 90 seconds to answer the question to the other two members of their triad. The nonpresenting members of the group are not allowed to speak. If the presenter finishes early, the group sits silently and reflects. After 90 seconds, the teacher gives the cue for person two to speak, and after those 90 seconds person three gets their turn. Round 2 is done in the same format addressing the second question and with person two being the first person to present. Round three is the same with person three starting the dialogue. At the end of the process there is a ten-minute debrief that brings the ideas back together, and if the ideas have not already surfaced, the teacher has a chance to connect the poem to the idea of relationships. 1. What is the speaker saying in this poem? Keep in mind the title. 2. What examples of literary devices (metaphor, simile, personification) do we see? Why do we think they are used? 3. Based on the literary devices and word choice employed, what message/theme is the poet trying to relay? How do you know?
Reflection Time: 15 minutes	Open Inquiry Journal Reflection based on thinking occurring in class.

Figure 8.4 Immerse 1

Relationships

Immerse 2

Learning Goals
Process: Build background knowledge, connect to content, and discover interesting ideas.

Content: Students will begin to build context of the play *Romeo and Juliet* for future study. Students will begin to reflect on the nature of relationships as they read a number of poems.

Location: English Classroom
Team Members: English Teacher

Starter Time: 10 minutes	Read aloud and analyze the prologue of <u>Romeo and Juliet</u>. The prologue to <u>Romeo and Juliet</u> is read together and then a brief discussion of broad ideas occurs before sending students into Inquiry Circles to analyze the text.
Worktime Time: 30 minutes Text Analysis Inquiry Circles	In Inquiry Circles of 4, students analyze and break down the prologue of <u>Romeo and Juliet</u> to help them understand what they will be reading about in the play. Groups are assigned to one of the following parts: 1. Setting (What is the time and place of the story? How do you know?) 2. Characters (Who might the main characters be? What type of people are they? Rich or poor? Young or old?) 3. Plot (What do you anticipate the plot will be?) 4. Conflicts (What main conflict do you think the story will have? What are some other conflicts that may arise?) 5. Genre (What genre—tragedy, romance, comedy, etc.—do you think the play will be? Why?) For each part, the group must provide brief notes or a brief paragraph in response to the questions listed. One student is designated as the reporter and types up the notes or paragraph and submits them to this discussion board in the Learning Management System for everyone to view. Each group is graded based on the thoroughness of their response and the quality of their details (see Figure 8.6).

Figure 8.5 Immerse 2

Poetry In Voice 30 minutes	Poetry in Voice (www.poetryinvoice.com) is a program that encourages the love and live recitation of poetry in a competitive format. Our school participates in this program across all grades and has had some students move to the regional and national levels. Students access poems from www.poetryinvoice.com; however, they may also use another poem from a different site if they are not interested in participating in the competition. (See Figure 8.6) Students are given class time to find a poem and to complete the reflection. They are also allowed to change their poem if they find another one that they prefer later on in the process as long as they redo the reflection. The process is left quite open for students to interpret the relationships so that they can find a personal connection with or interest in the poem's topic. For example, "The Man He Killed" by Thomas Hardy allowed one boy to consider the implications of meeting a man in war who is your "opponent" versus bumping into the same man in a bar during a time of peace. As part of the poem selection process, students are asked to complete a Reading and Viewing Reflection on their chosen poem.
Reflection Time: 10 minutes	Inquiry Journal reflection must include pasting students' Reading and Viewing Reflection into their Inquiry Journals in addition to any other related thinking that might be occurring.

Figure 8.5 Immerse 2 (*Continued*)

POETRY IN VOICE

This year, we will be hosting an in-class competition for Poetry in Voice. Visit the Poetry in Voice website http://www.poetryinvoice.com/poems to find your poem. Your poem must meet the criteria below:

1. It must be 25 lines or less **or** pre-20th century.
2. You must be able to justify how it relates to relationships.
3. You must be able to memorize it!
4. It must be personally interesting to you.

Once you have chosen your poem, you will post the title and author of the poem and a brief reflection. You will type your reflection into the text box below and copy it into your Inquiry Journal as well. Your reflection must include the items listed below. You will be graded according to the rubric attached.

- the title of the poem and its author
- how it incorporates the idea of relationships
- why you are interested in the poem
- 1 or 2 literary devices or uses of diction that stand out to you and why

Poem Selection			
Criteria	**Ratings**		**Pts**
Connection to Relationship	Student clearly identifies the relationship in the poem and explains it. The student provides evidence of the relationship and clearly justifies its legitimacy as a relationship. 3 pts	Student identifies a relationship in poem but lacks clear evidence or justification for why this can be considered a relationship. 2 pts	Student discusses concepts relating to relationships, but doesn't identify a specific relationship in the poem. 1 pts	**3 pts**
Personal Interest	Student shows a clear interest in the author, the content of the poem, and/or the relationship identified. The student convincingly explains this personal interest. 3 pts	The student shows some interest in the author, the content of the poem, and/or the relationship identified. There is some evidence that the student has a personal interest in the poem. 2 pts	The student shows little interest in anything to do with the poem. The poem seems to have been selected at random. 1 pts	**3 pts**
Use of Literary Devices and Diction	The student chooses two literary devices or examples of specific diction and clearly analyzes their importance in the poem. 3 pts	The student chooses one literary device or example of specific diction and describes its importance in the poem. The analysis may lack specific details. 2 pts	The student does not identify any literary devices or examples of specific diction. OR The student does not analyze the identified literary devices or examples of specific diction. 1 pts	**3 pts**
			Total Points: 9

Figure 8.6 Poetry in Voice

Explore

Relationships

Explore 1

Learning Goals
Process: Explore interesting ideas, look around, and dip in.

Content: Students will locate poetry resources in the Learning Commons. Students will understand how to use EasyBib and its annotation function as their Inquiry Log. Students will explore poems that connect them to the theme of relationships.

Location: Learning Commons
Team Members: Teacher Librarian, English Teacher

Starter Time: 15 minutes	The bulk of the class time is used for students to Explore the physical and digital collections in order to select and better understand their poems. In the starter the librarian introduces 3 key tools and resources for Exploration. 1. Areas of the physical book collection that address poetry collections and criticism 2. Specific databases 3. Larger search tools are also addressed in a brief review in order to set students up for the research that they will need to do in connecting their particular interests in relationships with their poem and <u>Romeo and Juliet</u>. 4. The Inquiry Log is introduced by using EasyBib (which, at the time of this writing, is about to become Imagine Easy Scholar) to create annotated bibliographies. EasyBib is a tool that most students will have used in previous years, so a review is all that is necessary.
Worktime Time: 45 minutes	Students are encouraged to browse, look around, and dip into multiple resources from the physical and digital collection available in our Learning Commons to better understand their poems.
Reflection Time: 15 minutes	Reflection is entered into the Inquiry Journal based on any connections to interest or ideas that were made with poetry or poetry criticism read during the class.

Figure 8.7 Explore 1

Relationships

Immerse 3

Learning Goals
Process: Build background knowledge, connect to content, and discover interesting ideas.

Content: Students will read and comprehend Shakespearean language. Students will build an understanding of the nature of the different relationships present in Act 1 of *Romeo and Juliet*.

Location: English Classroom
Team Members: English Teacher

Starter Time: 5 minutes	The idea of mind mapping has been used prior to this unit as a way of visualizing the connections between ideas. The students are used to using pencil and paper to explore and demonstrate the closeness of each relationship using proximity and lines. An example of the kind of mind map that the students create can be found in Figure 8.9.
Worktime Time: 60 minutes	While watching the movie version of Act 1 of <u>Romeo and Juliet</u>, the students individually create a mind map of the relationships that exist. This is a long act in the play, and this activity takes much of the period to sketch what can be multiple iterations of the students' mind maps. (See Figure 8.9)
Reflection Time: 15 minutes Inquiry Journal	Students complete an Inquiry Journal entry based on observations and connections made in the Act 1 relationship mapping exercise. Journal Prompt: "What did you notice about the relationships you mapped in Act 1? Be explicit and provide details in your explanation."

Figure 8.8 Immerse 3

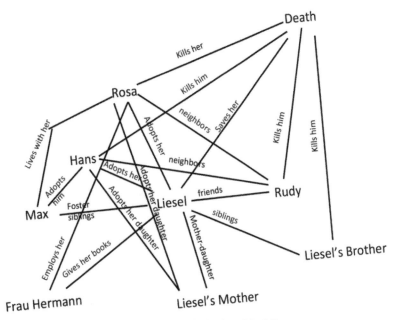

Figure 8.9 Sample Relationship Map

Immerse

Relationships

Immerse 4

Learning Goals
Process: Build background knowledge, connect to content, and discover interesting ideas.

Content: Students will select and analyze poems for tone and diction. Students will begin to understand how a poet uses tone and diction to express ideas about relationships.

Location: English Classroom
Team Members: English Teacher

Starter Time: 10 minutes	The students make their final decision about the poem that they wish to use for this unit. This poem is used as their <u>Poetry in Voice</u> entry if they are choosing to enter that competition, and is otherwise used for the analysis and reflection process that occurs in this and the next few classes. The choice of this poem does not bind the student to a particular research topic, and the poem itself may or may not end up being used as a resource in the eventual research.
Worktime Time: 50 minutes	The students are asked to write a 1–2 paragraph analysis focusing on the author's word choice and how that conveys the speaker's tone toward the subject and dictates the audience's mood when reading or listening to the poem. Students specifically focus on the author's tone and the audience's mood toward the highlighted relationship.
Reflection Time: 15 minutes	Inquiry Journal reflection based on connections made through study of poem and theme of relationships.

Figure 8.10 Immerse 4

Relationships

Explore 2

Learning Goals
Process: Explore interesting ideas, look around, and dip in.

Content: Students will explore the concept of relationships and continue to find personal connections.
Location: Learning Commons
Team Members: Teacher Librarian, English Teacher

Starter Time: 5 minutes	These 2 classes really begin the more individual exploration of connecting personal interests/curiosities with the theme of relationships. Students are reminded of the Inquiry Log (EasyBib) as their research organizer and are given time to take their exploration in their own direction.
Worktime Time: 60 minutes	The classes are informal and unstructured with the 2 teachers circulating and talking with students about their interests and ideas. The teachers' role in this process is to support students in clarifying their thinking and stimulating new ideas when a student is stuck as well as to focus thinking when a student feels overwhelmed. Students are encouraged to go back to their previous Inquiry Journal entries to pick up ideas that they recorded in previous classes and to keep the Inquiry Journal open to record new thinking as they work through their Explore process.
Reflection Time: 10 minutes each session	Students reflect in journals about what was interesting and new ideas that are surfacing about relationships as they look around. Inquiry Journal Prompt: "What relationships are interesting or important to you? What makes them important? Where have you experienced relationships like this in your life? What are you finding out about relationships that might be interesting to share with others?"

Figure 8.11 Explore 2

Relationships

Immerse 5

Learning Goals
Process: Build background knowledge, connect to content, and discover interesting ideas.

Content: Students will refresh their text analysis skills with focus on diction and irony. Students will deepen their understanding of their chosen poem through preparation for their final presentation.

Location: English Classroom
Team Members: English Teacher

Starter Time: 20 minutes	Students are given the roles of Benvolio, Mercutio, and Romeo for the in-class reading of Act 1, Scene 4. The scene is read aloud by the students.
Worktime Time: 30 minutes Inquiry Circles Inquiry Community	Once the scene is read, the class breaks into Inquiry Circles, groups of 3. Each Inquiry Circle works together to find examples of ironic statements and specific diction (phrasing or words) that helped the audience to understand the scene. In so doing they will describe the relationship between the three characters in each scene. They have 5 minutes to complete this task, and then they report their findings back to the Inquiry Community. The Inquiry Community discusses the irony and diction as well as what students noticed about the relationships present in this scene. The remainder of the class is devoted to the practice of students' <u>Poetry in Voice</u> poems.
Reflection Time: 15 minutes Inquiry Journals	Inquiry Journal reflection connecting ideas around <u>Romeo and Juliet</u> discussion and poetry study. How might these new ideas serve to inform others that surfaced during previous Explore session?

Figure 8.12 Immerse 5

Relationships

Immerse 6

Learning Goals
Process: Build background knowledge, connect to content, and discover interesting ideas.

Content: Students will deepen their understanding of how Shakespeare treats the relationship between Romeo and Mercutio. Students will review and practice writing text analysis in multiparagraph form using a theme statement.
Location: English Classroom
Team Members: English Teacher

Starter Time: 5 minutes	The English teacher introduces the question, "How does Shakespeare use metaphorical language to contrast Romeo's current mood to that of his friends?"
Worktime Time: 65 minutes Inquiry Circles	In Inquiry Circles, groups of 4, students do a sample outline for the analysis on the prompt: "How does Shakespeare use metaphorical language to contrast Romeo's current mood to that of his friends?" They then have 20 minutes to share and discuss as a class. Next, students complete the following assignment: "Based on your own understanding and our discussion of Act 1, Scene 4, write a 2–3 paragraph composition that answers the following question: 'How does Shakespeare's use of rhetorical devices help the reader to understand the relationship between Mercutio and Romeo?' "Organize your ideas using the Point Example Explain chain (PEE Chain) (See Figure 8.14). Give two or three examples per paragraph to fully develop your answer. Ensure that you clearly explain all of your ideas. The criteria for your composition are as follows: • There is a clear thesis statement/point that dictates the topic for the composition. • There are at least two direct and relevant quotes to support the response. • Quotes are integrated correctly into the writer's own sentences. • Each quote is clearly explained to support the thesis statement/point. • There is a sense of an ending to the composition; a concluding statement (a sentence that wraps up the ideas clearly) is provided to link all of the ideas back to the thesis statement."
Reflection Time: 5 minutes	The assignment today serves doubly as a reflection on content.

Figure 8.13 Immerse 6

Make a **Point**, provide an **Example** or **Evidence**, and **Explain**

Create a PEE chain

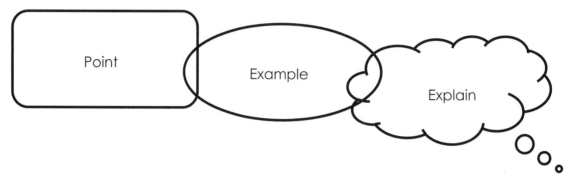

POINT:

The playwright, William Shakespeare, hints to us that Mercutio and Romeo have been good friends for a while and know each other quite well. During their conversation Mercutio uses many puns and metaphors that come off as somewhat taunting yet supportive.

EXAMPLE:

This is shown to us when Romeo is reluctant to go to the feast. After the event with Rosaline that left him heartbroken, Mercutio tells him that "[he is] a lover. Borrow Cupid's wings, / and soar with them above a common bound" (I.iv.17–18).

EXPLAIN:

Mercutio is using Cupid's wings as a symbol for love and in a way telling Romeo to look at love from a different viewpoint on his next search for a significant other. Mercutio, knowing Romeo's situation, understands that Romeo will find another lover soon enough and is encouraging him not to get too down on himself and to have a night of fun at the Capulets' feast.

Figure 8.14 Point Example Explain Chain

Immerse

Relationships

Immerse 7

Learning Goals
Process: Build background knowledge, connect to content, and discover interesting ideas.

Content: Students will watch and listen for understanding of plot development. Students will explore the concept of romantic relationships through examining the relationship between Romeo and Juliet.

Location: English Classroom
Team Members: English Teacher

Starter Time: 30 minutes	Yesterday students worked on an analysis of rhetorical devices used by Shakespeare. Today they have time to complete the analysis from the previous class. Once it is complete, they turn to a partner and gain feedback from a peer by doing peer edits, using yesterday's criteria (see Figures 8.12 and 8.13). Students then revise their initial work.
Worktime Time: 50 minutes Inquiry Community	As an Inquiry Community, watch Act 2 of <u>Romeo and Juliet.</u> A 10-minute Inquiry Community debrief follows the viewing around these questions: • How do we define romantic relationships? • Focusing on their behavior in the scene, is the relationship between Romeo and Juliet an example of a true romantic relationship? Why or why not? • What might be a better example?
Reflection Time: 15 minutes	Inquiry Journal reflection exploring romantic relationships based on what was watched, adding information about any other ideas students noticed or thought of regarding relationships.

Figure 8.15 Immerse 7

Immerse

Relationships

Immerse 8

Learning Goals
Process: Build background knowledge, connect to content, and discover interesting ideas.

Content: Students will watch and listen for understanding of plot development. Students will identify and analyze characters' roles in relationships. Students will identify and analyze conflicts resulting from relationships.

Location: English Classroom

Team Members: English Teacher

Starter Time: 10 minutes	Students will use the Pair-Share process to review the relationships in the first two acts of <u>Romeo and Juliet</u> and determine which demonstrate actual love. They need to be able to defend their choices.
Worktime Time: 45 minutes Inquiry Circles	Review all of the relationships encountered thus far in the play to determine which might relate most closely to those that students are looking at in their Explore phase. Students are given 15 minutes in Inquiry Circles to discuss these connections with their peers. Finally, they are asked to look at conflicts resulting from these relationships in their Inquiry Circles. They have another 15 minutes for this process.
Reflection Time: 15 minutes	Inquiry Journal reflection connecting ideas around <u>Romeo and Juliet</u> discussion. In particular, students are asked to reflect on the relationship with the ideas that they are looking at in their Explore sessions.

Figure 8.16 Immerse 8

Explore

Relationships

Explore 3

Learning Goals
Process: Explore interesting ideas, look around, and dip in.

Content: Students will explore relationships of interest from different angles. Students will accurately document research and information using an annotated bibliography for an Inquiry Log.

Location: Learning Commons
Team Members: Teacher Librarian, English Teacher

Starter Time: 10 minutes	At the beginning of the class, the students are encouraged to reflect on the types of relationships that they are finding most interesting. To expand their ideas outward, we introduce the idea of the types of professionals who study these types of relationships. "Think about a professional that might be interested in the relationships you are uncovering. Pair with a partner to talk about the potential list of professionals that you are considering (e.g., psychologists, scientists, artists, historians, coaches). Share some ideas and connections with the Inquiry Community." Finding the work of these people may inform students' research choices.
Worktime Time: 60 minutes Inquiry Log	Students continue to explore resources and enter them into the Inquiry Log. Students are also advised that they will be heading toward the Identify phase and will want to start thinking about specific directions that their research could take. The Inquiry Journal is a place to record ideas, stop and jot, ask questions, and record other thinking.
Reflection Time: 15 minutes Inquiry Journal	• How interested are you in this idea that you are exploring? • What are you finding easy to do? • What are you finding hard to do? (Questions adapted from the SLIM Reflection. See the CiSSL website, http://cissl.rutgers.edu/images/stories/docs/slimreflectionsheet.pdf)

Figure 8.17 Explore 3

Immerse

Relationships

Immerse 9

Learning Goals
Process: Build background knowledge, connect to content, and discover interesting ideas.

Content: Students will view and understand the development of mentoring relationships in *Romeo and Juliet*.

Location: English Classroom
Team Members: English Teacher

Starter Time: 10 minutes Inquiry Journal	Journal Topic: "How do mentors impact individuals? Reflect on how this exists in or impacts your own life."
Worktime Time: 50 minutes Inquiry Community	Together watch Act 3 of <u>Romeo and Juliet</u> in the Inquiry Community. Students are asked to pay attention to and focus specifically on who acts as a mentor within the act and how effective he or she is in this role. A 10-minute debrief discussion occurs using the guiding question "How do mentors impact individuals?" We focus particularly on the characters of Friar Lawrence and the Nurse in this conversation.
Reflection Time: 15 minutes	Inquiry Journal with a focus on the mentors or on individual experiences, <u>Romeo and Juliet</u>, or anything connected to their Explore ideas.

Figure 8.18 Immerse 9

Relationships

Immerse 10

Learning Goals
Process: Build background knowledge, connect to content, and discover interesting ideas.

Content: Students will discuss and analyze the connection between an individual and his or her mentor.

Location: English Classroom
Team Members: English Teacher

Starter Time: 15 minutes	The class reads Act 3, Scene 3 of _Romeo and Juliet_ together.
Worktime Time: 50 minutes Inquiry Community Text-Based Seminar Protocol (NSRF)	The class then enters into a Text-Based Seminar protocol. (See Figure 8.20) This is a structured Inquiry Community discussion that focuses discussion specifically on the text itself. Students must refer to the text to change the course of the discussion. The protocol regulates time given to each person to speak. The prompting questions for the protocol are: • What examples do we have in our own lives? • What examples do we have in _Romeo and Juliet_? • Are the mentors in _Romeo and Juliet_ effective? Do they try to do what is best for their mentees or do they serve their own purposes? Why or why not? • Why is the relationship between a mentor and a mentee reliant on trust and respect? • What are the qualities of a good mentor?
Reflection Time: 15 minutes	Inquiry Journal on what have you learned about relationships thus far and what from today's discussion connects with your ideas about relationships.

Figure 8.19 Immerse 10

NSRF®
National School Reform Faculty®
Harmony Education Center

Text-Based Seminar Protocol

NSRF, Spring 2015

Facilitation Difficulty: 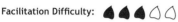   20-50 min., depending on time available   Up to 15    No preconference

Purpose — To increase understanding around a complicated or deep text, based on a focusing question that is genuine and/or useful. Use of this protocol will guarantee that the entire group will be engaged in the inquiry. Good for students and adult learners who already have some experience with protocols.

Time — 20-50 minutes, depending on time available and participants' familiarity with the protocol.

Facilitation tips — As coach, you have two primary tasks: posing the focusing question and keeping the group focused without pushing any particular agenda. Because this activity is less structured than many protocols, it can be challenging to lead for those unfamiliar with protocol structure. These tips might make the job easier:

- Take time to craft a meaningful focusing question to be revealed in the meeting. You're striving to push the thinking of all the participants, to invite them to recognize and challenge their own assumptions. Your question should require close reading of their notes in the text and allow many aspects of the text and different opinions to be discussed. You may want to select a provocative quote from the text itself and create a focusing question around it.

- It's helpful to prepare a few follow-up questions to insert as needed. These questions might refocus participants toward a different perspective, in case you have a group that's slow to become fully engaged in the seminar. You may also create new followups that arise from the conversation itself.

- Some participants feel driven to fill silences and see the seminar as more of a debate than an equal sharing of perspectives. Some are inclined to express opinions independent of the text. Usually, a reminder of the protocol rules will pull them back on task. If those reminders aren't sufficient, introduce one of your follow up questions and/or extend invitations to people who have not yet spoken in order to put the group back on track.

- It is sometimes useful to keep running notes of the conversation and to periodically summarize for the group what has been said.

Preparation — Ensure that all participants have received the text, read it and marked important ideas in advance. Bring chart paper and a marker to post the focusing question.

Steps:

1. **Setup** — (5 min.) Review the purpose of the Text-Based Seminar. Also remind the participants that they should:

   - Work from the text rather than expressing opinions without a page reference

   - Strive to enhance and deepen their understanding

   - Watch their airtime so they can learn as much from listening as speaking

2. **Reflect** — (5 min.) Chart the focusing question and give the group five minutes to silently review their notes and the text with this question in mind. If they haven't already, participants can highlight sections of the text that are meaningful to them.

Text-Based Seminar Protocol page 1 of 2

Figure 8.20 NSRF Text-Based Seminar Protocol

From *Guided Inquiry Design in Action: High School*. Leslie K. Maniotes, Editor. Santa Barbara, CA: Libraries Unlimited. Copyright © 2017.

3. **Remind** — (2 min.) Inform or remind the participants that your job is to:

   - Keep the conversation on target, so you may remind the group about the focusing question if people's comments start wandering, or interject another question.

   - Make sure that air-time is shared. This means that you may keep track of who's already spoken and invite participation from those who have not yet spoken.

4. **Instruct** — (2 min.) Instruct participants that each time they want to bring up a new topic, they must first refer to a passage in the text, citing page number and paragraph placement on the page. Subsequent people who speak to that point do not need to reference that passage again. However, when a participant wishes to move on to another topic, they must ground their comment in the text by referencing the appropriate page number and location of the passage on that page, and then read the passage before making the new point.

5. **Begin** — (15-30 min.) Set the clock based on the time available for the Protocol, and invite some-one to begin addressing the focusing question. As coach, if you like, you may identify and verbalize themes developed through the protocol.

6. **Debrief and reflect** — (5 min.)

   - *Which quotes or ideas in the text did not strike you as important in your first reading that feel much more important now that you've discussed them?*

   - *How did you feel about the requirement to quote a particular passage rather than simply express your opinions related to the text?*

   - *Did you notice anyone stating something contrary to your beliefs, and if so, did they encourage you to think differently or "dig in deeper" to bolster your own ideas?*

   - *Did the protocol feel more like teaching or training (pointing you towards a specific outcome) or more like facilitation (revealing the complex thoughts of the group)?*

Text-Based Seminar Protocol page 2 of 2

Figure 8.20 NSRF Text-Based Seminar Protocol (*Continued*)

Relationships

Learning Goals
Process: Pause and ponder to identify the inquiry question.

Content: Students will synthesize information to determine a focus for the project.
Location: Learning Commons
Team Members: English Teacher, Teacher Librarian

Starter Time: 5 minutes	The concept of a Driving Question is reviewed with the Inquiry Community. "For our relationships project, you will identify a Driving Question that will drive your inquiry. Today you will follow the steps (See Figure 8.22) to complete this task, and submit your notes that you take."
Worktime Time: 50 minutes Inquiry Journal Inquiry Chart	The students are given much of the class to reread their Inquiry Journals and annotated bibliography and note on a separate piece of paper all questions that they recorded or that occurred to them as they read. They then create (Inquiry Chart) another mind map of their questions in an effort to identify key themes/ideas in their reflections. Finally, students draft a Driving Question that clearly articulates the direction of their future research. Teachers circulate and check in with students as they work. Sample Driving Questions from our students were: • "How is the relationship between political superpowers such as countries or parties (Democrats, Republicans) similar to the relationship between the Capulets and the Montagues?" • "What characteristics make up a good leader in a relationship?" • "What are the most important aspects of having a successful relationship?" • "Why do people feel the need to have relationships in their lives even though they know that there will be problems involved?"
Reflection	Student notes are used as the reflection for today.

Figure 8.21 Identify

Identify

<u>Steps to Identify a Driving Inquiry Question:</u>

1. Open up a notepad or Word document on your computer. You can also take notes by hand.

2. Read through your Inquiry Journal entries. Write down all of the questions you listed in your entries and any questions that come up as you reread them. Try to list as many questions as possible.

3. List any other questions you still have about relationships.

4. Take the questions you have and arrange them into a mind map or a categorized list. Be sure that you try to group the questions together by similarities as much as possible. A mind map might work best so that you can draw connections between questions that may not necessarily be in the same category.

5. Analyze the groups of questions you have formed and identify the group you are most interested in researching further.

6. Based on the questions you have in that group, write one concise, specific driving question. Your question should address the idea that relationships are impacted by various factors.

Figure 8.22 Steps to Identify an Inquiry Question

Relationships

Gather

Learning Goals
Process Goal: Gather important information, go broad, go deep.

Content Goal: Students will deepen their understanding of their chosen topic.

Location: Learning Commons
Team Members: English Teacher, Teacher Librarian

Starter Time: 30 minutes Aha! Protocol (NSRF)	Students begin the Gather stage by completing the Aha! Protocol to get feedback on their driving questions and help brainstorm their next steps from their peers. (See Figure 8.24) Students are given a worksheet for the Aha! Protocol and divided into Inquiry Circles of three groups of seven. There are 6 questions on the worksheet, and each question is answered during a three-minute timed round. After each round, the students pass the paper around so that feedback is provided by five different peers. The first student records his or her driving question and why it is interesting, and each subsequent student provides feedback based on this student's driving question. The questions (in order) are: 1. What is your driving question? Why is it interesting to you? (Completed by the student who is asking the driving question.) 2. Have you had a similar question? What was your question? How does your question compare with this classmate's? (Completed by Student 2) 3. Why do you think this question is interesting and significant? What could make it more interesting and/or significant? (Completed by Student 3) 4. What questions do you have to help your classmate think more deeply or differently about the driving question? Try to list questions that will help your classmate gain a better understanding of the topic. (Completed by Student 4) 5. What other questions or ideas can you add based on the other driving questions that you have already read today? (Completed by Student 5) 6. What next steps, ideas, resources, or anything else do you think your classmate should consider? (Completed by Student 6) Students are then given 10 minutes to discuss ideas and questions raised during the protocol. This discussion happened as a whole class activity to share and compare ideas, but it can also be a small group discussion within the groups of seven.

Figure 8.23 Gather

Worktime Time: 60 minutes 3 sessions	The students are given three classes to gather the information that they need to support their identified inquiry topic. Before beginning research, the students are required to complete and submit a Research Plan. The Research Plan consists of: 1. Driving question 2. 3–5 research questions 3. Justification for the research questions 4. A list of sources from the Immerse and Explore phases that can be used to help answer the research questions 5. A list of potential source types and information that will need to be found to help address the research questions 6. A schedule/plan for how the student will approach the Gather process based on the time given During the Gather classes, the teachers circulate and have conversations with each student multiple times over these classes in order to address specific issues as they arise.
Reflection Time: 15 minutes / class	Students complete an Inquiry Journal entry at the end of each class, reflecting on the ideas they have considered, what connections they see, and their progress in responding to their Research Questions and, ultimately, their driving question.
Notes:	Adapt the Worksheets in Figure 8.24 by using these questions. 1. My driving question and why it is interesting to me. 2. Have you had a similar question that you have considered? What was your question? How does your question compare with this classmate's? 3. Why do you think this question is interesting and significant? What could make it more interesting and/or significant? 4. What questions do you have to help _____ think more deeply or differently about the driving question? (Try to list questions that will help your classmate gain a better understanding of the topic.) 5. What other questions or ideas can you add based on the other driving questions that you have seen today? 6. What next steps, ideas, resources, or anything else do you think _____ should consider?

Research Plan

What is your driving question?
What are your research questions? (You must have 3–5 questions.)
How do these research questions help you to answer your driving question?
Which sources from your annotated bibliography can you use to help answer your research questions?
What other types of sources or information from sources might you need to find to answer your research questions?
What are your next steps for research? Write out an actual research schedule for yourself to manage your time. You will have three entire classes on (dates) to research, so please plan accordingly. Your research notes are due (date) at the beginning of class.

Figure 8.23 Gather (*Continued*)

NSRF®

National School Reform Faculty®
Harmony Education Center

Aha! Protocol

Courtesy of The Coltrain Group, by Michele Mattoon

Facilitation Difficulty: 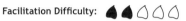   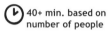 40+ min. based on number of people   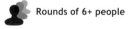 Rounds of 6+ people    No preconference

Purpose — To increase and strengthen meaning gleaned from a speaker presentation, video, or dramatic performance, to share and extend that meaning within a group, and to apply the meaning to one's personal experience.

Group size — Can accommodate any size group, ideally in tables of six or more people.

Preparation — Print the Aha! Protocol Worksheet for each participant and make sure everyone has a pen.

Steps:

1. **Setup** — (4 min.) Direct participants to sign their name at the top of the worksheet and write down in box #1 an "Aha!" moment they had sometime during the previous event (a speaker's presentation/ video/performance/etc.). Explain that, because these papers will be shared with others at each table, everyone should try to write legibly and as specifically as possible within the space. Their "Aha!" could include things like:

    a. A new idea to try

    b. A revelation about something they'd tried before

    c. A connection between two different ideas

    d. A key understanding they didn't know before

    e. An insight into themselves, their way of working, a colleague, a process, etc.

    Also have them write some notes in box #1 related to why this moment was an "Aha!" for them. For the purpose of this protocol, "why" needs more explanation than "what."

2. **Write and pass** — (3 min.) Have everyone pass their paper clockwise/to the person on their left. Instruct the group to read the original person's answer in box #1 (their "Aha!"), and then answer the question in box #2, "Has something like this happened to you? What was it?"

3. **Rounds** — (3 min. per section-total 12 min.) Direct the group to pass the papers again clockwise/to their left. With this and every subsequent turn, instruct them to read the original person's answer to #1 (the original "Aha!") and then answer the question in the next open box (#3, #4, #5, then #6). Caution everyone not to read the sections between the original post in box #1 and the empty box they're about to complete until they've answered their question, or they might run out of time.

4. **Read** — (3 min.) After all six boxes have been completed by different individuals, pass the papers back to the original writers/worksheet owners. Each person silently reads all the comments added to their paper.

5. **Discuss** — (12 min.) Each table should pick a person at their table to take notes, and someone who will share out important points to the whole group in Step 6. Each table should discuss the points that stood out to them.

6. **Share out** — (15 min.—about 1 and ½ minutes per table) Tables share out to whole group.

Aha! Protocol page 1 of 2

Figure 8.24 NSRF Aha! Protocol

From *Guided Inquiry Design in Action: High School*. Leslie K. Maniotes, Editor. Santa Barbara, CA: Libraries Unlimited. Copyright © 2017.

7. **Debrief and reflect** — (2-5 min.)

- *How did it feel to consciously take time out to reflect and identify a specific realization?*

- *Which followup question helped push your thinking the most?*

- *Did any of the additions to your page or the original questions on pages from others in your group surprise you? Why?*

- *How did this protocol affect your group discussion and your understanding of the presented material?*

Aha! Protocol page 2 of 2

Figure 8.24 NSRF Aha! Protocol (*Continued*)

Aha! Protocol Worksheet

Courtesy of The Coltrain Group, by Michele Mattoon
Use with the Aha! Protocol

My name:
Owner of the worksheet

1. My Aha! moment and why it was so important to me. (Write more about why than what.)

2. Has something like this happened to you or occurred to you? What are my thoughts around it?

3. Was this Aha! moment also significant to you? Why or why not?

Aha! Protocol Worksheet page 1 of 2

Figure 8.24 NSRF Aha! Protocol (*Continued*)

From *Guided Inquiry Design in Action: High School.* Leslie K. Maniotes, Editor. Santa Barbara, CA: Libraries Unlimited. Copyright © 2017.

4. What questions* do you have for the owner of this worksheet to help them think more deeply or differently about that idea?

*If you have experienced the Probing Questions exercise, write probing questions here.

5. What insights can you add from any of the other people's Aha! moments you've read today?

6. What next steps, ideas, resources, or anything else do you have for the owner of this worksheet to consider?

Aha! Protocol Worksheet page 2 of 2

Figure 8.24 NSRF Aha! Protocol (*Continued*)

Create

Relationships

Learning Goals
Process: Reflect on learning. go beyond facts to make meaning, create to communicate.

Content: Students will deepen their understanding of their chosen topic in an effort to explain it to others. Students will deepen their understanding of the relationship between the medium of their presentation and the message.

Location: Learning Commons
Team Members: English Teacher, Teacher Librarian

Starter Time: 10 minutes	The topic of what the end product of the inquiry will be has been avoided up to this point in order to allow students to focus on developing the story that they need to tell about their research before they identify the best medium for telling that story. On the first day of Create, the students write a "Spark Notes"-style summary of their findings. Each presentation must include a visual and oral component that cannot be longer than 5 minutes. As the students have been presenting their research findings in traditional and less traditional media in Social Studies, English, and other courses since at least Grade 8, they will have an understanding of the kinds of opportunities that they have to present their work. Using a Pair-Share protocol, students explore how they might best tell their story with a partner. The Pair-Share discussion opens up an opportunity to explore more creative ways of presenting their stories that are appropriate and desirable.
Worktime Time: 60 minutes	Once the students have had a chance to establish a direction for their Create phase, they are given 3 classes to build their creation. As usual, teachers circulate to ensure that students are on track and that any issues in this phase are addressed appropriately and promptly.
Reflection Time: 15 minutes	Time is given at the end of each class to step back from the Create process to reflect on how things are going and make any notes for what might need to be addressed during and prior to the next class.

Figure 8.25 Create

 From *Guided Inquiry Design in Action: High School*. Leslie K. Maniotes, Editor. Santa Barbara, CA: Libraries Unlimited. Copyright © 2017.

Share

Relationships

Learning Goals
Process: Learn from one another, share learning, tell your story.

Content: Students will expand their understanding of the concept of relationships through connecting others' topics to their own.
Location: Learning Commons
Team Members: English Teacher, Teacher Librarian

Starter Inquiry Community	Two sections of classes are given time to share. Each student shares his or her project with the Inquiry Community.
Worktime A few sessions until all students have shared	There are 10 presentations each day. As speaking and presentation skills are part of the English Curriculum, it is important, in this case, for each person to have the opportunity to present his or her work to the large group. The audience members spend their time completing a peer evaluation of each presentation, looking for ideas that require more clarity, and asking questions to extend the discussion further. (See Figure 8.27)
Reflection Time: 10 minutes each session	Time is given to reflect in Inquiry Journals on the question, "What have I learned from the presentations of others that has added to the understanding of my own topic?"

Figure 8.26 Share

Relationships and *Romeo and Juliet*

Peer Evaluation Form

Evaluator:	Evaluatee:

Please evaluate your peer's presentation as accurately as possible. Provide any comments needed to justify your evaluation in the boxes provided or below the rubric.

	Definitely	Mostly	Not Really
Clarity of message **The information was presented clearly and was easy to understand.**			
Interest **The presentation was interesting to view and listen to. The presenter kept your interest for the whole presentation.**			
Relevance **The presentation clearly connected to relationships and presented a new and/or interesting perspective on relationships in our society.**			

Clarifying Questions:
What key information was missing from the presentation? What information needs to be included so that you understand the presentation better?

Extension Questions:
What follow-up questions do you have for the presenter to help you dig deeper into the topic? If the presenter were to continue the research, what question would you like him or her to ask next?

Figure 8.27 Peer Evaluation Form

Relationships

Learning Goals

Process: Evaluate achievement of learning goals, reflect on content, reflect on the process.

Content: Students will refine their understanding of their own research process. Students will deepen their understanding of relationships and their own particular topic as they synthesize and look for extensions of their knowledge.

Location: Learning Commons
Team Members: English Teacher, Teacher Librarian

Starter Time: 10 minutes Inquiry Community	The Inquiry Community is introduced to the idea that inquiry never ends. Although students have presented their final presentation, they may still have questions about their topic or the skills that they have developed. Today's class gets at the questions "So what?" and "What next?" and looks at the content of the unit they have just experienced and the process of their research and learning. Students are broken into groups to prepare for the following activity.
Worktime Time: 35 minutes Chalk Talk Protocol (See Figure 8.29)	The Chalk Talk protocol (see Figure 8.29) is used to generate a discussion around a final review of the entire unit and as a springboard to their final Inquiry Journal entry for the unit. The prompt questions are based on the broad questions "So what?" and "What next?" Chalk Talks are a way to generate documented discussion while giving equitable access to discussion time and putting the students who like to think before they respond on an equal footing with those who are always quick to jump in. Four stations are set up around the room, each with a large sheet of chart paper on a table and enough markers for each person to have access. On each piece of chart paper there is a prompting question. The questions are: 1. What big ideas have you learned about relationships, Shakespeare, _Romeo and Juliet_, or literature in general? Why is what you learned important? (So what? content) 2. What have you learned about yourself as a researcher? How will this impact you moving forward? (So what? process) 3. What questions still remain about your research into relationships and _Romeo and Juliet_ or the related topics of your research? What plans might you have to pursue these questions? (What next? content) 4. What struggles did you encounter in the research process itself? What plans might you put in place to improve your learning/research skills for future projects? (What next? process)

Figure 8.28 Evaluate

	Each group of four or five students starts the protocol at a different station and is given seven minutes to respond to the prompt at their station. They cannot talk, but they can write, draw images, check, draw connecting lines, circle, or in any other visual/written way respond to their prompt. After five minutes, they move to the next station to read the prompt question, read the previous responses, and contribute their own. This continues until each group has had a chance at each prompt. At the end of four rounds (one stop at each station by each group), a debrief discussion is held with the entire group to tease out big ideas and uncover thinking that may have occurred after a group had left a station.
Reflection Time: 30 minutes	Students are asked to post a final entry in their Inquiry Journal looking at how today's discussion is particularly pertinent in their own lives. They might reflect on what lessons they learned that might impact their own relationships, or they might discuss how their research topic helped them understand an issue better that was being addressed in another course or in another aspect of their lives. They might also reflect on the process and how this unit has improved their research skills or revealed an issue that may need to be dealt with in future research assignments.

Figure 8.28 Evaluate (*Continued*)

National School Reform Faculty®
Harmony Education Center

Chalk Talk Protocol

NSRF, Spring 2015

Facilitation Difficulty: 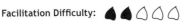 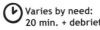 Varies by need: 20 min. + debrief   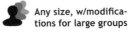 Any size, w/modifications for large groups    No preconference

Purpose — To silently reflect, generate ideas, check on learning, develop projects or solve problems. It can be used productively with any group. Because Chalk Talk is done in silence, it gives groups a change of pace, encourages thoughtful contemplation, and reduces the risk often felt in verbal conversations. A Chalk Talk can be an uncomplicated silent reflection or a spirited, but silent, exchange of ideas. It can solve vexing problems, reveal how much a group knows about a topic, get an entire project planned, or give a committee lots of information without any verbal sparring. It can be an unforgettable experience. Students love it — it's the quietest they'll ever be!

*Group size — See note after protocol for recommendations for large groups

Preparation — Large chalk board and multicolored chalk, or whiteboard and multicolored markers, or many pieces of chart paper taped together on the wall and multicolored markers. Ideally, write your question or topic in the center of the space but do not reveal it until after the setup.

Facilitation tips — During the protocol, your job is to remind everyone to stay silent and active. Do not allow them to return to their seats until the debrief (exempting those who are physically unable to stand). You may also write your own comments to push participants' thinking in new directions. If people's comments seem to be focused in only a few places, write down some new questions in blank spots.

Steps:

1. **Setup** — (5 min.) Explain that Chalk Talk is a silent activity that gets everyone out of their seats for the duration of the protocol. No one may talk at all, nobody should go sit down until prompted, and all "comments" should be written on the boards/papers instead of being spoken. When not writing, participants should be standing back from the wall, reading each other's comments and allowing others space to write. They may respond to comments by:

   - Adding related or contrasting thoughts alongside an existing comment

   - Drawing a line connecting two similar comments

   - Adding exclamations, stars, smiley faces, +1s, or other pictographs to a comment

   - Drawing a picture that symbolizes what they are thinking or feeling

2. **Question** — (1 min.) If you were unable to prep the room and pre-write the question(-s), do so now, in the center of the board, and draw a large circle around it for emphasis. Sample questions:

   - *What did you learn today?*

   - *So What? Or Now What?*

   - *What do you think about social responsibility and schooling?*

   - *How can we involve the community in the school, and the school in the community?*

   - *How can we keep the noise level down in this room?*

Chalk Talk Protocol page 1 of 2

Figure 8.29 NSRF Chalk Talk Protocol

- *What does the scheduling committee need to know?*

- *What do you know about Croatia?*

- *How are decimals used in the world?*

3. **Distribute** — (2 min.) Hand out pieces of chalk or markers to everyone, or place many pieces of chalk/markers at the boards and hand chalk/markers to several random participants to get the ball rolling.

4. **"Talk"** — (10-15 min.) Announce to the group that, *"The Chalk Talk is now open!"* Participants write as they feel moved. Chalk Talks tend to begin and end like corn popping. A few people will start writing at first. Then, more and more people will join until there is a flurry of activity for a time. Gradually, fewer and fewer people will contribute until there will only be one or two writing at a time. There are likely to be some pauses in writing activity. Breaks for reading and reflection are natural, so allow wait time before deciding it is over. When it's done, it's done! Invite everyone to return to their seats for the debrief.

5. **Debrief and reflect** — (5 min.)

- *What did you notice about the comments? Anything surprising? Any patterns?*

- *Why did we do this activity in silence?*

- *What, if any, next steps should be taken?*

- *What did you think of the activity? What worked, what didn't?*

- *How might you use this in your work?*

6. ***Big group option** — One Chalk Talk works well with up to 15 people. If you have a larger group, set up separate (adjacent or parallel) walls with different questions, one per 15 participants (e.g., two chalk talks for 16-30 people, three chalk talks for 31-45, etc.). Participants can then feel free to comment silently on any of the walls, reading and writing at will. If you have more than one Chalk Talk going simultaneously, expect to increase your time accordingly to allow for more interaction. Example questions for a multiple Chalk Talk experience:

- *What is experiential learning?*

- *What are the benefits of experiential learning?*

- *What are the obstacles around incorporating experiential learning into our curriculum?*

- *What supports do teachers need to effectively teach common core using experiential learning?*

Chalk Talk Protocol page 2 of 2

Figure 8.29 NSRF Chalk Talk Protocol (*Continued*)

From *Guided Inquiry Design in Action: High School.* Leslie K. Maniotes, Editor. Santa Barbara, CA: Libraries Unlimited. Copyright © 2017.

Romeo and Juliet and Understanding Relationships Unit Resources

Websites

Poetry in Voice. (2011). Poetry In Voice | A poetry recitation contest for high schools in Canada. Retrieved from http://www.poetryinvoice.com/

CiSSL Slim Reflection: http://cissl.rutgers.edu/joomla-license/impact-studies/57-impact-studies-slim

EasyBib: http://www.easybib.com

Film

Zeffirelli, F. (Director). (1968). *Romeo and Juliet* [Motion picture on DVD]. United Kingdom: BHE Films.

Poetry

Bradstreet, A. (1677). The author to her book. Retrieved from https://www.poets .org/poetsorg/poem/author-her-book

Databases

"Relationships" is a broad topic with many potential paths to content. Some databases used for this particular research include:

Academic Search Premiere by EBSCO
JSTOR
Literary Reference Centre Plus by EBSCO
Oxford Reference Online
Poetry and Short Story Reference Centre by EBSCO
Science in Context by Gale

Teaching Resources
NSRF Protocols: http://www.nsrfharmony.org/free-resources/protocols/a-z
Mindmapping: http://www.mindmapping.com

Figure 8.30 Unit Resources

Historical Thinking on Taking a Stand

9

Kathy Boguszewski

Each year, schools across the United States participate in an academic competition called National History Day (NHD). NHD's primary purpose is to excite students about all types of history while developing research, critical thinking, and communication skills. An additional goal is for students to recognize that history is a part of everyday life, not just something found in a textbook. By designing the course using the Guided Inquiry Design® process, we enable students to achieve remarkable academic growth through their research and development of creative presentations.

During the competition students select a topic related to an annual theme. This course content is based on the 2017 theme, "Taking a Stand." The course presented here is designed to be able to be adapted to the annual themes with some alteration in content.

This is an extensive project involving the phases of the Guided Inquiry Design process across an entire semester. The project is an excellent opportunity for language arts and social studies teachers to collaborate with the library media specialist (LMS) as an information professional and co-teacher. In our case, the class starts in September in order to help the students build a foundation, spread out the work, and manage their time. At Rock University High School, the class activities occur during a two-hour block of time, once a week. For this book, I chunked the activities into a more traditional high school schedule of 55 minutes.

Rock University High School (RUHS) is a public charter school in the School District of Janesville, Wisconsin, located on the UW–Rock County Campus. Rock University High School prepares future leaders, grades 10–12, with the skills essential to designing innovative solutions. Through a rigorous, personalized, and internationally focused program, RUHS students explore real-world applications and learn to be of service. Students gain confidence, recognize their potential, and deepen their understanding of one another and the world. Our graduates are inspired and empowered to craft their own futures.

For this unit we include due dates for selecting a topic, identifying questions, gathering information, creating meaning from the information, sharing what they learned, and evaluating the process and projects. Most of the work occurs during class time so that the library media specialist (LMS) and teacher(s) can guide students. When needed, teachers assist their students so they can be successful during this course. We included the Special Education and English Language Learning teachers as active collaborators with the Learning Team to help differentiate instruction as needed. There is an expectation that students will also need to spend

157

additional time on their own to explore and gather information and create their projects. The teachers inform parents by sending home letters of the expectations, due dates, and Open House celebration.

In our school, students and teachers use Google Apps for Education. This unit is written within that context. In some school districts, teachers' and students' Google accounts are in two separate domains. In our case, the LMS adds the students in the Young Historians class to her email contacts and adds each student to a new group titled Young Historians. The LMS also uploads all the class session PowerPoints to a Google drive folder titled National History Day. The LMS shares the Google drive folder with the students and Learning Team. This way, students can refer back to the class PowerPoints, as needed, throughout the semester-long course. These PowerPoints are available in read-only format using this link: http://tinyurl.com /GIDinAction/HS. In our case, independent students who want to participate in the National History Day competition, but who have a schedule conflict, can also refer to these PowerPoints. Independent students can also schedule face-to-face conferences with the teaching team and contact teachers via email.

Guided Inquiry Design®
Unit Overview
National History Day
2017 Theme—"Taking a Stand"

We chose this particular project in order to prepare our students for the rigors of a college education. Through the unit they practice how to prepare themselves for:

- College assignments that appear partially online and with the professor commenting on their work.
- Time management and the additional work outside of class needed for extended projects.
- The college-ready research process.
- The deep understandings of how primary sources paint various perspectives of historical context throughout American history.

Questions for the Learning Team:

- How can the research-based Guided Inquiry Design process enhance the National History Day (NHD) requirements and research strategies?
- What impact does the Guided Inquiry Design process have on the quality of projects that the students produce?
- How does the Guided Inquiry process sustain students in thinking like a historian, engage students in historical inquiry that has personal meaning, motivate them to understand historical context and people's firsthand perspectives of historical events, and assist students to gain a deeper understanding and appreciation of history?

The Team: English and Social Studies Teacher, Library Media Specialist, Special Education Teacher, English Language Learner Teacher.

Concept: Taking a Stand

Guiding Question(s): On what issues have people taken a stand? When, in history, have people taken a stand? What were the factors that caused them to speak out? What were the conditions under which they took a stand? What were the contributing factors in their ability to be strong in the face of opposition?

Learning Goals:
Students will demonstrate proficiency in the *College, Career, and Civic Life C3 Framework for Social Studies State Standards* and the *Standards for the 21st Century Learner,* as authored by the American Association of School Librarians. (See the Google folder **http://tinyurl.com/ GIDinActionHS-NHD** for a complete list of standards addressed at each phase.)

Timeline:
September—Students build an understanding of higher level thinking skills and build a relationship with classmates as they:

- Discuss and share an understanding of the Guided Inquiry process.
- Develop an effective argument strategy including purpose, method, audience, and voice.
- Frame an argument and show the importance of transition.
- Evaluate different types of primary source evidence.

Figure 9.1 Unit Overview

From *Guided Inquiry Design in Action: High School.* Leslie K. Maniotes, Editor. Santa Barbara, CA: Libraries Unlimited. Copyright © 2017.

- Differentiate between fact and opinion, inference and guessing, inductive and deductive thinking.
- Explain how statistics and political cartoons can be best inferred in an argument.
- Explain how and why two people can interpret an event differently with a focus on causation.
- Critique the merits of "18" specific suggestions in authoring a powerful argument.
- Interpret different types of visual imagery and how they can be used in an argument.
- Evaluate and critique the strengths and weaknesses of different arguments that were part of the Scottsboro Boys Trial.

October–January—Students work through the various stages of the Guided Inquiry process and determine how to share their learning through creating a documentary, exhibit, historical paper, performance, or website.

February—Parent Open House, School and Regional Competition.

April—if qualify: State Competition.

June—if qualify: National Competition in Virginia.

 **Open** Time: 4 Sessions @ 55 minutes each = 220 minutes	To gain an understanding of the theme for the year (Taking a Stand) and to open students' minds to the meaning of historical context, students analyze various historical maps depicting the movement of Native Americans from their native lands to reservations. They discuss taking a stand from various points of view (Native Americans, early explorers and pioneers, U.S. government and military, others). To gain a deeper understanding of historical context, students analyze 2 videos on current topics. They will also make connections within the videos to the NHD theme. One video is on the topic of education and the other is on innovation: 1. Sir Ken Robinson's video _Changing Education Paradigms,_ https://youtu.be/zDZFcDGpL4U 2. _History of Apple and the First iPhone: RIP Steve Jobs,_ https://youtu.be/BG4azxx1Xjl Students meet in Inquiry Circles to share their analyses and evidence for their claims and reflect on their thinking. Students use technology - rich Inquiry Tools to communicate (Google Drive, Google Docs, email, NoodleTools). They also share their thinking through writing in their Inquiry Journals and conversations in Inquiry Circles and Inquiry Communities.
 **Immerse** Time: 3 Sessions @ 55 minutes each = 165 minutes	Students gain a deeper understanding of the theme by studying sample compelling questions related to the theme. After hearing how to think like a historian, the students determine the difference between primary and secondary source examples. They review the elements of a thesis after viewing a National NHD-winning documentary project: _The Tiananmen Square Massacre: A Government's Encounter with Its People,_ https://youtu.be/fS6NoRWZv1w Students share their ideas on the thesis in that documentary. They also study how the images in the video reinforced the thesis and how the project relates to the theme Taking a Stand. Students participate in a jigsaw activity of analyzing primary sources and critique a political cartoon for its effectiveness in proving an argument. Finally, students immerse themselves in some of the curated historical resources that the LMS added to the RUHS Destiny Homepage.

Figure 9.1 Unit Overview (*Continued*)

 **Explore** Time: 2 Sessions @ 55 minutes each = 110 minutes	Students analyze why <u>Rough in the Bunch: Appalachia's Rayon Girls Fight for the Right to Strike</u>, https://youtu.be/trqO6QhtMxo, was a NHD winner. They then further explore the resources that the LMS added to the RUHS Destiny Homepage. As they locate resources on topics of interest, they use the Stop and Jot document in their Inquiry Journal to track their reading strategies. They gather in Inquiry Circles to share their findings.
 **Identify** Time: 3 Sessions @ 55 minutes each = 165 minutes	Students meet in Inquiry Circles to determine the advantages and disadvantages of working on an individual or group project. They review the notes they took the day before in their Stop and Jot. They then determine a manageable topic. Students look for clues in their notes for developing an overarching compelling question and supportive questions. They show evidence that they are thinking like a historian as they develop their questions. The LMS guides the students through registering in the school's NoodleTools account, creating a project, and sharing the project with the teachers.
 **Gather** Time: 3 Sessions @ 55 minutes each = 165 minutes 1 Session: All-Day Field Trip to Public Library	Students are guided through a minimum of 4 sessions. One session is at the public library where the reference librarians share how to gather information from reference books, the online catalog, the shelves, and the online resources. The students learn how to locate primary source newspaper information from print indexes and microfilm. They learn how to make copies when needed. The LMS models how to identify keywords and synonyms, how to use Boolean logic when connecting words and concepts, and how to locate information on the state database as well as school district–purchased databases. Students gain proficiency using NoodleTools (which follows the Cornell Note-Taking Strategy) for citations and notes. A judge from the National History Day state and national competition gives the students tips on narrowing their topic. The judge, LMS, and teacher conference with students on narrowing their topic choices.
Create Time: 4 Sessions @ 55 minutes each = 220 minutes	Students create their thesis and organize their notes using a traditional outline format in NoodleTools or by creating a visual chart or storyboard. They determine their presentation category. Students participate in webinars from National History Day on how to create a website using the NHD Weebly account. They participate in face-to-face workshops for iMovie, exhibit design, performance directing, and writing historical papers. Tutorials have also been added to the RUHS Destiny Homepage: https://sdj.follettdestiny.com/common/servlet/logout.do?tm=

Figure 9.1 Unit Overview (*Continued*)

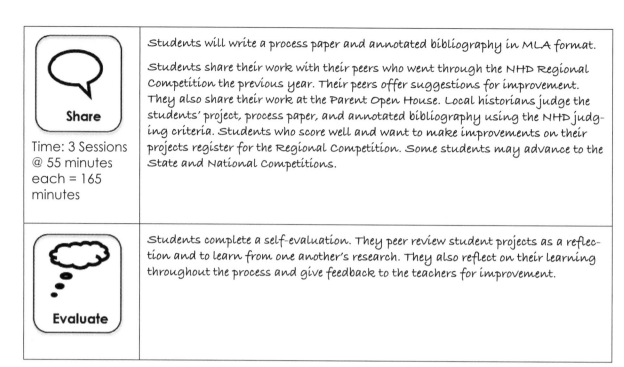

	Students will write a process paper and annotated bibliography in MLA format.
Share Time: 3 Sessions @ 55 minutes each = 165 minutes	Students share their work with their peers who went through the NHD Regional Competition the previous year. Their peers offer suggestions for improvement. They also share their work at the Parent Open House. Local historians judge the students' project, process paper, and annotated bibliography using the NHD judging criteria. Students who score well and want to make improvements on their projects register for the Regional Competition. Some students may advance to the State and National Competitions.
Evaluate	Students complete a self-evaluation. They peer review student projects as a reflection and to learn from one another's research. They also reflect on their learning throughout the process and give feedback to the teachers for improvement.

Figure 9.1 Unit Overview (*Continued*)

National History Day

Session 1

Learning Goals
Process: Invitation to inquiry, open minds, stimulate curiosity on the theme Taking a Stand.

Content: Students will wonder about how to think like a historian and about how the theme Taking a Stand relates to early American history.

Location: Library or classroom with WiFi access and every student has access to a laptop.
Team Members: History and/or English Teachers, Librarian, Special Education Teacher, English Language Learning Teacher, and/or Reading Specialist

| Starter

Time:
20 minutes | Welcome students to the National History Day Project and this year's theme: Taking a Stand.

Open their minds to thinking like a historian and historical context through exposing them to various Internet resources on American History. Begin with an analysis exercise on historical maps. Divide the class into 5 Inquiry Circles. Explain the Jigsaw activity. Each Inquiry Circle member will read, take notes in his or her Inquiry Journal on page 3, and share reflections on one of the categories under the Annenberg site: 1 group of 2 students will read "From Sea to Shining Sea." Four groups of 4–6 students will read and take notes on the content from "Indians," "Colonists," "Nation Explodes," "50 States."

They will follow the Inquiry Circle Protocol

• Choose
　• Facilitator—asks questions and keeps group on track
　• Scribe or Reporter—writes all interesting facts and ideas and shares in larger group
• Each member reads and shares notes.
• Each member listens and adds to the conversation.
• Report back to Inquiry Community on their Reflections.

Annenberg Learner Interactives United States History Map. Indians. Internet, Feb. 14, 2016. https://www.learner.org/interactives/history map/indians.html |
| Worktime

Time:
20 minutes | Continue historical context and theme analysis. In Inquiry Circles students reflect upon what they are thinking as they view the movement of Native Americans across the map of North America in the sites below.

States and Territories of the United States of America: 1700–1960. Internet. Feb. 14, 2016. http://edudemic.com/wp-content/uploads /2012/07/changingusa.gif |

Figure 9.2 Open 1

Inquiry Circles Inquiry Journal	Interactive Time-Lapse Map Shows How the US Took More Than 1.5 Billion Acres from Native Americans. http://www.slate.com/blogs/the_vault/2014/06/17/interactive_map_loss_of_indian_land.html
	"What do you notice? What do you see as the interactive map moves across time? Take sides and discuss from the Native Americans' point of view and the explorers' and pioneers' point of view.
Inquiry Community	"Think about the theme, Taking a Stand. Write in your journal on page 4 a reflection on the theme and the maps you analyzed. What are you thinking about? How could the theme connect with what you learned?
	"Ask the Inquiry Community what questions this raised for them. Some questions you can use to think about this conversation are: What if there were no boundaries? Why did people separate into groups? What if people were only separated by geographical boundaries such as water and mountain ranges? How about today? How does technology traverse boundaries?"
	LMS hands out sticky notes to each Inquiry Circle.
	"When and why did people go beyond their boundaries, take risks, take a stand, and make a change that altered the world as they knew it?
	"Write a different answer on each sticky note. Team members will organize the sticky notes into common themes on the whiteboard."
	Students write in their Inquiry Journals on the Notecatcher page (page 4)
	• Write thoughts on which ideas, people, or historical time periods resonate with your passions. • What vocabulary do you not understand? • What questions do you have? • What are you wondering about? Is there an idea or connection you are making with a passion for learning more? • Which area excites you the most? • What cultures, locations, sciences, sports, the arts speak to you?
	Students then share their thoughts in an Inquiry Circle.
Reflection Time: 10 minutes	"Reflect on this year's theme, Taking a Stand, and the maps you analyzed. What are you thinking about?"
Notes:	Collect the Inquiry Journals after each class session to see who is on track and who needs assistance. Grading on the 1–4 scale helps students understand that their time during class is valued.
	• 4—went above and beyond in your notes and reflections • 3—completed all the notes and reflections • 2—completed 3/4 of the notes and reflections • 1—completed less than 3/4 of the notes and reflections

Figure 9.2 Open 1 (*Continued*)

National History Day

Session 2

Learning Goals
Process: Invitation to inquiry, open minds, stimulate curiosity on historical context of the theme Taking a Stand.

Content: Students will discuss questions tied to the theme and how the historical context applies to the current topic of Education Reform.

Location: Library or classroom with WiFi access and every student has access to a laptop.

Team Members: History and/or English Teachers, Librarian, Special Education Teacher, English Language Learning Teacher, and/or Reading Specialist

Starter Time: 5 minutes	Ice Breaker Activity: LMS groups students into Inquiry Circles. Students explain what period in American history interests them the most and why.
Worktime Time: 35 minutes Inquiry Journal	View Sir Ken Robinson's video <u>Changing Education Paradigms</u> on YouTube: https://youtu.be/zDZFcDGpL4U After viewing the video students will independently think and write answers to the questions in their Inquiry Journal. (pages 4–5) • Define paradigm. • As you view the video, write any questions that come to your mind. • What is the historical context of education reform efforts? • How does Sir Ken connect with your own experiences? • What surprised you about his information? • What techniques did he use to go beyond facts and connect with you? • What stand does Sir Ken take on education?
Inquiry Circles Inquiry Community	Discuss examples of questions that are tied to the theme: Taking a Stand. Inquiry Circle: Individuals in the circle start the thinking process during "Think, Pair, Share" activities. Pick 2: • What are examples of people taking a stand that led to unforeseen consequences or seminal moments in history? • What are examples of scientists or engineers taking a stand that led to new cures or safer modes of transportation? • How did people taking a stand on ideas, beliefs, or theories change events? For example, how did people utilize the press, radio, television, the Internet, social media to take a stand on issues and inform the public? • How did artists take a stand on events and what were the results?
Reflection Time: 10 minutes Inquiry Community	Students share their journal entries with their Inquiry Circle. After small groups share ideas, the reporter is asked to share their thoughts with the Inquiry Community.
Notes:	Students see how documentary examples relate to the theme.

Figure 9.3 Open 2

Open

National History Day

Session 3

Learning Goals

Process: Invitation to inquiry, open minds, stimulate curiosity on historical context of the theme, Taking a Stand.

Content: Students discuss how historical context applies to the current topic, technology, and how the theme Taking a Stand relates to the video.

Location: Library or classroom with WiFi access and every student has access to a laptop.

Team Members: History and/or English Teachers, Librarian, Special Education Teacher, English Language Learning Teacher, and/or Reading Specialist

Starter Time: 2 minutes	"Today we'll think about another topic, The evolution of technology in relation to the theme Taking a Stand."

Worktime
 	
Time:
35 minutes
 	
Inquiry Circles
 	
Inquiry Journal
 	
Inquiry Community
	View the video <u>History of Apple and the First iPhone: RIP Steve Jobs</u> on YouTube, https://youtu.be/BG4azXx1Xjl
	
	Notecatcher in Journal—page 5
	
	• What was the historical context for the iPhone invention?
	  • What was the timeline? Who were major contributors or inventors? What technology preceded it?
	  • What social or economic events influenced or were influenced by the iPhone? (pop culture, music piracy, personal safety)
	• What bigger themes in history do you think are connected to the development of the iPhone?
	• What stand did Steve Jobs take in this video?
	
	After the students watch the video they write the answers to the questions in their Inquiry Journals.
	
	Review the Inquiry Circle Protocol:
	• Choose
	  • A Facilitator—asks questions and keeps on track
	  • A Scribe and Reporter—writes all interesting facts and ideas and shares in larger group
	• Each partner shares own ideas
	• Each partner listens and adds to the conversation
	
	The students convene in the Inquiry Circle. The Facilitator, Scribe, and other students follow the protocol as they share their thoughts.

Reflection Time: 18 minutes	After small groups share ideas, the reporters are asked to share their thoughts with the Inquiry Community.

Figure 9.4 Open 3

National History Day
Information Literacy Deep Dive

Session 4

Learning Goals
Content: Students will know and understand the tools that will support this process, information location and use, and will reflect on how these tools will play a role in their learning.
Location: Library or classroom with WiFi access and every student has a computer.
Team Members: Librarian, History Teacher(s)

Starter Time: 5 minutes	"Today we will be setting you up with the technology, human resources, and tools that will serve as a support system for you during this entire process."
Worktime **Google Apps** Time: 15 minutes	The librarian models how to use the school district's Google apps for education. The National History Day (NHD) folder has been shared with the students in the class and with the teaching team. The folder includes all the NHD PowerPoints, Student Journal, and other NHD documents. The students open their SDJ Google Account email and go to their Google Drive where they create a new folder titled "Young Historians." They go to their "Shared with me" section under "My Drive." Move the NHD shared folder to My Drive into the Young Historians folder.
Inquiry Journal Time: 5 minutes	Students gain an understanding of how they will use the Inquiry Journal during the course. The LMS presents to the students how using the available PowerPoints for each session will help them to stay on track with the various activities throughout the class time. If they miss a class, they can refer to the PowerPoint in their Google Drive folder. The Inquiry Journal, in print format, is handed out to each student. Overview of the content of the Inquiry Journal: • Table of Contents • Notecatchers • Stop and Jot and Inquiry Log • Tips and Possible Topics • Inquiry Journal Prompts • Pair Share Protocols • Reflections

Figure 9.5 Information Literacy Deep Dive

From *Guided Inquiry Design in Action: High School*. Leslie K. Maniotes, Editor. Santa Barbara, CA: Libraries Unlimited. Copyright © 2017.

Cornell Note-Taking Strategy Time: 10 minutes Inquiry Circle	The students study how the Cornell Note-taking strategy (See Figure 9.6 from page 7 in the NHD Journal) can help them gain an understanding of new information and can guide them through their note-taking/thinking process. The students review and discuss in Inquiry Circle: • What elements of the template are helpful? • What elements might be a challenge? • Which elements make the most sense to use when you take notes?
Inquiry Toolkit 6 Cs Time: 5 minutes	The teacher or LMS shares the 6 Cs of the Inquiry Toolkit that they will use during the course: 1. Collaborate—learn from one another in Inquiry Communities 2. Converse—discuss interesting ideas, meaningful questions, and emerging insights in small Inquiry Circles 3. Compose—write and reflect in Inquiry Journals 4. Choose—keep track of info in Inquiry Logs 5. Chart—Visualize, organize, synthesize ideas 6. Continue—Sustain the inquiry process to completion
Reflection Time: 15 minutes Inquiry Circle and Inquiry Community	Reflection for Session 4 in Inquiry Journal—page 32 • What am I now wondering about from the past sessions and conversations I had with peers? • What new thoughts or ideas do I have? • What connections am I making with my experiences? • What topic or topics am I thinking about that would interest me for the project? Students share their reflections with their Inquiry Circle. Reporters take notes of topics and interests and write them on the whiteboard. They circle common topics and LMS takes a picture of the choices.
Notes:	

Figure 9.5 Information Literacy Deep Dive (*Continued*)

Cornell Note-Taking Template

Name: Date:	Topic / Essential Question:

Bibliography: Use MLA (Humanities Research)

Vocabulary:	Questions: Think Like a Historian **Lower Level:** What, Who, When? **Higher Level:** How, Why, Cause and Effect, Ramification, Change and Continuity, Turning Points, How can we learn from the past? How can we view events through others' eyes?	Notes: Name of expert. Page numbers if print source. Hyperlink if Internet. Use quotations when copying text. Paraphrase new information or ideas. Write facts.

Reflections: How did the new information relate to what I already know? What is the agenda or background of the source? Were the ideas facts or opinions? Do the facts or opinions appear to be biased? What was surprising to me? What is the significance of the facts or opinions in history? Why is the information important? How can I apply the facts or opinions to my questions? What is beyond the ideas that stimulate me to research further?

Figure 9.6 Cornell Note-Taking Template

From *Guided Inquiry Design in Action: High School*. Leslie K. Maniotes, Editor. Santa Barbara, CA: Libraries Unlimited. Copyright © 2017.

National History Day

Session 1

Learning Goals
Process: Students will build background knowledge, connect to content, and discover interesting ideas on the NHD theme.

Content: The students will review quotes and possible topics based on the NHD theme. They will build an understanding of how to "Think Like a Historian" by analyzing the differences between resources.
Location: Library or classroom with WiFi access and every student has a laptop.
Team Members: History and/or English Teachers, Librarian

Starter Time: 15 minutes	Return Inquiry Journals and explain scores: • 4—went above and beyond in your notes and reflections • 3—completed all the notes and reflections • 2—completed 3/4 of the notes and reflections • 1—completed less than 3/4 of the notes and reflections Reflect on the introduction to the project: - 2 Post-it Notes • Jot down 1 idea about the NHD project that fascinates you. • Jot down a question you have about the project. Round Robin—Share your thoughts by placing notes on the whiteboard under "Fascinates Me" and "Questions I Have." Students organize "Fascinates Me" thoughts into common themes and LMS answers the students' questions.
Introduce "Think Like a Historian" Time: 5 minutes	The LMS shares how to "Think Like a Historian" • Interrogate the evidence • Build a case • Look for bias
Worktime Time: 30 minutes	Review Theme—Taking a Stand (2017) Share and post definition and quotes on Taking a Stand. Individuals choose one. Reflect on the meaning in the context of who said it: • Courage is what it takes to stand up and speak; courage is also what it takes to sit down and listen. <u>Winston Churchill</u> • <u>Those who stand for nothing fall for anything.</u> <u>Alexander Hamilton</u>

Figure 9.7 Immerse 1

Inquiry Circles	• *Get up, stand up, Stand up for your rights. Get up, stand up, Don't give up the fight. Bob Marley* • *Freedom and justice cannot be parceled out in pieces to suit political convenience. I don't believe you can stand for freedom for one group of people and deny it to others. Coretta Scott King* Share with Inquiry Circle. Share examples of compelling questions that relate to the theme: • As people took a stand in the way they think and act, what changes have occurred in religious beliefs? Students analyze an interactive map showing growth of religions worldwide over time. • How did the Little Rock Nine take a stand with the Central High School students in 1957 and change the shape of the civil rights movement in the 1960s? • How did Les Paul's stand on sound influence blues, alternative, and heavy metal music? Discuss what qualities make these questions compelling.
Time: 10 minutes	**Primary and Secondary Resources** LMS reviews the difference between Primary and Secondary Resources: • Who is the author and when was it published? • Did the person live at the time of the event or learn about the event later? • Biography vs. Autobiography Check for understanding—Students use thumb up/thumb down to vote on whether certain sources are primary or secondary sources: • Text of 19th Amendment from National Archives • Book published in 2005 on Women's Suffrage • Website developed by a librarian on events leading up to the passage of the 19th Amendment • A pamphlet published in the late 1890s warning about the dangers of giving women the right to vote • Photograph of a woman protesting for the right to vote from the early 1900s • A political cartoon published in a 1919 newspaper on women voting. • An encyclopedia article covering the topic of Women's Suffrage

Figure 9.7 Immerse 1 (*Continued*)

From *Guided Inquiry Design in Action: High School.* Leslie K. Maniotes, Editor. Santa Barbara, CA: Libraries Unlimited. Copyright © 2017.

Reflection Time: 5 minutes	What am I wondering about or what new ideas do I have today? Page 32, Session 1 in Inquiry Journal
Notes:	Other Compelling questions for examples: • How did John Muir's stand on preserving the environment influence people to look at the National Parks differently? • How did Gaylord Nelson's stand on the environment plant the seeds for Earth Day and environmental changes in the cities? • How did Harley Davidson take a stand on how people explored the country? • How did Golda Meir's stand on peaceful negotiations with the Palestinians shape her leadership in Israel? • How have labor unions' stands on working conditions shaped the health and financial stability of workers in the United States?

Figure 9.7 Immerse 1 (*Continued*)

From *Guided Inquiry Design in Action: High School*. Leslie K. Maniotes, Editor. Santa Barbara, CA: Libraries Unlimited. Copyright © 2017.

National History Day

Session 2

Learning Goals
Process: Build background knowledge, connect to content, and discover interesting ideas.

Content: Students will critique a National History Day winner, looking for elements that meet the criteria for a documentary.

Location: Library or classroom with WiFi access and every student has a laptop.
Team Members: History and/or English Teachers, Librarian

Starter Time: 5 minutes	*"Today we will examine and critique a National History Day documentary winner using the National History Day judging criteria located on the Wisconsin National History Day website."*

Worktime
Time: 25 minutes
	Review elements of a thesis:
	
	  • *An informed argument*
	    • *What is evidence to support your argument?*
	  • *What would an opposing view be?*
	    • *What would be evidence to support the opposing view?*
	  • *Which argument is stronger and why?*
	
	Reflect while viewing documentary, 5 minutes
	
	Review the questions from NHD Journal, page 8 (Figure 9.9) that students will think about while viewing the NHD national documentary winner.
	
	Watch documentary, 10 minutes
	
	The students watch and reflect on <u>The Tiananmen Square Massacre: A Government's Encounter with Its People.</u> https://youtu.be/fS6N0RWZv1w
	
	View documentary again. In partners, one person counts the number of primary sources and the other counts the seconds between the script narration and the changing of pictures.
	
	Analyze documentary techniques, 10 minutes
	
	Students capture thoughts in the Notecatcher section of the NHD Journal, page 8, after watching the video. (Figure 9.9)

Figure 9.8 Immerse 2

Jigsaw and Inquiry Circle	**Protocol**, 15 minutes
Inquiry Community	Share the Document Analysis website from the National Archives. http://www.archives.gov/education/lessons/worksheets/index.html Students determine which document analysis they will study. Group students by their choices. Inquiry Circle Protocol: • Choose a facilitator to keep team on track and a reporter. • Read, think, and take notes. • Share notes in Inquiry Circle. • Reporter jots down the thoughts of the group. • Reporter—plan to share in 10 minutes. Inquiry Community—"What knowledge did you gain that your peers would want to know?"
Reflection Time: 5 minutes Inquiry Community	In Inquiry Journal use the prompt to reflect on today's thinking. "When I heard or read about _____ it made me think about ___." Round Robin—Share your Reflections.
Notes:	Remember to collect Inquiry Journals from students.

Figure 9.8 Immerse 2 (*Continued*)

Tiananmen Square Documentary

1. What is the historical context?

2. What stand did the students, military, and government take during the events?

3. What is the thesis?

4. How did the students use primary sources to demonstrate proof of the thesis?

5. How does the documentary show analysis and interpretation of the events?

6. How is the topic significant to history and what conclusions are drawn?

7. How did the music contribute to the theme?

8. How did students give credit to resources?

9. What did you learn from watching this example?

Figure 9.9 Tiananmen Square Documentary Notecatcher

Immerse

National History Day

Session 3

Learning Goals
Process: Build background knowledge, connect to content, and discover interesting ideas.

Content: The students will analyze political cartoons and then focus on diving into Destiny and Web Path Express, the school district's online catalog and the National Archives website. They will use the Stop and Jot for sites they might return to later.
Location: Library or classroom with WiFi access and every student has a laptop.
Team Members: History and/or English Teachers, Librarian

Starter Time: 5 minutes	Entrance Card Hand an index card to each student as they arrive. Students will write reflections for the following questions: 1. What do you remember most about viewing the <u>Tiananmen Square Documentary</u>? 2. When you analyzed various primary source documents, what was most helpful?
Worktime Time: 45 minutes Inquiry Circles Inquiry Community	**Political Cartoon Analysis**, 15 minutes "In your Inquiry Circle, share thoughts on the sample cartoon, <u>Welcome to all!</u>, 1880, http://www.loc.gov/pictures/item/2002719044/ "What stand is the artist taking? Are you persuaded to go on the Ark or stay home?" Next, explore historical context on the Immigration Timetable, http://www.libertyellisfoundation.org/immigration-timeline • What wars were occurring in the world around 1880? • How does knowing the timeline help you gain a deeper understanding of the cartoon? Discuss further what the cartoon might be saying. Reporter shares with the Inquiry Community what the group discovered. **Analyze Further: Political Cartoon 2**, 15 minutes Students will study the Cartoon Analysis Checklist (http: teachinghistory.org)

Figure 9.10 Immerse 3

Stop and Jot	Students review various cartoons with a partner using the following sources:
	• President Franklin Delano Roosevelt Political Cartoons http://www.nisk.k12.ny.us/fdr/FDRcartoons.html • Herblock's Political Cartoons from Library of Congress http://www.loc.gov/exhibits/herblocks-history/presidents.html Have students choose 1 cartoon and analyze the cartoon using the checklist as a guide. They will share their analysis of one cartoon with the Inquiry Community.
	Online Resources, 15 minutes LMS will model how to locate online resources that have been curated on school's Destiny: Homepage. Students will focus on Web Path Express and the National Archives website. Stop and Jot (page 10 in NHD Journal. See Figure 9.11) Students use Stop and Jot to show evidence of locating valuable resources. Students will be assessed on their Stop and Jot work: • 2 resources for 1 point • 3 resources for 2 points • 4 resources for 3 points • 5 and over for 4 points
Reflection Time: 5 minutes	"List further ideas or interests that you have and that you may want to explore."
Notes:	It is critical that students take the time to Stop and Jot on any resource that they think is interesting. Collect the journals after each class session to see who is on track and who needs assistance.

Figure 9.10 Immerse 3 (*Continued*)

Stop and Jot

Source:	
Page number or URL	Ideas and questions

Source:	
Page number or URL	Ideas and questions

Adapted with permission from Kuhlthau, Maniotes, and Caspari. *Guided Inquiry Design: A Framework for Inquiry in Your School.* Libraries Unlimited, 2012.

Figure 9.11 Stop and Jot

Explore

National History Day

Session 1

Learning Goals
Process: Explore interesting ideas, look around, and dip in.

Content: Students will analyze another NHD National Winner. They will spend time exploring curated resources and district databases. They will think and share their thoughts in Inquiry Teams.

Location: Library or classroom with WiFi access and every student has a laptop.
Team Members: History and/or English Teachers, Librarian

Starter Time: 5 minutes	Give students time to reflect on their Inquiry Journal. "What are you interested in? Has your thinking changed?" Students might start changing their ideas about what they are interested in.
Worktime Time: 45 minutes Inquiry Log	Students analyze why <u>Rough in the Bunch: Appalachia's Rayon Girls Fight for the Right to Strike</u> was a NHD winner. Students take notes in their NHD Journal, page 11 (See Figure 9.13). Next, students begin the research process. Today they will explore resources. As they browse, and read, relax, and reflect, they will come to see multiple perspectives and concentrate on how the resources bring questions to mind that are tied to the NHD theme. **Teacher shares 2017 sample topic choices,** 10 minutes Students read the 2017 Taking a Stand topic choice examples (pages 13–14 in NHD Journal), http://tinyurl.com/GIDinActionHS-NHD Students take notes on their interest in the topic choices in their Inquiry Journal. Students explore the curated resources and keep an Inquiry Log (see http://tinyurl.com/GIDinActionHS-NHD). They will keep track of all resources in the Inquiry Log and track their reading strategies on the log.
Reflection Time: 3 minutes	In Inquiry Journal: "What was interesting to you today? What is standing out in the things you browsed?"
Notes:	Use the Inquiry Log through the Gather phase. The Inquiry Log is different from Stop and Jot. Students can use the log in their NHD Journal or in an electronic version in their Google folder.

Figure 9.12 Explore 1

Rough in the Bunch Video

1. What is the historical context?

2. What is the thesis?

3. How did the student use primary sources to demonstrate proof of the thesis?

4. How does the documentary show analysis and interpretation?

5. How is the topic significant to history and what conclusions are drawn?

6. How did the student give credit to resources?

7. What did you learn from watching this example?

8. Which elements made this documentary a National Winner?

9. How does this documentary relate to the theme: Taking a Stand?

Figure 9.13 *Rough in the Bunch* **Video Notecatcher**

INQUIRY LOG

Use this Inquiry Log from the **Explore** stage through the **Create** stage.

	Explore	**Gather**
Track your choices through the inquiry.	As you explore, check the box if you may use the source for your inquiry. ✔ "Maybe"	As you gather, check the box if you will use the source for your inquiry. ✔ "Use it"
Track the reading strategies you use.	As you explore, place an **x** after the sources you dipped into.	As you gather, mark an ***** after the core sources you read deeply.

Cite all your sources.

	Source Citation	Maybe ✔ / Dip in x	Notes: What makes it useful?	Use it ✔ / Go deep *
1				
2				
3				
4				
5				
6				
7				
8				
9				
10				

Used with permission from Kuhlthau, Maniotes, and Caspari, *Guided Inquiry Design* (2012).

Figure 9.14 Inquiry Log

Explore

National History Day

Session 2

Learning Goals
Process: Explore interesting ideas, look around, and dip into resources within an online database.

Content: Students will spend time exploring BadgerLink and adding resources to their Inquiry Log. They will think and share their thoughts in Inquiry Circles.

Location: Library or classroom with WiFi access and every student has a laptop.
Team Members: History and/or English Teachers, Librarian

Starter Time: 10 minutes	**BadgerLink Searching Tips** Today the class spends the session exploring resources in Badger-Link, Wisconsin's online resources portal. The LMS shares tips on how to search BadgerLink. The students gain an understanding of how to look for the citations in the articles and how to email resources to their account. The students gain an understanding of how to search for primary and secondary history resources.

Worktime
Time: 45 minutes
Inquiry Log
Think, Pair, Share
 	
Inquiry Circle
 	
Inquiry Community
	Students explore the various BadgerLink resources and use the Inquiry Log to track sources. Track reading strategies in the Inquiry Log.
	
	Pair Share (See Figure 9.16). Think first—review Inquiry Log.
	
	Each partner shares own ideas and reactions.
	
	Each partner listens and gives feedback. See protocol (Figure 9.16).
	
	Inquiry Circle Protocol
	
	Choose Facilitator—asks questions and keeps team on track.
	
	Scribe and Reporter—writes all interesting facts and ideas and shares in larger group.
	
	Each individual shares:
	
	    a. What sources they would like to dip into further
	    b. Why they think they might be useful
	
	The Reporter shares the ideas discussed in the Inquiry Circle.

Reflection Time: 5 minutes	"What I am wondering about or what ideas do I have at this stage of the process?" "When I dipped into it, it made me think about____." (Page 33 in NHD Journal) Process reflection: "How is the Inquiry Log working for me?" "What could I start to do differently?"
Notes:	Students in our course switch from the Inquiry Log to NoodleTools once they start the Gather Stage.

Figure 9.15 Explore 2

Explore—PAIR SHARE PROTOCOL

Use your Stop and Jot and complete this notecatcher as a guide for this conversation with a partner.	
Which sources seemed most valuable? Write down what was interesting. Why was it interesting?	This is interesting … This is interesting because …
Read over what you wrote and write ideas you would like to tell someone else.	I would like to tell _____ about …
Pair Share **Partner A**: Shares **Partner B**: Listens and takes notes **Partner B**: Shares **Partner A**: Listens and takes notes	Share with your partner and take notes on what you are hearing. Telling helps to clarify ideas for forming a good inquiry question.
Partners exchange notes.	Read your partner's notes. They will give you insight for forming inquiry questions.
Reflect on what you found interesting and how you described it to your partner. Think about possible questions for further exploration.	Write three possible questions that you would like to explore further. 1. 2. 3.

Adapted with permission from Kuhlthau, Maniotes, and Caspari. *Guided Inquiry Design: A Framework for Inquiry in Your School*. Libraries Unlimited, 2012.

Figure 9.16 Explore—Pair Share Protocol

Identify

National History Day

Session 1

Learning Goals

Process: Pause and ponder to identify an inquiry question and decide direction.

Content: Students will review notes, share the advantages and disadvantages of group or individual projects, choose a manageable topic, and gain knowledge in "Thinking Like a Historian."

Location: Library or classroom with WiFi access and laptop computers.
Team Members: Social Studies and/or English Teachers, Librarian, Special Education Teacher, English Language Learner Teacher, and/or Reading Specialist

Starter **Reflect** Time: 5 minutes	Enter ticket: Give students time to pause and reflect on their ideas from the past sessions. Hand them a notecard and ask them to write their names and to list 3 ideas or activities that opened their minds during the Open, Immerse, and Explore Sessions. Have them hand in the notecards.
Worktime Time: 45 minutes Inquiry Journal	**Group or Individual Project**, 10 minutes The LMS will guide the students to determine if they prefer working in a group or as individuals during the research process and project creation and sharing stage (Page 18 in NHD Journal, see Figure 9.18). They will respond in their Inquiry Journal and share ideas in the Inquiry Circle, then chronicle responses in their Inquiry Journal on Individual or Group Project Advantages and Disadvantages (Inquiry Chart Figure 9.19). **Think Like a Historian**, 5 minutes The students will begin to show evidence that they are Thinking like a Historian. LMS reviews "How to Think Like a Historian" • What questions do we ask of the past? • How? What? Where? Why? Who? • How can we find answers? • How do we evaluate the evidence? • What matters? Historians' tools of Inquiry: • Cause and effect • Change and continuity • Turning points • Through people's eyes • Using the past to make sense of the present

Figure 9.17 Identify 1

From *Guided Inquiry Design in Action: High School.* Leslie K. Maniotes, Editor. Santa Barbara, CA: Libraries Unlimited. Copyright © 2017.

	The students will begin to determine a manageable topic. "What aspects of a historical topic excite you the most?" (Page 20 in NHD Journal—see Figure 9.20.) Students will review their notes with their shoulder partner to see if there are clues in them for developing an overarching compelling question and supporting questions as they consider the questions posed in Figure 9.20.
Reflection Time: 5 minutes	Reflect in Inquiry Journal: "What are some questions I have formulating in my mind regarding my project?"
Notes:	LMS reminds students that all PowerPoints are on their Google Drive that the teacher shared with them. If they miss class, they are expected to get caught up before the next class.

Figure 9.17 Identify 1 (*Continued*)

Learning How I Learn
How Do You Prefer to Work?

1. Do you prefer to work alone or with a group? Why or why not?

2. Do you enjoy being a group leader? Why or why not?

3. Do you enjoy being a group partner? Why or why not?

4. Do you keep on schedule? Why or why not?

5. Are you a last-minute planner? Why or why not?

6. Do you enjoy acting? Why or why not?

7. Do you love writing? Why or why not?

8. Do you enjoy working with technology? Why or why not?

9. Do you enjoy working with your hands? Why or why not?

Figure 9.18 Learning How I Learn—How Do You Prefer to Work?

Group Project

Advantages	Disadvantages

Individual Project

Advantages	Disadvantages

Figure 9.19 Inquiry Chart

Inquiry Chart to Identify

What Aspects of a Historical Topic Interest You the Most?

Time period?

Local, state, national, world history?

Cultures, locations, sciences, sports, the arts?

Famous people and how they took a stand?

• What is your topic?	• Are there adequate primary sources?
• How does your topic interest you?	• Is the topic credible as a historical topic?
• Is it too broad?	• What evidence have you discovered so far on various points of view on why the topic matters through a historical lens?
• How might you narrow the topic?	• What is the historical context of your topic?

Figure 9.20 Inquiry Chart to Identify

Identify

National History Day

Session 2

Learning Goals
Process: Pause and ponder to identify an inquiry question and decide their direction.

Content: Students will understand how to choose a topic. They will identify their compelling overarching question and their supporting questions.

Location: Library or classroom with WiFi access and laptop computers.
Team Members: Social Studies and/or English Teachers, Librarian

Starter Time: 15 minutes	**Hooking to an Inquiry Topic**—15 minutes Students determine how to hook their topic through an emotional, intellectual, and problem-solving lens. They write responses in their Inquiry Journal. (Page 21 in NHD Journal.) See lesson from: Empire State Information Fluency Continuum. http://schools.nyc.gov/NR/rdonlyres/1A931D4E-1620-4672-ABEF-460A273D0D5F/0/EmpireStateIFC.pdf
Worktime Time: 30 minutes	**Basic and Advanced Levels of Inquiry**—10 minutes Students consider the differences between the basic and advanced inquiry levels and how including both levels in their thinking process helps them to gain the thinking skills of a historian. They answer the questions in their Inquiry Journal (See Figure 9.22). **Selecting Compelling Research Questions**—20 minutes Guide the class through the steps in the protocol or have students work in pairs to answer the questions in Column 1 by reflecting on examples in Column 2 (See link above for more information). (Pages 23–24 in the NHD Journal)
Reflection Time: 5 minutes	"Write a draft of your compelling question in your Inquiry Journal."
Notes:	The librarian or teacher uses many exemplars from National History Day Guides.

Figure 9.21 Identify 2

Gaining the Thinking Skills of a Historian

Basic Questions	Advanced Questions
Where and when was your topic occurring?	Historical context—what else was occurring at the time that was related to your topic?
Who were the major historical figures?	What caused the people to be courageous and take a stand? What were the results?
How did they prepare to take a stand?	What changed as a result of their taking a stand?
What challenges did they encounter?	Why is your topic significant?

Figure 9.22 Gaining the Thinking Skills of a Historian

Identify

National History Day

Session 3

Learning Goals

Process: Pause and ponder to identify an inquiry question and decide direction.

Content: Students will evaluate their compelling questions and register in the school's NoodleTools account.

Location: Library or classroom with WiFi access and laptop computers.

Team Members: Social Studies and/or English Teachers, Librarian

Starter Time: 20 minutes http://schools.nyc.gov /NR/rdonlyres/1A931D4E -1620-4672-ABEF-460 A273D0D5F/0/Empire StateIFC.pdf (p. 10:2) *(Empire State Information Fluency Continuum. New York City Department of Education, 2015.)*	**Formative Assessment: Criteria for Compelling Questions—** 20 minutes Students analyze and assess their questions and enter them in the shared Google Doc. It is beneficial to include the Criteria for Writing Compelling Questions in the Inquiry Journal. They can refer to it as they write their questions. Students will consider the Criteria for Writing Compelling Questions and compare to their own possible questions. (See link) Students will share their draft questions with a shoulder partner, discuss, and get feedback using the question "How do your questions and your partner's questions meet the criteria?" They will revise their questions as needed.
Worktime Time: 35 minutes	LMS shares a doc titled <u>Topic Choices 2017-NHD-RUHS</u> in the Google National History Day folder with the class. Students open the doc. The columns are marked:

Name	Group or Individual Project	Historical Interest	Broad Topic	Narrow Topic	Compelling and Supporting Questions	Thesis

Type of Project	Documentary	Exhibit	Paper	Performance	Website

	LMS shares exemplar on Women's rights. NoodleTools—20 min. The Librarian demonstrates how to log in to the school's NoodleTools account, how to create a new project, to share the project with the teachers, to use the bibliography and notecard tools. Students will enter their compelling question on their Project Dashboard in NoodleTools.
Reflection Time: 5 minutes	"In addition to your compelling question and supporting questions, what other questions are beginning to formulate in your mind?" I need help with ____ (Page 33 in NHD Journal)
Notes: NoodleTools	NoodleTools follows the Cornell Note-Taking Protocol. National History Day requires an annotated bibliography, in alphabetical order, with primary and secondary sources separated, which can be accomplished using NoodleTools in MLA format.

Figure 9.23 Identify 3

National History Day

Session 1

Learning Goals
Process: Gather important information, go broad, and go deep.

Content: Review compelling and supporting questions, choose keywords for searching in online databases, use Boolean logic tips, continue note-taking and annotating bibliography in NoodleTools.
Location: Classroom with WiFi access and laptop computers.
Team Members: Social Studies and/or English Teachers, Librarian

Starter Time: 10 minutes	**Review Compelling Questions** The students will review their compelling questions on the shared Google Doc. The LMS made comments and suggested possible changes students could consider for their compelling questions ahead of class. The questions must relate to the theme "Taking a Stand." **Keywords Presentation** The LMS models how to choose keywords from the compelling questions in order to search for further information online.
Worktime Time: 40 minutes Inquiry Journal Inquiry Circles	**Keyword Catcher**, 20 minutes The LMS shows the shared Google Doc titled <u>Topic Choices 2017-NHD-RUHS</u> via the projector. The students choose their own keywords from their questions and use the "Keyword Catcher" (Figure 9.25) to capture their thoughts on words, synonyms, dates, and people for searching. Students answer the questions in their Inquiry Journal and enter names of people they can email or contact. Students share their ideas in the Inquiry Circle for feedback. **Boolean Logic Tips and worktime**, 20 minutes The LMS will share Boolean logic tips for searching online databases. Students will begin going deeper into their sources using NoodleTools to capture their notes and bibliography citations. They will also begin to curate primary source pictures, voices, music, documents, maps, etc. in their Google folder. They will add those sources to their Bibliography in NoodleTools. The note-taking and annotating bibliography process will continue for 2 more class sessions.
Reflection Time: 10 minutes	Students complete Inquiry Journal prompts (Figure 9.26). Students summarize the important information for the Inquiry Community.
Notes:	The librarian or teacher guides students through the Gather phase by conferencing with the students and commenting on their notes in NoodleTools. It is critical to build a relationship with the students by either emailing them additional source information or listening to their frustrations as they search for the most reliable sources.

Figure 9.24 Gather 1

Keyword Catcher

Topic :

Keyword	Synonyms	Dates	People

- What types of primary sources exist for your topic?
- Where have you looked for information?
- Where will you look for more information?
- Make a list of people you want to contact via email or personal interview. Would they be a primary or secondary source?

Name	Contact Info	Expertise	Primary Source	Secondary Source

Figure 9.25 Keyword Catcher

Gather Inquiry Journal Prompts

Inquiry Journal Prompts	Reflections
How is NoodleTools working for you?	
Write three new ideas you learned in today's session.	I learned that 1. 2. 3.
Write about something that surprised you.	I was surprised that
Write something that you already knew about. Tell how you know.	I knew that
List ideas that you want to know more about.	I would like to know more about
How can my teacher help me?	

Adapted from Kuhlthau, Maniotes, and Caspari. *Guided Inquiry Design: A Framework for Inquiry in Your School*. Libraries Unlimited, 2012.

Figure 9.26 Gather Inquiry Journal Prompts

National History Day

Session 2

Public Library All-Day Field Trip and NHD Judge Visit
Learning Goals
Process: Gather important information, go broad, go deep.

Content: Students learn about how to use the public library to gather historical information.

Location: Hedberg Public Library and classroom with WiFi access and laptop computers.
Team Members: Social Studies and/or English Teachers, Librarian

Total Time at Library: 5 hours and 15 minutes **Starter** 9:00 Time: 30 minutes	Students will meet at our local Hedberg Public Library to gain knowledge from reference librarians on where they can go to gather information. Students arrive at 9:00 and meet near Circulation Desk. The reference librarians review historical context, primary and secondary sources, and where students can gather information from the library resources. The students use the microfiche and microfilm machines as they gather information from historical newspapers and magazines. Young adult and reference librarians give a tour of the library. They spend time in the Janesville Room, where they see where local history is stored and accessed.
Worktime 9:30–10:30 (60 minutes) **Presentation**	Students gather in the Computer Lab after the tour. Using the shared Google Doc that indicates the students' topics and questions, the reference librarians model where to locate and gather information from the New York Times Paper Index, reference books based on historical topics, and other primary sources in the reference section. The librarians then model how to search for information on students' topics using the online library catalog, databases, and other well-known digital primary sources. They also demonstrate how Google can be helpful in locating primary sources.
Introduce NHD Judge 10:30	NHD judge shares tips from a judge's perspective and confers with students and groups. Students sign up for conference times with the judge and the teachers in 15-minute blocks of time.
Formative Assessment 10:35–11:35	The teacher, school librarian, and reference librarians then assist students in locating information from the various locations in the library in print, microfiche, and microfilm formats. Students will begin to use NoodleTools to document their sources and take notes. Some students may change their minds on their topic due to lack of primary source information or based on other information they find. Conference with public librarians, teacher, and school librarian on inquiry questions and where students can locate information.

Figure 9.27 Gather 2

From *Guided Inquiry Design in Action: High School*. Leslie K. Maniotes, Editor. Santa Barbara, CA: Libraries Unlimited. Copyright © 2017.

Continued Research 12:35–3:00 Time: 2 hours and 25 minutes	Students continue gathering information, checking out materials, and making copies. **Formative Assessment NoodleTools** Librarian will grade NoodleTools work using the following scoring system: 4: 9 or more sources 3: – 6–8 sources and notes 2: 4–5 sources and notes 1: 3 sources and notes minimum
Notes:	The librarian or teacher guides students through the Gather phase by conferring with the students and commenting on their notes in either the NoodleTools or Google Docs format.

Figure 9.27 Gather 2 (*Continued*)

Gather

National History Day

Session 3

Learning Goals
Process: Gather important information, go broad, and go deep.

Content: Continue note-taking and annotating bibliography and conference with teachers.

Location: Classroom with WiFi access and laptop computers.
Team Members: Social Studies and/or English Teachers, Librarian

Starter Time: 10 minutes	Entry Ticket: Students reflect on time spent at Hedberg Public Library. Each student has an index card. Students write their names on the card and 3 activities that helped them at Hedberg Public Library. "What suggestions do you have to improve your time at the library?"

Review
Time: 10 minutes
	Students continue to take notes and create an annotated bibliography in NoodleTools. LMS reviews bibliography steps. Refer to Noodle-Tools Support Center for more tips. (NoodleTools.com)
	
	NoodleTools places Bibliography in alphabetical order (Primary and Secondary Sources)
	
	   – in MLA Format
	   – Indicate Primary, Secondary under the Description Tab
	   – Annotation in the Citation Box
	
	Notes need to include
	   – Quotations
	   – Paraphrases or summaries of information
	   – My ideas—your reflections or next steps after you read the info
	   – Images

Worktime Time: 30 minutes	Students continue to research. LMS and teacher circulate among students and offer assistance. LMS helps students to locate experts who can add primary source information to their research. For example, the local historical society archives helped a student researching trench warfare during World War I. They have artifacts of trench art, helmets, food rations, diaries, letters, and pictures of local soldiers who served. Another student researching how Title 9 impacted athletics for local girls and coaches before, during, and after the 1970s was able to delve into yearbooks, local newspapers, and interview retired teachers and coaches.
Reflection Time: 5 minutes	"What challenge did you face today and how did you resolve it?"

Figure 9.28 Gather 3

National History Day

Session 4

Learning Goals
Process: Gather important information, go broad, and go deep.

Content: Continue note-taking and annotating bibliography and conference with teachers.

Location: Classroom with WiFi access and laptop computers.
Team Members: Social Studies and/or English Teachers, Librarian

Starter Time: 2 minutes	LMS reminds students that the entire time is to be spent gathering information. This is the last day in class for gathering information and notes. Students continue to take Notes and create an annotated bibliography in NoodleTools.
Worktime Time: 45 minutes	Students continue to research. LMS and teacher circulate among students to confer with and offer assistance to students. LMS helps students to locate experts who can add primary source information to their research. Students can meet in Inquiry Circles to share resources and ideas.
Reflection Time: 8 minutes Inquiry Community	Share initial thoughts on projects with the Inquiry Community. "How do you plan to share the knowledge you are gaining?"

Figure 9.29 Gather 4

Create

National History Day

Session 1

Learning Goals
Process: Reflect on learning, go beyond facts to make meaning, and create to communicate.

Content: Students will draft a thesis and collaborate with a partner to ensure it meets the criteria.

Location: Library or classroom with WiFi access and every student has a laptop.
Team Members: History and/or English Teachers, Librarian

Starter Time: 5 minutes	Present the agenda and inform students of NHD Ask an Expert webinar series. Remind students of 5 NHD presentation categories: • Documentary, Exhibit, Paper, Performance, Webpage Students have entered their category on shared Google Doc titled <u>Topic Choices 2017 NHD</u>.*
Worktime Time: 40 minutes	**Thesis Presentation**, 10 minutes Thesis Addresses a specific topic: • Expresses student's informed opinion about the past based on evidence • Evaluates the significance of the topic in history • The "So what?" **Exemplars**—Share exemplars of good, bad, and ugly thesis statements: • Earth Day was first celebrated in April 1970 and we still celebrate it today. • Earth Day was a revolution for the environment and changed everything. • Beginning as an exchange of ideas at a teach-in about environmental issues, Earth Day represented the reaction of many people to changes in the environment and increased public and governmental demand for reform, marking the start of the modern environmental movement. Share one more exemplar: • The Bennett Law, which made English the only permissible language for public and private education in Wisconsin, was enacted in 1890 and later repealed. • In response to dramatic changes in immigration, the 1890 Bennett Law was a major reform in education that, although later repealed, laid the foundation for a continued exchange of ideas over the role of education and language assimilation of immigrant children.

Figure 9.30 Create 1

Inquiry Chart	**Draft Thesis,** 20 minutes–
	Students use the Crafting a Thesis Inquiry Chart (Figure 9.31) in their Inquiry Journal to write their thesis and include other points needed to prove their thesis.
	Students draft their thesis and include connection to the theme, facts, opinions, whose point of view.
	Inquiry Partner feedback—10 minutes
	Work together with a partner to get and give input.
	• Can your compelling question be crafted to a thesis statement? • Is the thesis specific enough? • Does it address the topic's significance in history? • Does it have an opposing viewpoint? • Can you see the theme connection?
	Students add thesis to shared Google Doc and NoodleTools Dashboard.
Reflection Time: 5 minutes	In Journal on page 34 students write: • What was most helpful today? • What else do I need to do to be prepared to start my project next week?
Notes:	*At this point the teacher will know how many exhibit boards to order from NHD website or can purchase them at a local Office Supply Company.

Figure 9.30 Create 1 (*Continued*)

My Thesis

Evidence I Need to Prove My Thesis	Connection to Theme

Categories of Facts	Categories of Opinions	Whose Point of View

Figure 9.31 Crafting a Thesis with Supporting Evidence

From *Guided Inquiry Design in Action: High School*. Leslie K. Maniotes, Editor. Santa Barbara, CA: Libraries Unlimited. Copyright © 2017.

Create

National History Day

Session 2

Learning Goals
Process: Reflect on learning, go beyond facts to make meaning, create to communicate.

Content: Students will organize Information in an outline, NoodleTools, or on an Inquiry Chart.

Location: Library or classroom with WiFi access and every student has a laptop.
Team Members: English Teachers, Librarian, History Teacher

Starter Time: 5 minutes	Present the agenda and inform students that today they will organize information. **Organize Information Options:** "There are many ways to organize your information. How do you decide which is the best way? Do you know what method you prefer?" LMS asks class which format works best for them and their project: Traditional outline, storyboards, pictures, mindmapping, graphic organizers, text, music, voice
Worktime Time: 40 minutes	**NoodleTools** LMS shows class how they can access the power of NoodleTools through the • Help: Tutorials and guide (http://www.noodletools.com/helpdesk) • Users Guide • Notecards and outline **Outline** LMS shares option for a traditional outline. (We wanted all students to have access to this information so they would know what an outline at this level looks like and how to use one.) (See example in the Google folder.) **Inquiry Chart** The other option is to draw an Inquiry Chart. Examples are shared in the PowerPoint slide. Students draft their outline in NoodleTools, Google Docs, or on an Inquiry Chart. They hand in materials to the teacher, who will comment that day so students have immediate feedback. **More Guidance**—5 minutes "Go to National History Day Folder in Google Drive. Read over the Contest Rule Book and handouts."
Reflection Time: 5 minutes	In Journal on page 34 students write: • What was most helpful today? • What else do I need to do to be prepared to start my project next week?

Figure 9.32 Create 2

Create

National History Day

Session 3

Learning Goals
Process: Reflect on learning, go beyond facts to make meaning, and create to communicate.

Content: Students will view exemplars, summarize their work, and provide feedback and support to their partner.

Location: Library or classroom with WiFi access and every student has a laptop.
Team Members: History and/or English Teachers, Librarian

Starter Time: 5 minutes	Teacher returns the students' work and students review these and reflect on teacher's/librarian's comments.
Worktime Time: 40 minutes	Review winning examples from NHD website. Once students have reviewed examples, they engage in worktime on creating their presentations. The LMS and teacher guide students through their project creations. Students will begin projects during class the next day. **Create—Pair Share Protocol—Inquiry Partner**, 20 minutes Review Create—Pair Share Protocol (Figure 9.34). Students write their thoughts first: • With a partner—first student listens to partner on what he or she wrote and gives input. • Then students reverse roles and partner shares what he or she wrote. • Both partners take notes as they listen.
Reflection Time: 5 minutes	**Show NHD *Ask an Expert* Video** National History Day <u>Ask an Expert</u>—Highly recommend that students register and watch the webinars or view past webinars on YouTube. "Where are we with our projects?" Share Round Robin.
Notes:	**Homework—Website Webinar**, 10 minutes View NHD Website Webinar—complete webinar on your own time. Even if some students do not plan to create a website as a project, this will give tips for all projects.

Figure 9.33 Create 3

Create—Pair Share Protocol

Pair Share Prompts	Go Beyond the Facts to Make Meaning
As you reread notes and review your journal, think about what you have learned about your inquiry questions. Write what these ideas make you think about regarding your inquiry question.	I learned I think
Read over what you have written in your outline and write what you would like to tell someone else about.	I would like to tell about
Pair Share **Partner A**: Shares **Partner B**: Listens and takes notes **Partner B**: Shares **Partner A**: Listens and takes notes	Share with your partner and take notes on what you are hearing. Telling helps to clarify what you have learned and helps you draw out your own ideas and opinions about your inquiry questions.
Partners exchange notes.	Your partner's notes on your telling can give you insight into the meaning of what you have found out and for adding ideas of your own to share what you have learned about your inquiry questions.
Reflect on what you learned and how you described it to your partner. Think about creative ways to share your learning with the other students.	Now write what you learned about your inquiry questions, adding your own thoughts. You also can note some ways to share your learning with others.

Adapted from: Kuhlthau, Maniotes, and Caspari. *Guided Inquiry Design: A Framework for Inquiry in Your School*. Libraries Unlimited, 2012.

Figure 9.34 Create—Pair Share Protocol

Create

National History Day

Session 4

Learning Goals
Process: Reflect on learning, go beyond facts to make meaning, and create to communicate.

Content: Students will examine the criteria and design their projects with the success criteria in mind.

Location: Library or classroom with WiFi access and every student has a laptop.
Team Members: History and/or English Teachers, Librarian

Starter Time: 15 minutes	**Rule Book**—10 minutes Students study National History Day Contest Rule Book and Judging Criteria for their project category. **Review**—5 minutes—Upcoming Schedule • More time to create project • Create process paper and annotated bibliography • First Draft for peer review and then revise • Present to seniors who will evaluate projects based on Judging Criteria • Parent Open House and School Judging by teachers and guest judges • Self-reflection and feedback—Register for Regional Competition
Worktime Time: 35 minutes	Worktime to begin designing their chosen format • Documentary, Exhibit, Website, Paper, Performance Script Depending on schedules, more time can be allocated to work on projects during class.
Reflection Time: 5 minutes	"Where are we with our projects? What's challenging? What help do you need?"
Notes:	Students may use their own time to complete their projects.

Figure 9.35 Create 4

Create

National History Day

Learning Goals
Process: Learn from one another, share learning, and tell your story.

Content: Students will write process paper and annotated bibliography.

Location: Library or classroom with WiFi access and every student has a laptop.
Team Members: History and/or English Teachers, Librarian, Special Education Teacher, English Language Learning Teacher, and/or Reading Specialist

Starter Time: 10 minutes	**Students begin to compose their process paper.** The process paper allows judges to get insights into students' specific topics and processes. **Process Paper Requirements** Explain the requirements for a process paper. Requirements are described here: http://www.wisconsinhistory.org/ Review the requirements for writing the process paper. (http://www.wisconsinhistory.org/pdfs/nhd/witopicsfulllist.pdf). LMS reviews annotated bibliography requirements.
Worktime Time: 40 minutes	Students review Inquiry Journal and NoodleTools to reflect upon their process as they begin writing their process paper. A template is shared in Google Docs. Students copy the template, name it their name—Process Paper, and move it to their Young Historians folder on their Google Drive. Share with teachers. If they have been using NoodleTools, they need to update their annotations for each citation.
Reflection Time: 5 minutes	"What was your biggest challenge today and how did you or will you remedy it?" Share in the Inquiry Community.
Notes:	The LMS and teacher guide students through the writing of the process paper and the annotated bibliography.

Figure 9.36 Create 5

Share

National History Day
Share with Peers for Critique

Session 1

Learning Goals
Process: Learn from one another, share learning, and tell your story.

Content: Students will share within the Inquiry Community and will be critiqued by their peers in order to make needed revisions.
Location: Library or classroom with WiFi access and every student has a laptop.
Team Members: History and/or English Teachers, Librarian, Special Education Teacher, English Language Learning Teacher, and/or Reading Specialist

Starter Time: 10 minutes	The teachers and LMS assist the students in designing the space and make sure the technology is working. The class sets up presentation stations at school.
Worktime Time: 40 minutes	**Presentations to Peers** Students present their work to the seniors who participated in National History Day the previous year. Seniors critique the students' work using the NHD Judging Criteria located on the NHD website. The forms vary by category, but overall they have same criteria for evaluating projects: Historical quality of the work (60%), connection to theme (20%), clarity of presentation (20%), and rules compliance.
Reflection Time: 10 minutes	Reflect in Inquiry Journals: "How was sharing with the seniors helpful to me? What did I learn about myself through this? What did I learn about getting feedback? What did I learn from the feedback? What will I change?"
Worktime on their own	**Revise** The students revise their projects based on the input from their classmates, and the seniors' experience and critique.
Notes:	Send a note home to parents inviting them to an open house.

Figure 9.37 Share with Peers

Share

National History Day
Share with Parents at Open House

Session 2

Learning Goals
Process: Learn from one another, share learning, tell your story.

Content: Students will share with the larger learning community. If their presentation qualifies for NHD Regional Competition, they will share with others in Madison, WI.
Location: Library or classroom with WiFi access and every student has a laptop.
Team Members: History and/or English Teachers, Librarian, Special Education Teacher, English Language Learning Teacher, and/or Reading Specialist

Starter Time: 10 minutes	LMS serves refreshments at the open house. The LMS and teachers welcome the parents and explain the purpose of the open house. They have previously sent a letter home inviting the parents.
Open House Time: 90 minutes	Students share their revised work at the open house where local historians will judge their work based on the National History Day judging forms. Students will share their process paper, annotated bibliography, and projects. They will share • What they have learned about their topic, • What they have learned about themselves, • What they are most proud of, • What their biggest challenge was and what they would do differently next time. The judges will share their judging critiques with the students and parents. Those who score well and desire to go to Regionals will discuss with parents what they need to do to qualify. They will have a week to make changes to their projects.
Reflection	In Inquiry Journals: "What have I learned about the process, my product, and from the feedback I've gotten?"

Figure 9.38 Share 2 with the Community

Evaluate

National History Day

Learning Goals
Process: Evaluate achievement of learning goals, reflect on content, and reflect on process.

Content: Students will evaluate their thinking process and give feedback to the teachers.
Location: Library or classroom with WiFi access and every student has a laptop.
Team Members: History and/or English Teachers, Librarian, Special Education Teacher, English Language Learning Teacher, and/or Reading Specialist

Starter	The starter includes refreshments and sets a celebratory tone.
Worktime Time: 30 minutes	**Reflections** Students reflect using the following questions on an index card (see Figure 9.40). Students complete Self-Reflection on Inquiry (found on page 159 [Figure 11.12] in <u>Guided Inquiry Design</u> [2012]).

Reflection
Time: 20 minutes
	Feedback
	
	Students will give recommendations to their teachers for
	
	    1. Improving the inquiry process
	    2. Improving peer evaluation
	    3. Improving parent open house
	    4. Other recommendations (see Figure 9.41)
	
	Students hand in Inquiry Journals. Teachers will grade and return.

Notes:	The librarian scores the process daily by collecting and returning the Inquiry Journals at each class. The librarian and teachers score the final projects as a culminating activity. There is no final exam for this course. The Learning Team meets to evaluate the various activities and determine what to alter for the next year, based on time restraints and student feedback. The team discusses whether they need to make changes to the instructional design and what were unique characteristics of this group of students that affected the design and implementation. We designate a note-taker and attach the notes to the course design for reference next year.

Figure 9.39 Evaluate

Reflect on Your Learning

- In what ways did you learn to use writing as a thinking tool?

- In what ways did the journal support your learning through this process?

- How did charts help you?

- What were your challenges and in what ways did you move forward, continuing through any tough spots?

- Where and when did you feel that you were able to dig deeper into the inquiry?

- How were collaboration and idea sharing with your Inquiry Circle useful to you?

Figure 9.40 Reflect on Your Learning

Student Recommendations for the Learning Team

Recommendations for Improving the Inquiry Process	Recommendations for Improving Peer Evaluation
Recommendations for Improving Parent Open House	Other Recommendations

Figure 9.41 Student Recommendations for the Learning Team

National History Day Unit Resources

All Unit Resources online: http://tinyurl.com/GIDinActionHS-NHD

Student Resources Accessed throughout the Course
Open Sessions

Annenberg Learner Interactives United States History Map. Indians. Internet. February 14, 2016. https://www.learner.org/interactives/historymap/indians.html

History of Apple and the First iPhone: RIP Steve Job. YouTube video, October 6, 2011. https://youtu.be/BG4azxx1Xjl

Onion, Rebecca and Claudio Saunt. *Interactive Time-Lapse Map Shows How the US Took More Than 1.5 Billion Acres from Native Americans*. The Vault: Historical Treasures, Oddities, and Delights. Slate Group. Internet. February 14, 2016. http://www.slate.com/blogs/the_vault/2014/06/17/interactive_map_loss_of_indian_land.html

Robinson, Ken. *Changing Education Paradigms*. YouTube video, October 12, 2010. https://youtu.be/zDZFcDGpL4U

States and Territories of the United States of America: 1700-1960. Internet. Feb. 14, 2016. http://edudemic.com/wp-content/uploads/2012/07/changingusa.gif

Immerse Sessions

Abelson, Aaron, Hyunho Lee and Carter Wang. *The Tiananmen Square Massacre: A Government's Encounter with Its People*. YouTube video, January 8, 2011. https://youtu.be/fS6NoRWZv1w

Document Analysis Worksheets. National Archives. http://www.archives.gov/education/lessons/worksheets/index.html

Herblock's Political Cartoons. Library of Congress. http://www.loc.gov/exhibits/herblocks-history/presidents.html

Immigration Timeline. http://www.libertyellisfoundation.org/immigration-timeline

President Franklin Delano Roosevelt Political Cartoons. Niskayuna High School. http://www.nisk.k12.ny.us/fdr/FDRcartoons.html

Religions of the World Animated Map. http://www.businessinsider.com/map-shows-how-religion-spread-around-the-world-2015-6

Explore

Grace, Emma. *Rough in the Bunch: Appalachia's Rayon Girls Fight for the Right to Strike*. You Tube, July 9, 2014. https://youtu.be/trqO6QhtMxo

General Research Links to Open Source Resources

Badgerlink. (Wisconsin Residents) http://badgerlink.dpi.wi.gov/
Google Scholar. https://scholar.google.com/
Project Gutenberg—Free eBooks. http://www.gutenberg.org/
Smithsonian American Art Museum. http://americanart.si.edu/

Create and Writing Resources

NoodleTools. http://www.noodletools.com/
Google Sites Tutorial. https://sites.google.com/site/mflynchsites/
iMovie Tutorial. https://www.msu.edu/course/tc/243/iMovie%20Tutorial.pdf
Live Binder. http://www.livebinders.com/welcome/home
Purdue University OWL. https://owl.english.purdue.edu/
Soundzabounds. http://www.soundzabound.com/?

Figure 9.42 Unit Resources

University of North Carolina at Chapel Hill Writing Center. http://writingcenter
    .unc.edu/handouts/
Web Creation Tools. http://www.craighighschool.org/lmc/web-tools
Weebly—How to Create Your NHD Weebly Account. http://nhd.org/entering
    -contest/creating-an-entry/website/nhd-web-site-registration-guide/#tab-id-1
Weebly Tutorial. https://youtu.be/slgv3tTYYqQ
Wordle. http://www.wordle.net/
Writing Process Paper. http://www.wisconsinhistory.org/Content.
    aspx?dsNav=N:4294963828-4294963805&dsNavOnly=N:1120&dsRecordDetails
    =R:CS3643

Historical Resources

American Archive of Public Broadcasting. http://americanarchive.org/
American Journeys. http://www.americanjourneys.org/
California Online Archives. http://oac.cdlib.org/
Cesar Chavez Foundation. http://www.chavezfoundation.org/
Chicano/a Movement. http://depts.washington.edu/civilr/mecha_intro.htm
Chronicling America. http://chroniclingamerica.loc.gov/
Civil Rights in the U.S. http://spartacus-educational.com/USAcivilrights.htm
Eyes on the Prize: American Civil Rights Movements 1954–1985. http://www.pbs
    .org/wgbh/amex/eyesontheprize/story/03_schools.html
Forced Labor: A New System of Slavery. http://www.nationalarchives.gov.uk
    /pathways/blackhistory/india/forced.htm
Gaylord Nelson and Earth Day. http://nelsonearthday.net/
Gilder Lehrman Institute of American History. https://www.gilderlehrman.org/
Historic Documents: U.S. State Department. https://history.state.gov/
Historic Newspapers. http://chroniclingamerica.loc.gov/
Historical Recordings: Library of Congress. http://www.loc.gov/jukebox/
History Matters: George Mason University. http://historymatters.gmu.edu/
Lewis and Clark Expedition. http://www.pbs.org/lewisandclark/index.html
Library of Congress. https://www.loc.gov/
Library of Congress Primary Source Sets. http://www.loc.gov/teachers/
    classroommaterials/primarysourcesets/
Library of Congress: Prints and Photographs. http://www.loc.gov/pictures/
Livingstone Online—Website Exemplar. http://www.livingstoneonline.org/
Martin Luther King Center. http://www.thekingcenter.org/
National Archives. http://www.ourdocuments.gov/index.php?flash=true&
National Archives: Primary Source Analysis. http://www.archives.gov/education
    /lessons/worksheets/index.html
National History Day. http://nhd.org/
National History Day Judging Forms. http://www.wisconsinhistory.org/Content
    .aspx?dsNav=Ny:True,Ro:0,N:4294963828-4294963805&dsNavOnly
    =N:4294963828-4294963805&dsRecordDetails=R:CS3027&dsDimensionSearch
    =D:Judging+criteria,Dxm:All,Dxp:3&dsCompoundDimensionSearch=D:Judging
    +criteria,Dxm:All,Dxp:3
National History Day Past Winners. http://nhd.org/contest-affiliates/examples/
National Parks History. http://www.nps.gov/history/stories.htm
Nelson Mandela Foundation. https://www.nelsonmandela.org/
Olympic Committee Archives: Univ. of Illinois. http://archives.library.illinois.edu
    /archon/?p=collections/controlcard&id=4719

Figure 9.42 Unit Resources (*Continued*)

Olympic Studies Centre. http://www.olympic.org/olympic-studies-centre
Olympics Team USA. http://www.teamusa.org/
Orphan Train Project. http://www.rootsweb.ancestry.com/~wiorphan/sitemap
    .html
PBS Learning Media. http://www.pbslearningmedia.org/
Political Cartoons: Franklin Delano Roosevelt. http://www.nisk.k12.ny.us/fdr
    /FDRcartoons.html
Political Cartoons: LOC Herblock's History. http://www.loc.gov/exhibits/herblocks
    -history/presidents.html
Political Cartoons: LOC (Library of Congress). http://www.loc.gov/teachers/class
    roommaterials/themes/political-cartoons/set.html
Political Cartoons: The New Yorker. http://www.newyorker.com/cartoons
Recollection Wisconsin. http://recollectionwisconsin.org/
Rock County Historical Society. http://www.rchs.us/
Scottsboro Boys Trials. http://law2.umkc.edu/faculty/projects/ftrials/scottsboro
    /scottsb.htm
Smithsonian Institute. http://www.si.edu/exhibitions/
Teaching History. http://teachinghistory.org/
University of Wisconsin Digital Collections. https://uwdc.library.wisc.edu/
Voices of Democracy. http://voices-of-democracy.org/
Wisconsin Electronic Reader. http://digicoll.library.wisc.edu/WIReader/Contents
    .html
Wisconsin Historical Society Online Collections. http://www.wisconsinhistory.org/
Wisconsin Pioneer Experience. https://uwdc.library.wisc.edu/collections/WI
    /wipionexp/
World Digital Library. https://www.wdl.org/en/
Yale University Photogrammar. http://photogrammar.yale.edu/

School and Public Library Resources

Rock University High School Destiny Home Page. https://sdj.follettdestiny.com
Hedberg Public Library. http://www.hedbergpubliclibrary.org/research_data
    bases.html

Teacher Resources

NoodleTools. http://www.noodletools.com/
*College, Career, and Civic Life C3 Framework for Social Studies State Standards:
    Guidance for Enhancing the Rigor of K–12 Civics, Economics, Geography, and
    History:* National Council for the Social Studies, 2013. http://www.socialstudies
    .org/c3
Empire State Information Fluency Continuum. http://schools.nyc.gov/NR
    /rdonlyres/1A931D4E-1620-4672-ABEF-460A273D0D5F/0/EmpireStateIFC.pdf
Standards for the 21st Century Learner. American Association for School Librar-
    ians, 2007. http://www.ala.org/aasl/sites/ala.org.aasl/files/content/guideline
    sandstandards/learningstandards/AASL_LearningStandards.pdf
Standards Connections by GID phase NCSS C3 & AASL in the Google folder
    https://drive.google.com/drive/u/0/folders/0BxC4U0GzSaOGc1N2LW5RR3VxTnc

Figure 9.42 Unit Resources (*Continued*)

The World Is Not Flat: Explore the World, Choose Your Adventure

Buffy Edwards

"This project makes me get outside my comfort zone. I like it," "You are asking us to think," and "I like the freedom to pick a topic and project format that I want." These are statements students made about their Guided Inquiry Design® senior project, statements that were certainly affirming to the collaborative planning team. The idea for this unit, "The World Is Not Flat: Explore the World, Choose Your Adventure" developed during a Guided Inquiry Design professional development institute in our district, Norman Public Schools, Norman, Oklahoma. During the fall of 2015 Norman Public Schools provided 3 three-day training institutes for teams comprised of a combination of instructional coaches, librarians, teachers, grade level teams, content area teams, and gifted resource teachers from each of the district's 24 schools. The institutes were led by Dr. Leslie Maniotes, author of *Guided Inquiry Design*.

The expectation from the district leadership was that teams who attended the Guided Inquiry Design Institute would develop a unit that could be taught during the 2015–2016 school year. The collaborative team for this unit was comprised of a teacher from language arts, science, social studies, and art, and the librarian. The goal of the collaborative team was to develop a multidisciplinary Guided Inquiry unit that would allow students the opportunity to earn credits in multiple content areas. This instructional unit could not be done in isolation, so it is with great appreciation and admiration that I dedicate this chapter to the amazing collaborative team of Jessica London, language arts teacher; Chris Jones, science teacher; Kent Nicholson, social studies teacher; and the English IV students. These students opened their hearts to learning and many were transformed by this experience. I also want to say thank you to Norman Public Schools for providing this incredible professional development opportunity with Dr. Maniotes.

Dimensions Academy High School is part of a K–12 alternative school. Students who attend are not successful in the regular school setting for various reasons and work primarily toward credit recovery. The students are capable of learning and experiencing success but have challenges that keep them from realizing their own potential. There is a focus on developing the student as a whole, offering them social, emotional, and academic support.

Planning

Instruction at Dimensions had traditionally been more self-paced because of the academic needs of the students. Students generally work through course materials in worksheet-driven packets, so the idea of a Guided Inquiry Design unit was a major paradigm shift for the team and school. The team agreed that moving to a Guided Inquiry Design should be implemented because of the possibilities of hands-on learning, engaging students more in their own learning, and allowing students to earn credits in multiple content areas at the same time—something that had never been done in the district before. The team had to consider the fact that in any given class there may be students who need credits in various content areas. (See Figure 10.1.) For example, in a science class there may be students who need biology and physical science, and in social studies some students who need history and world history or economics. The most challenging part of developing the unit was understanding how the unit could offer students the opportunity to earn credits in multiple content areas. The team recognized that this was very different, but also saw the potential for helping students recover credits for courses they had taken and failed or taken and did not complete.

After much discussion the collaborative team concluded that language arts standards would be integrated throughout all content areas and, depending on the credit needs of individual students, the content focus would be more emphasized in the area where the student needed credits. Students in English IV are required to complete a major research project, so the team agreed that the majority of the unit would be done during that hour while one-to-one ongoing conferencing with the content area teachers would be necessary.

The unit was designed so students could earn credits or partial credits according to their specific needs. Figure 10.1 shows a sample of the varied credit needs of different students and illustrates how credits potentially could be earned in multiple content areas. The depth of the student project dictated whether an adequate number of standards were met to earn the needed credit.

Student	Science	Social Studies	Math	Art
Student 1		World History	Geometry	
Student 2		U.S. History 2	Geometry	
Student 3	Anatomy Physiology	Government U.S. History Oklahoma History	Geometry Algebra I	Art
Student 4	Biology Anatomy Physiology	U.S. History	Geometry Algebra 1	Art

Figure 10.1 Sample of Varying Needs for Academic Credit

Understanding that students in alternative education often lack successful educational experiences, the collaborative team knew that it would be necessary to build background knowledge to fill in any gaps as well as scaffold students' understanding of the concept behind the guiding question, "What impacts and influences are found around the world?" Additionally, the team understood that because Guided Inquiry Design was so different from the norm at this school, everyone involved would need to be patient, understanding, and flexible. Challenges that the team anticipated dealing with during the unit were student attendance, attitudes toward learning, motivation to complete the project, and students' willingness to stretch themselves academically.

To facilitate the planning and implementation of the unit beyond the time at the Guided Inquiry Design Institute, the team had several collaborative planning sessions in person and relied heavily on Google Docs to collaboratively organize instructional material.

Implementation, Instruction, and Inquiry Tools

This unit was a nine-week project during spring semester. At the start, the dynamics of the students ranged from somewhat motivated to totally shut down and almost nonparticipatory, and as the unit moved through **Immerse**, **Explore**, and **Identify**, there were times when the students seemed to have more anxiety instead of curiosity. It was also difficult for students to share or discuss ideas, findings, and their feelings in Inquiry Circles. The team attributed this to the fact that students had been conditioned to a prescriptive style of assignment, and students' expectations were low. Because the unit was designed to offer the possibility of multiple credits, the team felt that **Open**, **Immerse**, and **Explore** should be extended to encompass content from all subject areas to demonstrate how the overarching idea of the unit, "What impacts and influences are found around the world?" could be connected across disciplines. During the **Immerse** phase, a field trip to an art museum proved to be a personal, social, and cultural experience. It was also educational because most of these at-risk students had not been exposed to these types of opportunities and experiences.

Working through the Guided Inquiry Design process really forced students outside their comfort zones because they were so conditioned to prescriptive assignments. Students initially were excited, but as they had more choice and voice, they experienced disequilibrium with the idea that they had so much freedom in terms of topics and the project format. The team used Inquiry Circles to discuss these feelings and how this project was so different from what they were used to completing, and the team reassured students that it would all come together. Students were uncomfortable and exhibited feelings of frustration and confusion. Some students really struggled identifying and creating good questions. They had the idea, knew what they wanted to learn more about, but could not get the question captured. With a shoulder partner, students used question cubes to create questions and share with each other. Question cubes provided a scaffold where students used the question stem to enable them to form quality questions out of their general topic or interests (see Figure 10.2).

Figure 10.2 Question Cube

Additionally, an inside-outside circle-sharing protocol, modeled in the Guided Inquiry Design institute, allowed students the chance to share their questions with several peers, which in turn helped them further internalize their topics. The team does feel that students being outside their comfort zone urged them to ask questions about the unquestionable—to really stretch their own learning. This notion is supported by Holmes (2015; see Figure 10.25) in that the feeling of uncertainty helps strengthen students' ability to let curiosity drive their investigation. To the students, taking time to **Immerse**, **Explore**, and **Identify** seemed as if it was "taking a long time to get started," but in reality the students were gaining valuable background knowledge and making personal Third Space connections with topics of interest. Students were anxious because, by habit, they expected to be given a topic for research and jumped ahead to looking up information, missing the focus of **Immerse** and **Explore** to look widely for what was interesting to them. Once they were able to **Identify** a topic and questions that they really connected with, their interest increased even more. According to Kuhlthau (2004; see Figure 10.25), students often feel anxious in the process until they are able to identify their topic and focus, and this was certainly the case at Dimensions. As the Guided Inquiry Design process continued, students started to become more involved in their learning. Exit slip responses to "How are you feeling?" included curious and fascinated, amazed, inspired, and eager. During **Identify** students worked closely with the content area teachers for guidance to ensure they would meet standards and earn needed credits.

It seemed that a feeling of trust was developing with the students. They were relaxing and trusting their own judgments, but more importantly, they were trusting the Guided Inquiry Design process. **Gather** was a little more challenging for students because they were having to stretch themselves to locate information on much higher level thinking and questioning than they were used to. The team recognized that for some students, note taking was natural but for others, it was a barrier.

To eliminate the barrier, teachers worked with certain students needing specific help. The team did a little "hand holding" to keep them on track and to provide a successful experience, which kept them motivated. Students were asked to locate specific types of information about their topic—a timeline, a poem, a newspaper article, online website, database article—and this helped move them comfortably into gathering. During **Gather** students used a vision board/Inquiry Chart to really bring their ideas together. This was a visual representation capturing and organizing their ideas. **Gather** covered more time than anticipated because of some internal school challenges, but it did not derail the unit at all. Because they had so much say in the format of the final project, students had the chance to really explore each possibility, and for many, the choices were new and different.

Once the students selected their format, the **Create** process went well. New energy and excitement was evident, and students seemed genuinely engaged in the project and their learning. In fact, several students were becoming meta-cognitively aware of their own learning, recognizing that they needed to go back to **Gather** to fill in some information gaps. Sharing projects was a celebration of success, and students really rallied and cheered each other on. The evaluation of the products was a very proud moment for both teachers and students. As students shared their projects we saw smiles, pride in what they had accomplished, and most importantly, improved self-confidence. Student self-assessments clearly demonstrated that they were uncomfortable at the start of the unit, saying that they were stressed and confused, but were confident and excited about their project by the end. It should be noted that for some students the accomplishment of finishing this Guided Inquiry Design project was a milestone: not only did they earn multiple credits, it also meant they would graduate.

Learning Through the Process

The Guided Inquiry Design process provides a wonderful platform for collaboration and co-teaching. A unit of this complexity would not have been possible without true teamwork and flexibility. The librarian and language arts teacher worked side-by-side throughout the unit co-teaching while the content area teachers were extremely flexible meeting with students throughout the unit as needed. Conferring with students was an important part of the process, one that was ongoing and allowed the students to converse with teachers, share their ideas, make connections across the curriculum, internalize their knowledge, and find those Third Space connections. It was absolutely critical that students confer with content area teachers regularly. This was an opportunity for guidance in really developing a project that met standards in multiple content areas.

Introducing the unit with **Open**, the use of international webcams and online videos really helped set the stage and pique curiosity. Most of the students had never been outside of their city, so observing the Seven Wonders of the World and geometric marvels was very awe-inspiring. In fact, in the final self-assessment one student shared that she saw something on the first day of **Open** that made her curious, and that is what she built her project around. Looking at locations around the world via international webcams, students used Inquiry Journals to reflect and make observations, followed by Inquiry Circle discussions: What did you observe? What made you wonder? Using the multidisciplinary approach, **Immerse** further developed background knowledge through a visit to an art museum, which provided an experience of looking at artwork from around the world. We chose to visit an art museum because for many of the students it was a first experience, and it gave them the opportunity to observe art from around the world to further their depth of background knowledge around the unit's guiding question. The **Explore** phase was done through stations. Observing students interacting and engaging with resources, the team realized that some of the students lacked confidence in their skills to dip into topics and were gravitating to using Google. This was when the team took time to reteach. Recall that many of these students have not had positive or successful academic experiences. Throughout the unit the team reminded themselves that reteaching and taking time to pause was a vital part of the students' emotional journey, and it was necessary and vital to the success of the overall unit.

As the unit moved on to **Identify**, the team noted that students were starting to talk more to

Figure 10.3 Providing Feedback

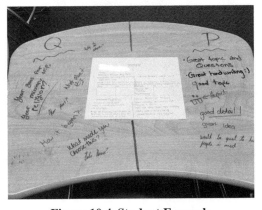

Figure 10.4 Student Example

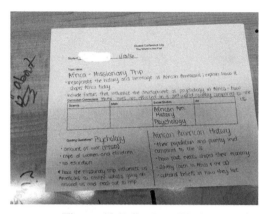

Figure 10.5 Student Work

one another about their topics and what they really wanted to focus on for their project. It appeared that many were even starting to enjoy the journey! During this stage, students were challenged to provide feedback to one another's student conference log using a two-part feedback carousel, a question and praise. Students rotated around the room offering feedback written on desktops with vis-à-vis pens. Students were engaged while interacting and providing invaluable peer review.

Gathering information started out with traditional paper and pencil, because that is what students were accustomed to using, but transitioned to Google Docs. The team wanted to infuse the unit with opportunities to develop digital 21st-century learning skills. So, throughout, there was the use of technology, Google Docs, online resources that allowed students to reach outside the classroom and school, personal learning devices, and skills that would prepare them for college and career.

Gathering concluded and transitioned into **Create** with students developing a vision board/ Inquiry Chart; basically, this was a visual representation of their outline. Students were asked

Figure 10.6 Vision Board/Inquiry Chart

to expand the outline they created into a storyboard that included pictures and keywords for the information their project would cover. The language arts teacher suggested that we take the time to do this because many of the students were very visual learners, and it was time well spent. In one-to-one student conferencing, students were asked to share their vision board and tell why they included what they did. Hearing the students talk about their vision boards and identify deep, rich, concrete thoughts about their topics was exciting. It was evidence that during the process phases **Immerse**, **Explore**, and **Gather** they had internalized knowledge and made new connections. Creating the vision board, organizing the ideas and thoughts, and having to verbalize them really brought the project together (see Figure 10.6). Students seemed excited again, eager to make sure the depth of information would meet the multicredit options and to move on to **Create**. With the completion of the vision board/Inquiry Chart, students were ready to select the format that best matched the purpose of their project.

The team created a sample product presentation with examples of the possible project formats from the **Create** choice board (see Figure 10.7). As possible project formats were presented, short Inquiry Circle discussions followed, allowing time for students to talk about how a particular project format would be a good match for their topic. At the beginning of the unit students were very worried about what the final product would be and why they "just couldn't do a PowerPoint" or write a paper. That uneasiness and uncertainty seemed to have been replaced with confidence: confidence in themselves and the potential for what they could create. Doubt and "settling for PowerPoint" was replaced with motivation to create historical newspapers,

Create Choice Board

Documentary	Comic Book/GN	Movie/ Travel Channel	Facebook Page
Short Story	Podcast	Historical Newspaper	Ad Campaign
Website or Blog	Infomercial	Infographic	Script
Grant	Proposal	Travel Agent Itinerary	Cultural Experience
Letter to the President	Diorama	Poem	Reference Book

Figure 10.7 Create Choice Board

websites/blogs, dioramas, a documentary, infographics, and travel channel videos using the video studio and green screen.

Students were at various places moving from **Gather** to **Create**, working on posters, computers, and notebook paper, getting themselves organized. On this particular day of the unit an observer shared, "I was just at Norman High School and it looked very similar there." Recall that students completing this unit are *at-risk alternative education students* fully engaged in their own learning and excited about an academic project. In Inquiry Circles, students reviewed grading rubrics. There were no traditional research papers or PowerPoints, but rather there were creative projects that demonstrated student achievement and mastery of content, earning them credits in multiple content areas. Products included historical newspapers, short stories, a diorama, a blog capturing the emotions of the psychological effects of living in an impoverished country, an online interactive poster about Syria and the guiding question of "What makes a country poor?" and a travel agent as a personal tour guide in Brazil. As students shared, the team observed with pride and amazement. Teachers were extremely pleased with what students had created.

Hands-on learning and student conferences were reported in the self-assessment to be the most beneficial in supporting student learning. Most students felt nervous, confused, and anxious at the start, but all shared that they were glad they did the project using a Guided Inquiry Design approach. For some students, selecting the topic was most challenging, and this was not a big surprise. Most students recognized that they had challenged themselves beyond their own expectations. The teachers felt that the quality of the projects was far superior to anything done in the past and that students were able to earn multiple credits where needed.

Reflection and Evaluation

The team felt overall that the unit was extremely successful and was confident that the foundation for a culture of inquiry had been established. It was noted that attendance improved and that students were motivated by the opportunity to earn multiple credits. As with any instructional unit, changes will be made to improve the process. For the most part, the necessary changes have to do with the length of time spent on a phase. One thing that we hoped to do was Skype with schools around the world, but unfortunately, this did not work out. This may be done in place of a couple of the webcams in the future, as well as using Twitter and other social media to connect with experts or natives around the world.

During this time frame, students were very concerned about the difference between traditional research papers and this project. Extending **Immerse** to include all the content areas meant extended time. In the next Guided Inquiry Design unit, students will be better prepared, knowing what to expect. **Explore** was challenging for students because they all wanted to start note taking—this is what they were accustomed to, so it is no surprise. Next time, we will emphasize the inquiry stance using something like a Stop and Jot form so students learn how to **Explore** without gathering information. **Gather** also took longer than anticipated because time was spent teaching students how to use Google Docs and other online tools. The team was pleased with the creativity and quality of the products students created and appreciated the candor of their evaluation and self-assessment. Most importantly, it was evident that the students' attitudes toward learning had changed. The climate in Mrs. London's fourth-hour English IV class showed a remarkable change from negative to positive and from a dread of school to true excitement about school. Students were smiling and talking more, exhibiting positive attitudes toward learning, collaborating with one another when someone needed help, and even joking with teachers. The social studies teacher shared, "The Guided Inquiry Design unit was really a leap of faith but as I have conferred with students one-on-one you could really see how students were involved in their own learning and it was great." But perhaps quotes from students give the most accurate evaluation.

In the beginning, it was a difficult concept to grasp, but after a while, things began to fall into place. The final outcome was definitely worth the time and effort. —Ashlyn

Starting a project from square one, building on a simple idea and creating an interesting, yet complex, subject matter and explanation has given me the confidence to prepare for college work expectations. —Ceridwen

Even though this project has been stressful and complex, it has given me the opportunity to explore new information and think outside the box. —Marissa

By using guided inquiry, it has helped me by bringing me outside of my comfort zone and has let me explore new things. —Kaitlyn

At first, this project was hard and stressful, but I'm confident that the final product will be worth it. —Tiffany

This process of learning has been an experience. It makes you more responsible for your work, rather than having people telling you what they expect. You learn how to organize and situate yourself. —Harjeet

Guided Inquiry Design®
Unit Overview
"The World Is Not Flat"

The Team: Language Arts, Science, Social Studies, Art Teachers, and Librarian
Concept: Cultural, societal, historical, scientific, and economical views are multifaceted and different around the world.

Guiding Question(s): What are the cultural, societal, historical, scientific, and economic influences that impact events, places, and people around the world?

Learning Goals:
Students will ask an important question about a place in the world to learn about its impacts and influences. Students will synthesize new information and create and share a final project.

The World Is Not Flat is a nine-week multidisciplinary Guided Inquiry Design unit that allows students the opportunity to earn credits in multiple content areas. The unit took place at an alternative school where instruction had been traditionally worksheet packet–driven. The Collaborative Team took a leap of faith implementing a Guided Inquiry unit because it was such a different approach to instruction at this school. Students utilized a variety of resources to gather information and selected their final project format from a choice board of options.

 **Open**	Students discuss similarities and differences between schools, states, and the United States. Observations around the world are made via international webcams. Art, geometric wonders of the world, biomes, and 7 wonders of the world video clips are shown. Students use Inquiry Journals to reflect and record observations. Students share ideas and notations about their observations in Inquiry Circles.
 **Immerse**	Using computers and personal computing devices accessing online resources and Internet searching, students complete a timed "Locate and Find" hunt for notable locations around the world. As locations are identified, a star rating scale is used to indicate level of interest. Using a laminated world map, students find and note their locations with the most stars. Students visit a local art museum, focusing on art and artists from around the museum.
 **Explore**	Following directions on the task card, students explore highest ranked notable locations around the world from the Locate and Find. As they explore, citations are recorded on the Inquiry Log and topics of interest are noted on the Idea Log. Teachers model and review the use of online resources and how to evaluate websites. Students explore additional sources of information including primary source documents and experts. Individual student conferences start in this phase and continue throughout the unit.

Figure 10.8 Unit Overview

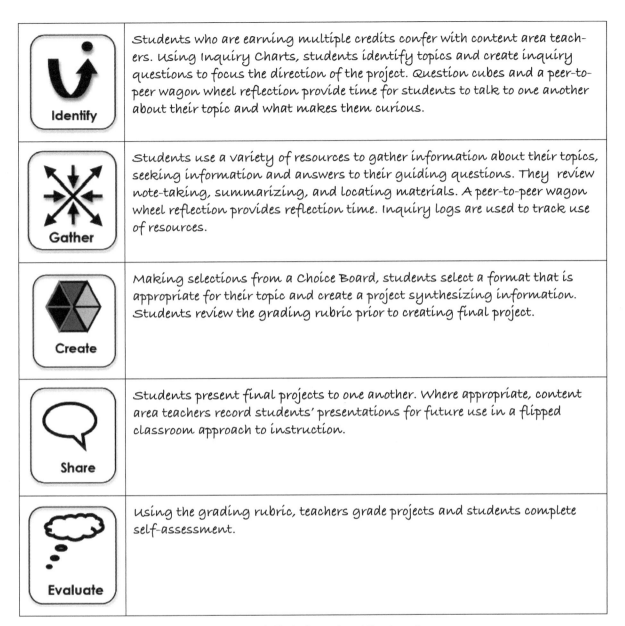

Identify	Students who are earning multiple credits confer with content area teachers. Using Inquiry Charts, students identify topics and create inquiry questions to focus the direction of the project. Question cubes and a peer-to-peer wagon wheel reflection provide time for students to talk to one another about their topic and what makes them curious.
Gather	Students use a variety of resources to gather information about their topics, seeking information and answers to their guiding questions. They review note-taking, summarizing, and locating materials. A peer-to-peer wagon wheel reflection provides reflection time. Inquiry logs are used to track use of resources.
Create	Making selections from a Choice Board, students select a format that is appropriate for their topic and create a project synthesizing information. Students review the grading rubric prior to creating final project.
Share	Students present final projects to one another. Where appropriate, content area teachers record students' presentations for future use in a flipped classroom approach to instruction.
Evaluate	Using the grading rubric, teachers grade projects and students complete self-assessment.

Figure 10.8 Unit Overview (*Continued*)

Open

The World Is Not Flat

Learning Goals
Process: Invitation to inquiry, open minds, stimulate curiosity about the world.

Content: Students will recognize influences and impacts around the world. Students will identify similarities and differences between schools, states, and the world.

Location: Language Arts Classroom
Team Members: Language Arts Teacher and Librarian

This **Open** session uses videos and virtual experiences from multiple content areas to get students thinking about the world in science, math, art, and social studies.

Starter Time: 20 minutes Inquiry Community	At the start of class display the world map and visit a location in the world via international webcam. "What do you see that is the same as where we live? What do you see that is different? How do the surroundings look different from our own?" Record responses. Using the school, state, country similarities and differences chart, open the discussion by comparing schools, states, and countries. As a group, consider: • Populations • Religions • Economics • Geography • Art • Personal experiences and connections to locations around the world
Worktime Time: 35 minutes Inquiry Circles	In groups, students will further open their minds by looking at video and virtual tours including geometrical wonders of the world, 7 wonders of the world, biomes of the world, and art masterpieces. Students record any questions and discuss what they see, what they are curious about, anything that piques their curiosity.
Reflection Time: 5 minutes	Using exit slips, students record 3 words that describe their thoughts and feelings about their observations and the unit overall.
Notes:	Students were interested and intrigued by webcams and watching how other populations live. It was beneficial to have a discussion about similarities and differences starting at school, then the state, and then the United States compared to other parts of the world.

Figure 10.9 Open

Immerse

The World Is Not Flat

Session 1

Learning Goals
Process: Build background knowledge, connect to content, and discover interesting ideas.

Content: Students will complete a locate and find scavenger hunt and identify geographic locations around the world. Using a star system, students rank locations to indicate their level of interest.

Location: Language Arts Classroom

Team Members: Language Arts Teacher and Librarian

This **Immerse** session has students investigating the geographic location of landmarks and points of interest using quick searches and online resources. This **Immerse** spanned two days.

Starter Time: 10 minutes Inquiry Journal Follow this link: http://tinyurl.com/GIDin Action-HS to see the full scavenger hunt	Show the world map and remind students of the guiding question: What impacts and influences are found around the world? In an Inquiry Circle, students view international webcams and reflect in their Inquiry Journals. Explain the Locate and Find scavenger hunt. (See example in Figure 10.11.) The locations on the scavenger hunt are wonders of the world, famous landmarks, or notable places from all over the world. Students may not be familiar with them. Remind students that even if they don't recognize or haven't heard of the location, they should read enough about them to note the location and indicate their interest on the star ranking. The more stars students mark, the higher their interest.
Worktime Time: 40 minutes Inquiry Circles	Using personal devices and desktop computers, students do quick searches to learn the geographic locations of places listed on the Locate and Find.. As students work through the list of locations, periodically ask them to share findings. Allow time for students to share what they have learned.
Reflection Time: 5 minutes	Answer Garden, https://answergarden.ch Students share reflections on locations that piqued their interest and reactions to what they learned on Answer Garden. Answer Garden allows students to share their thoughts and reflect in real-time Inquiry Circle participation and online brainstorming. (See Sample Student Answer Garden, Figure 10.12.)
Notes:	The Locate and Find hunt was very effective for immersing students in focusing on locations around the world. Comments included "the Sea of Stars blows my mind," "this looks like an imploded volcano," and "Can you give us more time?" It was noted that additional background knowledge was needed. Students were very engaged in this activity.

Figure 10.10 Immerse 1

Locate and Find World Scavenger Hunt (Sample List)
http://tinyturl.com/GIDinAction-HS

Landmark	Country	Interest Level
1,000-Year-Old Yew Tree		★ ★ ★ ★ ★
Abraham Lake		★ ★ ★ ★ ★
African Renaissance Monument		★ ★ ★ ★ ★
Ciudad de las Artes y las Ciencias		★ ★ ★ ★ ★
Dead Sea		★ ★ ★ ★ ★
Eiffel Tower		★ ★ ★ ★ ★
Free Spirit Spheres		★ ★ ★ ★ ★
Gehry Buildings at Medienhafen		★ ★ ★ ★ ★
Huacachina Oasis		★ ★ ★ ★ ★
Ice Cave		★ ★ ★ ★ ★
Machu Picchu		★ ★ ★ ★ ★
Museum of Islamic Art		★ ★ ★ ★ ★
Neuschwanstein Castle		★ ★ ★ ★ ★
Roman Colosseum		★ ★ ★ ★ ★
Taj Mahal		★ ★ ★ ★ ★

Figure 10.11 Locate and Find

Figure 10.12 Answer Garden

The World Is Not Flat

Immerse

Session 2

Learning Goals
Process: Build background knowledge, connect to content, and discover interesting ideas.

Content: Students will view and reflect on the art and objects in the Fred Jones Jr. Museum of Art collection.
Location: Language Arts Classroom and field trip to museum
Team Members: Language Arts Teacher and Librarian

In this **Immerse** session students visit a local art museum to view artwork from around the world to broaden their view.

Starter Time: 10 minutes Inquiry Journal	Show the world map and remind students of guiding question: "What impacts and influences are found around the world?" Students write in their Inquiry Journal about their expectations for the visit to the art museum. "What do you expect to see?"
Worktime Time: 3 hours	Students tour the Fred Jones Jr. Museum of Art on the University of Oklahoma Campus, http://www.ou.edu/fjjma.html Their permanent collection includes: "the Weitzenhoffer Collection of French Impressionism, the Eugene B. Adkins Collection of art of the American Southwest and Native American art, the James T. Bialac Native American Art Collection, 20th-century American painting and sculpture, ceramics, photography, contemporary art, Asian art, and works on paper from the 16th century to the present. Throughout the year, temporary exhibitions examine the art of various periods and cultures." http://www.ou.edu/content/fjjma/collections.html This museum was selected because of its proximity to our school, it provided a social experience outside of the classroom and school, and the exhibits represent cultures from around the world.
Reflection Time: 10 minutes Inquiry Circle and Inquiry Journal	Students discussed various art pieces from the tour and wrote a reflection in their Inquiry Journal about what stood out to them as it related to our concept of influences and impacts around the world.

Figure 10.13 Immerse 2

Explore

The World Is Not Flat

Learning Goals
Process: Explore interesting ideas, look around, and dip in.

Content: Students will explore ideas about notable landmarks and locations around the world as they browse through a variety of resources.
Location: Language Arts Classroom
Team Members: Language Arts Teacher and Librarian

Starter Time: 5 minutes Inquiry Journal	Students review their Inquiry Journal reflection on the art museum from yesterday. With a shoulder partner, students share what they noted from yesterday's work. As a class, students review the Locate and Find scavenger hunt creating a list of locations around the world that they ranked highest or were of interest to them.
Worktime Time: 45 minutes Inquiry Log	A task card with instructions and reminders about using online resources is provided (See Figure 10.15). Resources are arranged in stations where students explore topics of interest. As students explore, they Stop and Jot about points of interest in their Inquiry Log (See Figure 9.14) and on the Idea catcher (Figure 10.16). Station resources included nonfiction books, print atlases, Grolier Online, WorldBook Online, Britannica, CQ Researcher, and websites where appropriate.
Reflection Time: 5 minutes Inquiry Circle	Ask students questions: • What worked for you today? • What did not work for you today? • What will you change for tomorrow? Students talked about search strategies they used and which resources provided good information about their topic.
Notes:	Many students seemed to get lost in their own learning while exploring. Students showed more wonder and were very interested in the multicredit aspect and how their project would need to be developed to achieve this.

Figure 10.14 Explore

Task Card
Explore locations around the world

1. Use the Locate and Find (scavenger hunt) list of notable locations around the world to identify the locations you have ranked with the most stars.

2. Navigate to the online resource page of the Dimensions webpage and click on high school resources.

3. Look up your highest ranked locations in the resources listed below, noting any areas of interest or questions that you have on the Idea Log.

   • Grolier Online (school link)

   Note there are multiple encyclopedias within Grolier.

   • Use Britannica.

   Note the functionality for exploring on the right.

   • Access other resources listed as appropriate for your topic.

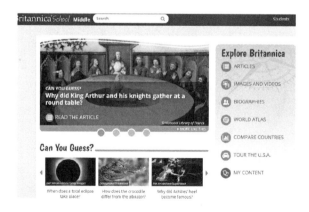

Figure 10.15 Task Card 1

Resource Stations	What did you look up?	What did you learn? **Stop and Jot**	How does the new info shift your topic?	Easy to use? How could you use the resource in your project?
Books Do you need to request some from other schools?				
Grolier Online • Lands and People • New Book of Knowledge • Grolier Multimedia				
Resource Stations	What did you look up?	What did you learn? **Stop and Jot**	How does the new info shift your topic?	Easy to use? How could you use the resource in your project?
WorldBook				
Safari Montage				

Figure 10.16 Task Card 2

Identify

The World Is Not Flat

Learning Goals
Process: Pause and ponder to identify their inquiry question.

Content: Students will develop probing questions about their topic. Students will use the Inquiry Log to guide their questions. Students will meet with content area teachers to discuss multi-credit projects and develop inquiry questions.
Location: Language Arts Classroom
Team Members: Language Arts, Librarian, Science, Art, and Social Studies Teachers

This **Identify** spanned several days to allow students time to develop outline, develop questions, and meet with content area teachers.

Starter Time: 5 minutes Inquiry Circle Inquiry Journal	Teachers discussed question creation with the Inquiry Community. "What is a good question?" Teachers model how to transform a question from basic knowledge level to a deep, robust, probing question.
Worktime Time: 30 minutes Inquiry Log Inquiry Circle	Students work individually to revisit Explore logs, journals, and task cards as needed while identifying inquiry questions. Students confer one-on-one with the team. **Question Cube** To assist in the development of questions, the team introduced the question cube. In Inquiry Circles, students had a set of two cubes—on each side of one cube a one-word question starter was written and on each side of the other cube, a verb was written. Students took turns rolling the dice to create the start of the question and then, referring to their notes, completed the question. Students discuss their topics and questions with content area teachers to ensure that the focus of each question will address appropriate standards to earn needed credits.
Reflection Time: 15 minutes	**Feedback Carousel** Using a desktop Feedback Carousel, students share their student conference sheets and questions with one another. Using a Vis-a-Vis pen, students record questions and praise on the desktop. (See Figure 10.18.)
Notes:	It was noted that students need additional scaffolding to develop quality questions. Question cubes were introduced during this phase and that helped tremendously. Desktop feedback was very successful and students offered one another excellent suggestions—and they loved writing on the desks!

Figure 10.17 Identify

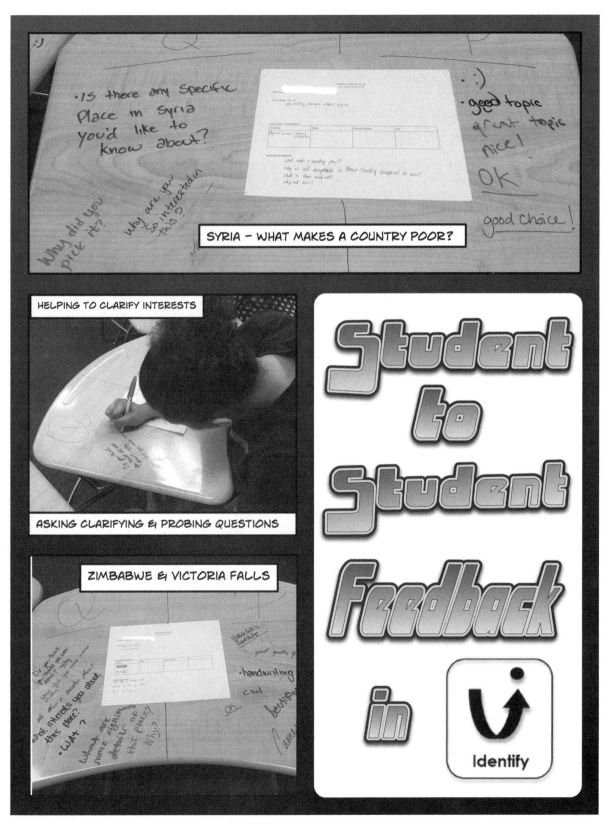

Figure 10.18 Student to Student Feedback

The World Is Not Flat

Learning Goals:
Process: Gather important information, go broad, go deep.

Content: Students will use, locate, and access resources in all formats (nonfiction, Internet, databases, online encyclopedias, etc.) and reflect on strategies of researching that work best and determine if gathered materials are appropriate for their research.

Location: Language Arts Classroom
Team Members: Language Arts Teacher, Librarian

This **Gather** phase lasted several days, allowing sufficient time for students to gather information to answer their research questions. Students were introduced to various Google Apps for Education including Google Docs, Slides, and EasyBib.

Starter Time: 10 minutes Inquiry Log	With a shoulder partner, students discuss their topic, their questions, and their plan for the Gather phase of researching. Students refer to their Inquiry Log and any notes already taken from the Stop and Jot.
Worktime Several Days Inquiry Logs	Ongoing throughout the several days of Gathering, continual reminders, modeling, conferencing, redirecting, assisting, and guiding are done. We used mini lessons and quick check-in how to's on: • Modeling note-taking • Highlighting keywords and phrases • Sharing curated resources • Demonstrating how to choose what's important to answer specific questions, and how to connect the new knowledge with what they already know • Searching strategies and specific resources as appropriate • Summarizing, paraphrasing, citing sources, and using quotes Arrange student conferences as needed, as students work to gather information using a variety of resources.
Reflection Time: 5 minutes	During the multiple days of Gather, several methods of reflection were implemented: Exit slips, response to prompt on Google Docs, and in Inquiry Circles asking the questions: What worked? What didn't? What will you change?
Notes:	Our students needed additional guidance on determining what was important and what information connected to their guiding questions. They also needed encouragement to keep digging and refining searches.

Figure 10.19 Gather

Create

The World Is Not Flat

Learning Goals
Process: Reflect on learning, go beyond facts to make meaning, create to communicate.

Content: Students will select a project format from the project Choice Board and synthesize the information gathered to build knowledge about their topic. Students will confer with content area teachers to verify that the depth of content meets standards as final projects are completed.

Location: Language Arts Classroom
Team Members: Language Arts, Science, Social Studies Teachers, and Librarian

This **Create** phase spanned several days while students created final projects. The first day of **Create**, students identified possible formats and explored how-to's. In the following days, students selected their format and developed the final project.

Starter Time: 15 minutes Inquiry Circle	After viewing the examples of possible projects, students choose three possible project formats from the Create Choice Board (See Figure 10.7). In Inquiry Circles, students discuss their choices. In the discussion, students share their rationale for why they selected those formats and how they fit with their particular question and content. Grading rubric and timeline are shared to help students stay on track. (See Figure 10.21.)
Worktime Time: 30 minutes	Once the project format was selected, students worked to create their final project.
Reflection Time: 5 minutes	Ask students: • What worked for you today? • What did not work for you today? • What will you change for tomorrow? Students were also asked about what they needed to continue their progress and finish their project. This was posed to them because the team felt they needed to assess and evaluate their use of time. The team saw the need to help this group of students to understand the importance of using time wisely.
Notes:	Students were engaged in the development of their projects. Some recognized they needed additional information and returned to Gather additional information as necessary.

Figure 10.20 Create

The World Is Not Flat—English IV Final Project Rubric

Organization	Criteria	Comments and evidence
	1 = does not meet 2 = meets 3 = exceeds	
Inquiry Journal Reflection Observations are recorded and reflective thoughts included		
Locate and Find Scavenger Hunt Complete and locations are ranked according to personal interest		
Inquiry Log Includes bibliographic information and/or URL		
Idea web Web developed to include broad topics, key-words, and Third Space ideas		
Guiding Question(s) Question(s) captures topic		
Green Light Topic Topic approved		
Outline Outline is complete and shows connected ideas		
Notes Evidence of information gathered in note format		
Annotated Bibliography Formatted according to MLA and includes resource description.		

Content	Criteria	Comments and evidence
	1/2/3	
English IV Grammar, punctuation, sentence structure, MLA format		
Science Evidence of standards in project		
Social Studies Evidence of standards in project		
Math Evidence of standards in project		
Art Evidence of standards in project		
Student Conferencing Form Completed and includes evidence of content area focus		
Presentation/Project		
Format Presentation is appropriate for the topic and audience		
Organization Information is presented in a logical sequence		
Quality of information Material included is relevant to the overall message/purpose, information is accurate		
Presentation Delivery is poised, controlled, and smooth; information is well communicated; visuals are well prepared		

Figure 10.21 Project Rubric

The World Is Not Flat

Learning Goals
Process: Learn from one another, share learning, tell your story.

Content: Students share projects for "The World Is Not Flat" unit with each other and Teacher Team.
Location: Language Arts Classroom
Team Members: Language Arts, Science, Social Studies Teachers, and Librarian. In addition, the school principal and counselor may also be invited.

Starter	Teachers welcome students to the "Celebration of Success" and congratulate them on their accomplishment of creating a finished senior project. Prior to the first presentation, students will be given the opportunity to ask any questions about the presentations. Teachers will review process and remind students about respectful audience skills while welcoming them to hear the final projects from their classmates. At the conclusion of all presentations, refreshments and snacks will be shared to celebrate the completion of the unit and the success of the students.
Worktime	Each student will share his or her presentation. All students share: • The name of their project • Why they selected the format that they did • The presentation • Briefly, what they are most proud of about their project As students present projects, the team uses grading rubric to assess.
Reflection	At the conclusion of all presentations, students will complete self-assessment.
Notes:	For our first round, the team and students chose not to expand the listening audience beyond the school principal and counselor. This may take place over two class periods to accommodate all presentations.

Figure 10.22 Share

The World Is Not Flat

Learning Goals
Process: Evaluate achievement of learning goals, reflect on content, and reflect on process.

Content: Students will complete a self-assessment reflecting on the process and the product.
Location: English IV Classroom
Team Members: English IV, Librarian, Science and Social Studies Teachers

Starter Time: 5 minutes	Students complete self-assessment. (See student self-assessment, Figure 10.24.) In Inquiry Circles, students talk about their project, their process, successes and challenges, and reflect using their self-assessment remarks as a guide.
Worktime Time: 15 minutes Inquiry Circle	Working in Inquiry Circles, use a line to map feelings students experienced across the process. Beginning Middle End Compare the shape of their line maps to the shape of Guided Inquiry Design Process. Have students connect to their own experience to note how it matched or ran counter to the process. Draw conclusions about their experiences and make generalizations and connections to the meaning of this to their own learning. Allow students discussion and sharing time to reflect on their learning and how they connected with content and topics.
Reflection Time: 20 minutes	Reflect on content learned and student perspective of "Impacts and Influence Around the World." As an exit slip, ask students to write a note to future students who will complete the senior project through a Guided Inquiry experience.
Notes:	See also the English IV teacher Standards Checklist page for assessment of English Language Arts Standards competencies. (See link in Unit Resources document, Figure 10.25.) There were opportunities to practice most of the OK ELA standards within this unit.

Figure 10.23 Evaluate

Student Self-Assessment Reflection

What feelings did you experience across the project?

Beginning	Middle	End

How would you use the feedback from the teacher to improve the next project?

Thinking back through the unit, what did you find most difficult?

Thinking back through the unit, what did you find easy to do?

What did you learn about your own learning during this project?

What advice would you give someone just starting a project like this?

What grade do you think you deserve on the project and why?

Figure 10.24 Self-Evaluate

Unit Resources—The World Is Not Flat

Google Folder Resources: http://tinyurl.com/GIDinAction-HS

Websites:
General
    Library of Congress
        http://www.loc.gov/
    Pics4Learning
        http://pics4learning.com/

Art
    Michelangelo, Sistine Chapel ceiling, 1508–1512 (Vatican)
        https://youtu.be/PEE3B8Fsuc0
    The Most Awe-Inspiring 3D Street Art from Around the World
        https://youtu.be/t0-qb0BWXn8
    International Webcams
        www.earthcam.com

Math
    9 Most Mathematically Interesting Buildings in the World
        https://www.google.com/url?q=http://www.tripbase.com/blog/9-most-mathe
        matically-interesting-buildings-in-the-world/&sa=D&ust=1454428715686000&usg
        =AFQjCNF8bPql87Rma6XFACqyrX-F_9wOwQ
    Wonders of the Geometric World
        http://prezi.com/dzwnvqnx2xgx/?utm_campaign=share&utm_medium
        =copy&rc=ex0share

Science
    BBC Documentary Trailer, *Life*
        https://youtu.be/IBws4yj7W1A
    Build a Biome
        http://cashmancuneo.net/biomes/biomebuil.swf

Social Studies
    Afghan Girl—*National Geographic* Cover
        http://ngm.nationalgeographic.com/2002/04/afghan-girl/index-text
    7 Wonders of the World
        https://youtu.be/Lka9A7IRYz8
    Time Is Nothing—Around the World in 343 Days (time lapse)
        https://youtu.be/UGnrT0F-lgs

Technology
    Answer Garden, https://answergarden.ch/
    Google Apps for Education
    Green screen and video recording equipment

Presentations:
Math
    Prezi—Wonders of the Geometric World
        http://prezi.com/dzwnvqnx2xgx/?utm_campaign=share&utm_medium
        =copy&rc=ex0share

Figure 10.25 Unit Resources

Online Encyclopedias and Databases:
Grolier Online
WorldBook Online
Britannica
CQ Researcher
Gale Virtual Library
Resources from EBSCOHost

Print Resources

Resources were available in the classroom for browsing as students progressed through the unit.

Chiarelli, B., Bebi, A. L., & Ravaglia, P. (1999). *The atlas of world cultures*. New York: Peter Bedrick Books.

Ching, J. (2010). *Jobs in green travel and tourism*. New York: Rosen Pub.

Concise atlas of the world. (1996). New York: Oxford University Press.

Corbishley, M. (1996). *The world of architectural wonders*. New York: Peter Bedrick Books.

Corrain, L., Galante, L. R., & Boni, S. (1997). *The art of the Renaissance*. New York: Peter Bedrick Books.

Curl, J. S., & Sambrook, J. J. (1999). *A dictionary of architecture*. Oxford: Oxford University Press.

Gabucci, A., Peccatori, S., & Zuffi, S. (2002). *Ancient Rome: Art, architecture and history*. Los Angeles: J. Paul Getty Museum.

Glancey, J. (2006). *DK Eyewitness Companions Architecture*. New York: DK Pub.

Milo, F., Cecchi, L., & Ricciardi, A. (1999). *The story of architecture*. New York: Peter Bedrick Books.

O'Gorman, J. F. (1998). *ABC of architecture*. Philadelphia, PA: University of Pennsylvnia Press.

Olson, N. (2008). *Pyramids*. Mankato, MN: Capstone Press.

PoemHunter.com: Poems—Quotes—Poetry. (n.d.). Retrieved March 14, 2016, from http://PoemHunter.com/

Salzmann, M. E. (2009). *Arctic Ocean to Zimbabwe: Geography from A to Z*. Edina, MN: ABDO Pub.

Scillian, D. (2003). *P is for passport: A world alphabet*. Chelsea, MI: Sleeping Bear Press.

Academic References from Chapter

Holmes, J. (2015). *Nonsense: The power of not knowing*. New York, NY: Crown Publishers.

How to Spark Curiosity in Children Through Embracing Uncertainty. (n.d.). Retrieved February 3, 2016, from http://ww2.kqed.org/mindshift/2015/10/21/how-to-spark-curiosity-in-children-by-embracing-uncertainty/

Kuhlthau, C. C. (2004). *Seeking meaning: A process approach to library and information services* (2nd ed.) Westport, CT: Libraries Unlimited.

Kuhlthau, C. C., Maniotes, L. K., & Caspari, A. K. (2015). *Guided Inquiry Design: A framework for inquiry in your school*. Santa Barbara, CA: Libraries Unlimited.

Maniotes, L. K., Harrington, L., & Lambusta, P. (2016). *Guided Inquiry Design in Action: Middle school*. Santa Barbara, CA: Libraries Unlimited.

Figure 10.25 Unit Resources (*Continued*)

Getting Started and Sustaining Change

Leslie K. Maniotes

Getting Started

If you are just getting started with implementing Guided Inquiry practice in your school, then this book should be a support. The units in these pages are examples. They are meant to inspire readers to think of the possibilities for Guided Inquiry in their own contexts, in a variety of content, and in a multitude of ways. Of course, you may want to take one or all of these units and try them out. If so, they are written in such a way that you can. In each of these units we have shown when and how the inquiry tools are used throughout the process and how they can be used for assessments and to drive interventions for learning. All the components are there for you to replicate or recreate in your own units.

From the beginning of developing Guided Inquiry, we have been hesitant to share whole units for fear that people would teach them as canned lessons and as the only way Guided Inquiry should look. This was not and never will be our intent. The true intent of this book is to give educators a picture of the wide variety of content and ways that Guided Inquiry can look from start to finish. We hope that these units will inspire you to design your own units. We know that education professionals with deep pedagogical and content knowledge have the intelligence and passion to create rich learning experiences for all children. The process and units described here are tools to support you to do that with clear intentionality.

We are all learning and growing this practice, even the authors of this book. So, when we talk about getting started, the best thing to do is find a team and try it out. Trying out a unit the first time can be a daunting task, so the units in the previous pages should remove some of that burden. For example, if you're not comfortable taking on all the tools, start with one in the first unit and try it. Then, slowly add more as you progress and deepen your understanding of the design and the flow of it. In essence, start where you are, and start small but intend to grow.

Risk Takers and Reflective Practice

In the first unit you try, pay attention to how students respond to the phases we describe. Compare their reactions to what is described in the ISP (Kuhlthau, 2004) and the bullets for each phase of the Guided Inquiry Design® process (Kuhlthau, Maniotes, and Caspari, 2012).

Take time in those first units to become very knowledgeable about the process itself. Raise your awareness to students' responding.

Take the stance of a reflective practitioner and pay attention to what was challenging for you as a team. Take time to meet and talk with your team about strategies to overcome the challenges that you faced. These conversations are the cornerstone to growing your practice within the Guided Inquiry Design. With these conversations you will be growing a culture of inquiry at your school, where you will begin to create common understandings and have evidence of how the practice supports student learning and engagement. Without the conversations you risk stagnation and—worse—having some people revert back to more traditional frames of research, which we know don't support student learning.

When questions arise, dip back into *Guided Inquiry Design* to reread and notice the subtleties of the phases as we describe them. We have had many people tell us that after teaching a few or even many units, going back into *Guided Inquiry Design* (Kuhlthau, Maniotes, and Caspari, 2012) has really helped them to understand a certain phase or tool on a deeper level than ever before. Other educators had "ah-ha" moments after rereading. They rediscovered the vital shift that "the first three phases before **Identify** are critical to the (success of the) unit." Or, "The first three phases are worth spending time in before jumping too soon into deeper research." Educators of inquiry learning benefit from opening up to learn about the process as they listen to and learn from teammates, colleagues, and students in a reflective practice.

Making a Commitment

The educators who are greatly successful are committed to using Guided Inquiry Design with fidelity. They trust the research behind the design and stick to it. That means sticking to the process and how the phases are designed as well as using some, if not all, of the tools throughout. All of this works together because it is grounded in the research about what we know about how students learn. The tools were born out of the research on strategies that students said helped them across the process (Kuhlthau, 2004). In turn, we created a system that reflected what students said worked. In that way, fidelity to the design is a support to implementation. Furthermore, having clear goals for implementation and being committed to practicing and improving on your own practice will get results. It's up to the team to keep the ball rolling. Making a commitment to engage in reflective conversations on implementation and design will have certain beneficial results.

Create Structures That Support Guided Inquiry Practice

Structures that support inquiry learning are also essential for its success. Getting flexibility in your schedule and common planning times are very important to your success. Make sure to take time for designing and planning together. Set yourself up for success, when getting started, by setting planning times on the calendar for the entire unit so the time is already scheduled for the team to meet periodically.

Sustaining Change

We believe all students benefit from this process and deserve high-quality instruction that provides opportunities to follow their interests within a subject matter and develop expertise through research and community learning. Sustaining change requires keeping momentum and continuing to develop your own practice and the schoolwide program. In this way, it is important to consider how your program is growing across the school and for all students. Consider the following questions: Do all students have access to this kind of learning in your school? Is it a privilege for gifted students or honors students? In this postindustrial age, all our students need the skills that we learn through inquiry (for more on this, see *Guided Inquiry* [Kuhlthau, Maniotes, and Caspari, 2015]).

Consider questions about equity and implementation: How are we systematically growing equitable Guided Inquiry practice across our school? How will we know when we have reached our implementation goal and can begin to work on sustaining the program?

Consider your goals: What are our goals or reasons for implementing Guided Inquiry Design? For what are we using Guided Inquiry? Name what you are hoping to accomplish. Some ideas on possible goals and ways to know if you are meeting them can be found in Figure 11.1.

Systems That Develop and Sustain Inquiry

Intentional planning for strategic development of the Guided Inquiry program is critical for the sustainability of a high level of implementation. It requires commitment. What we have found is that once people see the level of engagement in classrooms and the high level of rigor and quality sharing of learning that occurs through Guided Inquiry, it's easy to get more people on board. Most people want better learning for their students; they just aren't sure how to get there. Guided Inquiry provides that roadmap to success. When people see the impact on students, they want to join in.

A systems approach and thinking is often left to school leaders but is necessary to consider when you aspire to have equal access to inquiry for all students. Consider what systems are in place for implementing inquiry learning, assessing inquiry learning, and continuing our own professional development to support this practice.

A culture of inquiry can develop at a school through book clubs and rich discussion of the ideas. Coming together to use the same terminology and language around the practice builds your school as an Inquiry Community. Study groups and book clubs starting with *Guided Inquiry: Learning in the 21st Century* (Kuhlthau, Maniotes, and Caspari, 2015) help educators to understand the foundational knowledge behind Guided Inquiry and why it is important. Discussions around its importance include schoolwide goal setting for inquiry-based learning and determining what outcomes your staff is aiming for.

Once the vision, purpose, and goals are set, faculty can move to *Guided Inquiry Design* (Kuhlthau, Maniotes, and Caspari, 2012) to understand the process and the "how to." Reading this book together builds a common understanding of the approach, the language, and expectations. Reading these three books as a staff alongside professional development is one way to build a culture of inquiry and develop common understandings around student learning and teacher practice through inquiry.

Structures That Support Unit Design

Sometimes, in the hustle and bustle of the school year, it is challenging to find the needed time to sit down in Learning Teams to design a high-quality unit. Even once you know the value and phases of the Guided Inquiry Design process, it takes time and thought as a collaborative team to design and develop units of study. Leaders with a vision for inquiry in their school work to develop a schedule with teachers and librarians that includes time for designing units at strategic points across the year.

Examples of Implementation Goals
for Guided Inquiry

Goal We want to:	Component GI	Evidence we can collect How we know it is having an impact
Increase student engagement	Third Space	Track student interest level across and at the end of the process. Have students tell their story.
Impact rigor in content learning	Content	Learning Team compares the rigor of content learning from previous units to units following Guided Inquiry Design.
Embed information literacy into content area	Information Literacy	Determine the intended information literacy concepts and skills. Create performance indicators for those skills in use. Track information literacy skill use through the GID unit.
Increase critical thinking and collaboration	Social Skills	Intentional use of the structure of Inquiry Circles and Inquiry Community. Have students complete a collaboration checklist to reflect on their collaboration and thinking as related to grade level standards for speaking and listening.
Improve students' capability in independent research	Learning How to Learn	Use the SLIM reflection to have students reflect on how they are going through the inquiry process at checkpoints across the process.
Improve students' ability to communicate their learning to a wide audience	Literacy Competency	Use presentation checklists for self, peer, and Learning Team assessment of speaking and listening skills.
Increase interdisciplinary learning	Integrated Learning	Track the units that engage cross-disciplinary content. Determine interdisciplinary opportunities. Engage new collaborations at the school.
Develop an inquiry mindset across the school	Inquiry Practice	Gather data on teacher questions and student questions during lessons. Reflect together on findings in professional development time.

Figure 11.1 Examples of Implementation Goals for Guided Inquiry

Sometimes outside support is needed. The Guided Inquiry Design Institute was developed to support Learning Teams in gaining a deeper understanding of the practice and in taking time to design a unit. This professional development has been powerful for educator teams because they leave with a unit ready to teach, and implementation is boosted to the next level, because they have had the time to think it through with experts and team members outside the daily grind of school. No matter where you are in your understanding of the practice, the institute raises your level of implementation. The institute also builds capacity in the level of collaboration in the school, as all members of the team think and create together and reflect on roles for collaboration. Once back at school, teams report a higher level of collaboration. If you want more information on these institutes, contact Leslie Maniotes.

Professional Learning Communities for Reviewing Data and Reflection

Also critical for success are systems for progress monitoring and assessment of inquiry learning. Inquiry can be perceived as very open ended, and it can seem easy to lose track of learning goals. This doesn't have to be the case. The five kinds of learning can be measured and understood through careful progress monitoring within the unit. We cannot wait until the final product of inquiry to determine if or what students are learning. Systems for data analysis that support progress monitoring through inquiry will enhance successful implementation and give teachers the confidence to know what students are learning through each unit. With clear intention around the learning goals and routine systems to use the Inquiry Tools as data about student learning, teachers gain confidence in the rigor of student learning through Guided Inquiry.

It is important for the systems of the school to sustain teachers through professional development efforts. Effective teachers are highly reflective and are continually thinking how did my lesson go, and what can I improve upon for next time? They are clear on the learning objective and how that session supported that learning for students.

The learning team can support one another in reflecting and learning in powerful ways. Having teachers collaborate through inquiry builds capacity in the accountability system in the school as it connects groups of teachers who reflect together on student learning in meaningful ways. A system of Professional Learning Communities (PLCs), which provide a regular time for teachers working together in teams to reflect on inquiry practice alongside student learning through inquiry, supports teachers as they lean on one another and collaborate to develop together as reflective professionals within the practice of Guided Inquiry (DeFour, 2004).

Social Media, Networks, and Communities of Practice

Many educators are using social media to connect to educators all over the world. They are out there sharing best practices on a daily basis on Twitter, Facebook, Pinterest, and through more formal networks. These environments use searchable hashtags that link you to others engaged in the practice of inquiry learning. Hashtags like #inquiryed #guidedinquiry #GID can help you to find all kinds of resources and other educators teaching this way, sharing materials and ideas, any time, any day. Open networks can connect you to others and help you find a wider group to learn from.

Networks created around a community of practice can be even more fulfilling for professional growth and development. Bryk and colleagues (2015) recommend the use of a Community of Practice as a way to build upon what we know, continue conversation in the practice, and get us to our goal of higher student engagement and deeper learning as well as creating an inquiry culture in our schools. They explain that through networks our learning will accelerate by enabling a collective effort around a problem of practice. Communities of practice can be developed using Google+ or on Facebook for schools working to become an Inquiry Community. Districts and states have also supported the GID practice by creating online spaces where educators can share resources and session and unit plans that align with local and national standards. Our Guided Inquiry Design blog has become a community of practice and sharing as different educators take a week to describe their practice and their experience with Guided Inquiry Design and to reflect on challenges and growth (see more at http://52guidedinquiry.edublogs .org). All of these collective efforts are worth the time and investment as they enable reflective practice and sharing that benefits a larger community working toward a common goal of deeper learning in schools through an inquiry-based approach.

Webinars and Workshops

Professional development that supports what you are trying to do comes in so many forms. Another professional development avenue is through webinars and workshops. There are many webinars available on topics related to Guided Inquiry. Because there are so many components to the design, the webinars feature pieces of the larger whole. These can be watched individually, in small groups, or with the entire faculty. Facilitated discussions that follow the viewing enhance the learning and build bridges between members of the group around implementation of the ideas presented. Consider who will host the viewing, what questions might be most useful before the viewing, and arrange a time when all members can create an action out of the session for clear follow-up.

Finally, know that change takes time. Consider the levels of implementation that you would like to achieve as your goal. Create a roadmap to ensure your successful implementation toward those goals. We hope that this book has helped you along that path.

References

Bryk, A. S., L. M. Gomez, A. Grunow, and P. G. LeMahieu. (2015). *Learning to Improve: How America's Schools Can Get Better at Getting Better.* Cambridge, MA: Harvard Education Press.

DeFour, R. (2004). What Is a Professional Learning Community? *Educational Leadership, 61,* 8, 6–11. Alexandria, VA: Association of Supervision and Curriculum Development.

Kuhlthau, C. (2004). *Seeking Meaning: A Process Approach to Library and Information Services.* 2nd ed. Westport, CT: Libraries Unlimited.

Kuhlthau, C., L. Maniotes, and A. Caspari. (2012). *Guided Inquiry Design: A Framework for Inquiry in Your School.* Santa Barbara, CA: Libraries Unlimited.

Kuhlthau, C., L. Maniotes, and A. Caspari. (2015). *Guided Inquiry: Learning in the 21st Century.* 2nd ed. Santa Barbara, CA: Libraries Unlimited.

Index

About the Editor and Contributors

MARY KATHLEEN BOGUSZEWSKI (KATHY), MLS, has 50+ years in education. She was honored as a Herb Kohl Fellowship recipient for her collaborative work with high school teachers and students. She has presented at many conferences including the National Academy of Sciences in Georgetown on *Nontechnological Strategies to Keep Children Safe on the Internet,* and AASL on *Strategic Planning for Your School Library Media Program.* She is a National History Day coach whose students have placed at regional and state competitions. She earned her MLS at UW–Madison and has served as president of Beta Phi Mu, UW–Madison chapter.

ANITA CELLUCCI, MEd, President of the Massachusetts School Library Association, is the library teacher at Westborough High School. With several years' experience in libraries—from a large public library to elementary, middle, and high school libraries—Anita brings a wide range of understanding to the educational environment. Anita has a BA in American Studies from Lesley University, where her thesis relates to how libraries protect our First Amendment rights. She holds an MEd in Library Media Studies from Salem State University. She is a frequent speaker at conferences such as AASL, MLA, and MSLA as well as in local schools and libraries.

MARC CROMPTON, MLIS, is Head of the Senior School Learning Commons at St. George's School in Vancouver, British Columbia, where he has been on the faculty for 25 years. He holds an MLIS from San Jose State University and has a number of articles in *Teacher Librarian.* He has co-authored *Collection Development Using the Collection Mapping Technique* with Dr. David Loertscher. He blogs at http://mcrompton.ca/wordpress/adventures/

JEAN DONHAM, PhD, is retired Professor of School Library Studies, University of Northern Iowa. Earlier, she led the library/technology program for the Iowa City (Iowa) Community School District, then held a position as tenured Associate Professor at the University of Iowa School of Library and Information Science, and later directed the library at Cornell College, a selective liberal arts college in Mount Vernon, Iowa. She has published extensively in inquiry-based learning and high school to higher education transition.

MARCI D'ONOFRIO, MEd, is a Physical Science teacher at Westborough High School where she views her role as helping students to reflect on how science is an essential part of their daily lives. Before becoming an educator, Marci was an Environmental Engineer in Seattle, Washington, where she worked on projects for groundwater and soil restoration. She holds an undergraduate degree from Worcester Polytechnic Institute, majoring in Civil Engineering with an emphasis on Environmental Engineering. Marci received an MEd from Antioch University while teaching at a private middle school in Massachusetts.

BUFFY EDWARDS, PhD, has worked in school libraries for 28 years and believes in Guided Inquiry. Buffy is a Library Information Specialist for the Norman Public Schools and Teacher

Librarian for Dimensions Academy Alternative School in Norman, Oklahoma. She also contributes to the profession as an online adjunct university professor, teaching online graduate classes in school librarianship and teacher education preparation for more than 10 years.

HEATHER HERSEY, MLS, is currently the director of the Upper School Library at Lakeside School in Seattle. She has been a teacher librarian here since September 2011 after moving from New Jersey, where she worked at Hunterdon Central Regional High School as a librarian for eight years and English teacher for three years. She holds an MA in English from Seton Hall University and an MEd in English Education from Rutgers University, where she also completed her master's degree in Library Science in 2006. Her love of questions and her interest in the research process, especially how students use information, made becoming a librarian irresistible.

CAROL COLLIER KUHLTHAU, EdD, is distinguished professor emerita of Library and Information Science at Rutgers University. She was founding director of CISSL—Rutgers Center for International Scholarship in School Libraries. She is internationally known for her groundbreaking research on the information search process and the ISP model of thoughts, feelings, and actions in six stages of information seeking and use. Her published and authored numerous works include *Seeking Meaning: A Process Approach to Library and Information Services* (2nd ed.), *Guided Inquiry: Learning in the 21st Century*, and *Guided Inquiry Design: A Framework for Inquiry in Your School.* https://comminfo.rutgers.edu/~kuhlthau/index.html

LESLIE K. MANIOTES, PhD, is owner of BLV Consulting where she works with educational leaders to create systems for inquiry learning in schools and as Guided Inquiry Design's professional developer. She is a National Board Certified Teacher with more than a decade of classroom experience. Leslie has worked as a K–12 literacy specialist in Title 1 schools, and as administrator and teacher effectiveness coach in the Denver Public Schools. She holds a master's degree in Reading K–12 from the University of North Carolina at Greensboro and a doctorate in instructional curriculum in the content areas from the University of Colorado, Boulder. Leslie is co-author of the Guided Inquiry Series, including the titles *Guided Inquiry: Learning in the 21st Century, Guided Inquiry Design: A Framework for Inquiry in Your School,* and *Guided Inquiry Design in Action: Middle School. www.*guidedinquirydesign.com

JENNIFER TORRY is currently an English teacher and yearbook adviser at St. George's School in Vancouver. Jennifer completed her BA in English and French and Teacher Education at Lamar University in Beaumont, Texas, and she is currently pursuing a postbaccalaureate diploma at Simon Fraser University in Burnaby, BC.